José María de Jesús Carvajal

José María de Jesús Carvajal

The Life and Times of a Mexican Revolutionary

JOSEPH E. CHANCE

TRINITY UNIVERSITY PRESS
San Antonio, Texas

The publisher gratefully acknowledges the generous support of the Summerlee Foundation, Dallas, Texas, toward the publication of this book.

 Published by Trinity University Press
San Antonio, Texas 78212

Jacket design by Erin Kirk New
Book design by BookMatters, Berkeley, California
Map by Manuel Hinojosa

⊛ The paper used in this publication meets the minimum requirements of the American National Standard for Information Sciences — Permanence of Paper for Printed Library Materials, ANSI Z39.48–1992.

Library of Congress Cataloging-in-Publication Data

Chance, Joseph E.
    José María de Jesús Carvajal : the life and times of a Mexican revolutionary / Joseph E. Chance.
        p. cm.
    Includes bibliographical references and index.
    ISBN-13: 978-1-59534-020-7
    ISBN-10: 1-59534-020-3
    1. Carvajal, José María de Jesús, 1810–1874.   2. Mexico—History—19th century.   3. Texas—History—19th century.
4. Revolutionaries—Mexico—Biography.   5. Legislators—Mexico—Biography.   I. Title.
F1232.C32C43   2006
972'.04092—dc22   2005046603

10   09   08   07   06 / 5   4   3   2   1

To Juliet and Roman Rodriguez,
my grandchildren

Contents

Acknowledgments

I am indebted to many persons and organizations for the materials used in my study of José María de Jesús Carvajal. This biography could never have been completed without the help of the fine staff of the library at the University of Texas–Pan American. The interlibrary loan department worked wonders in locating the many obscure sources I needed. For their unceasing efforts, I give special thanks to Ruben Coronado, Alice Patino, Norma Romero, and Marisol Guerra. The staff at the circulation desk was very cooperative, and the smiling faces of Edna Luna and LuAnn Buchner always made any trip to the library a pleasant experience. All of these folks are truly a credit to the library and reflect the highest standards of service, which has always been the library's hallmark.

Several people opened their private libraries to me, sharing valuable documents and papers that would have been impossible to find anywhere else. I wish to thank Enrique Guerra of Linn, Texas; Verne D. J. Philips of Austin, Texas; Ahmed Valtier of Monterrey, Nuevo León; William Paul Burrier Sr. of Leakey, Texas; and Jack Jackson of Austin, Texas.

Without the translations of Spanish documents and letters, much valuable knowledge on José María Carvajal would have been lost to me. For their translations of Spanish-language documents and articles, I am indebted to Al Ramirez of Edinburg, Texas; Ismael Higareda and Jaime Herbert of Reynosa, Tamaulipas; and Dr. Hubert Miller of Edinburg, Texas. My dear wife, Carolyn, helped me to place the accent marks on Spanish names throughout the manuscript. My authority on Spanish orthography, the placement of accent marks, and the culture of northern Mexico was Lic. Hugo Morales Gutiérrez, who was raised in Camargo, Tamaulipas, and is Profesor Investigador at Universidad Autónoma de Tamaulipas.

Other archives and libraries were very helpful in furnishing materials pertinent to this biography. I wish to thank David Mycue of the Museum of South Texas History in Edinburg, Texas; Donaly Brice of the Texas State Library and Archives Commission in Austin, Texas; Anna Peebler of the Rosenberg Library in Galveston, Texas; Sandra Ragonese of the Historical Society of Pennsylvania in Philadelphia; Douglas Clenin of the Indiana Historical Society in Indianapolis; Dennis Northcutt and Kirsten Hammerstrom of the Missouri Historical Society in Saint Louis; R. Jeanne Cobb of the T. W. Phillips Memorial Library in Bethany, West Virginia; and the personnel of the Masonic Library in Waco, Texas.

Several individuals offered documents, articles, and their valuable advice and counsel. I especially acknowledge Dr. Jerry Don Thompson of Texas A&M International University in Laredo, Texas; Dr. Robert E. May of Purdue University in West Lafayette, Indiana; Dr. Jeffrey Mauck of Hickory, North Carolina; Stephen Butler, representing the Descendents of Mexican War Veterans, in Richardson, Texas; Mary Ramirez of Baytown, Texas; Grady Howell of Madison, Mississippi; Jose O. Guerra Jr. of Houston, Texas; Laurier B. McDonald of Edinburg, Texas; Ann Washington of McAllen, Texas; Bill Young and Dr. Anthony Knopp of Brownsville, Texas; Charles Spurlin of Victoria, Texas; Hugo Morales of Camargo, Tamaulipas; Esther P. Gonzales of Rio Grande City, Texas; Dick Heller of Mission, Texas; Bruce Cheeseman of Port Arthur, Texas; Eugene and Ernesto Everett Jr. of San Diego, Texas; and Rachel Chance of Austin, Texas.

Institutions that responded to requests for information include the Center for American History and the Benson Latin American Collection at the University of Texas at Austin, the Mississippi Department of Archives and History in Jackson, and the Virginia Historical Society in Richmond.

For aid with computers and printers, I give thanks to Dr. Monty Taylor and Gustavo Rivera of McAllen, Texas.

I am especially indebted to Dr. Andrés Tijerina of Austin, Texas, and Mary Lenn Dixon of Texas A&M Press for reading the manuscript and offering many valuable suggestions for revisions.

Finally I wish to thank Sarah Nawrocki and Barbara Ras of Trinity

University Press who saw me through a period of personal tragedy and did not abandon this project. David Peattie of BookMatters did a smooth and efficient job in overseeing the production of this book, and the sharp-eyed Amy Smith Bell put forth a magnificent effort in editing the manuscript.

Thanks to you all.

San Felipe de Austin

• San Antonio

T E X A S

Piedras Negras Eagle Pass

Nueces

Corpus Christi

C O A H U I L A   Laredo

• Monclova

Guerrero

Mier   Rio Grande City

Cerralvo   Camargo   Edinburgh

China   Reynosa   Brownsville

Matamoros

Monterey

Saltillo

GULF
OF
MEXICO

S⁰ Fernando

N U E V O   L E O N

TAMAULIPAS

N
W   E
S

Miquihuana   Ciudad Victoria   Soto La Marina

S A N   L U I S

S⁰ Bartolo

Tampico

San Luis Potosi

Tampacho

Tuxpan

Querétaro

Introduction

José María de Jesús Carvajal, the intellectual dreamer who sought social reform in Mexico, lived a life of struggle against the forces of the conservative Centralists of that republic. He led a pioneering effort for political reform in South Texas and northern Mexico; yet he is remembered by only a few contemporary historians—and then only for his leadership of a series of armed incursions into northern Mexico from Texas in 1851 and 1852 that came to be known as the Merchants War. The purpose of this book is to resurrect a memory of Carvajal and place him in his rightful position in the pantheon of those who molded the shape of the current Texas-Mexico border society.

Such a task cannot succeed without an examination of the turbulent nineteenth-century history of the border region of Texas and Mexico. During Carvajal's life, Texas progressed, in this order: from a Spanish royal colony to a state in the Republic of Mexico, from an independent republic to statehood in the United States, and from statehood in the Confederate States of America to, finally, a return to U.S. statehood. South of the Rio Bravo del Norte, after independence from Spain was gained, an internecine struggle for power between Conservatives and Liberals commenced that would dominate nineteenth-century Mexico. Carvajal's life cannot be fully understood without viewing him in the context of the rapidly changing politics that dominated Texas and Mexico.

In the early nineteenth century, Mexico was experiencing the last few decades of rule by the Spanish Crown. Spanish monarchial rule had created a byzantine system of bureaucracy that was unable to respond to the colonists' local problems; for example, a response to a request from an outpost in northern Mexico might take as long as a year for a round-trip. But this tedious process of top-down governance ground to a halt in 1804 when Napoleon Bonaparte invaded Spain, forcing the Spanish monarch, King Charles III, and his son, Ferdinand IV, to abdicate. Without the guidance and often hindrance coming from Madrid, officials in the New World discovered the obvious advantages of self-government.

An interim government, the Cortes de Cadiz, was created to govern Spain and its overseas possessions during the Peninsular Wars. In 1808 the Cortes de Cadiz created a Liberal constitution for Mexico, but the relaxation of centralized power came too late to assuage the restless Mexican people. Social foment had festered for years over the rigid caste system the Spanish monarchy had imposed on Mexican society. At the top of this caste system were the *gauchipines,* or peninsulars—those Mexicans born in Spain. This class occupied key positions in the central viceregal government, the high ecclesiastical positions, and controlled the overwhelming majority of foreign trade contracts. Mexican-born Spaniards, known as *creoles,* were next in the social structure and were generally miners and priests, managers and occasionally owners of haciendas, and holders of local municipal offices. At the bottom of the social structure were the so-called *mestizos,* the uneducated masses who performed the manual labor, serving as bonded servants. They were known as peons.

On 16 September 1810, Father Miguel Hidalgo voiced a cry for independence from the village of Dolores that triggered the revolutionary movement for the separation of Mexico from the Crown of Spain. The resulting revolution was political rather than social in nature. The aim of the revolution was independence from Spain and did not include the abolishment of the rigid caste system. A revolution for social change would commence in Mexico some hundred years later. The bloody revolution initiated by the now martyred Hidalgo continued until 1821, when the signing of the Manifesto of Iguala granted Mexico its independence.

With independence, a power struggle between two political philosophies would continue throughout the remainder of the nineteenth century. The Liberal Party, on the one hand, was inspired by the ideas of French political writers and the success of democracy in the United States. It espoused the establishment of a representative government and equality of all people before the law. Liberals generally distrusted the evils of a strong central government, preferring instead a diffuse distribution of power among local governments. The Conservative Party, on the other hand, were the peninsulars, the wealthy class of colonial Mexico, and their inheritors, who wished to retain their hereditary privileges. They felt that this could best be done by a strong central government or even the establishment of a monarchy. The clergy and the military, who wished to preserve the rights and privileges that had historically been granted by the Crown of Spain also came to be associated with the Conservatives. A central theme of nineteenth-century Mexican history is by and large the story of the Liberal-Conservative struggle for power.

After a brief flirtation with a constitutional monarchy, the balance of power in the Mexican Congress shifted to the Liberals. They produced a constitution for Mexico in 1824 that advocated a representative form of government. One of the first problems facing the new government was the nagging question of what to do with its vast northern territory of Texas. Little progress in the settlement of this region had been accomplished under Spanish rule. Only three villages of any size existed north of the Rio Bravo: San Antonio de Béxar in the center of the region, La Bahia to the east of San Antonio, and Nacogdoches to the north, all connected by a rude trail known as the Camino Real.

This large, unoccupied region, which did not have a well-defined northern boundary, was coveted by the United States, whose settlers were proceeding in an unrelenting path westward through the areas newly acquired as part of the Louisiana Purchase. Mexicans feared that their northern lands would soon be overrun by Anglo settlers claiming their vast vacant lands under the well-worn maxim that "nature abhors a vacuum." The Mexican government had attempted to colonize Texas with its own citizens but without much measurable success. No one living in the relatively settled area of Mexico lying south of the Rio Bravo wished to settle in the trackless wilderness north of the river. This area was teeming with warring Indian tribes who did not wish to see the land settled.

With few other alternatives the Mexican government decided to honor colonization contracts that had been granted earlier by the Spanish colonial government. One of the first of these contracts was given to Missouri empresario Stephen F. Austin under quite liberal terms. Austin carefully recruited his colonists from the United States, banning frontiersmen with no occupation other than hunting. He also called for "no drunkard, no gambler, nor profane swearer, no idler." In return for a pledge of allegiance to the Republic of Mexico and a promise to become Catholic, a family would receive 1,428 acres of choice land as well as freedom from Mexican taxes and import duties for ten years. By 1829, Austin wrote that "this is the most liberal and munificent Government on earth to emigrants."[1]

But the unprotected northern boundaries of Texas continued to invite illegal immigration, and the trickle observed in 1826 soon became a flood. This swarm of illegal aliens were of a decidedly different breed, fortune seekers and adventurers who moved onto vacant lands for which they had no title. The Mexican government responded in 1830 by canceling all emigration contracts and banning further settlement in Texas by citizens from the United States. But the impoverished government did not have the resources to enforce this law, and illegal immigration from the United States continued.

By 1835, fearing the loss of Texas and the Liberal policies that mandated the sale of church lands as well as restrictions being placed on the army, then president Antonio López de Santa Anna, the onetime Liberal, now affiliated himself with the Conservatives and moved to seize control of the government. His Conservative government assumed dictatorial powers and voided the guarantees of the Liberal constitution of 1824. In response to this usurpation of power, rebellion broke out in Texas in 1835. The struggle for Texas independence is well known, and by summer of 1836, the Lone Star flag fluttered in the breeze, proclaiming the new Republic of Texas to all.

The struggle to oppose the dictatorial control of Mexico by the Conservatives continued to be contested by the Liberals. From 1838 to 1840 the unsuccessful so-called Federalist Wars broke out in Mexico. But a strong conservative central government snuffed out resistance from the uncoordinated and poorly financed uprising and retained control of Mexico. Mexican hopes for the reconquest of Texas were dashed in 1845 by the annexation of that territory to the United States. A dispute over the ownership of those lands in Texas between the Nueces River and the Rio Grande triggered a series of armed confrontations that escalated into a formal declaration of war by the United States.

The rancorous debate between Mexican Conservatives and Liberals now temporarily ceased, and both parties closed ranks to oppose the U.S. invaders. U.S. forces, led by General Zachary Taylor, invaded northern Mexico and, after the capture of Monterrey, occupied that region until the end of the war. Resistance continued in northern Mexico throughout the remainder of the war with isolated Mexican guerilla actions in a hit-and-run campaign. A second thrust into Mexico through the city of Veracruz by the forces of General Winfield Scott culminated in the capture of Mexico City and the end of the war. The Treaty of Guadalupe Hidalgo, signed in 1848, marked the end of hostilities between the two countries, and the loss of half of Mexico's territory to the United States.

Unrest dominated postwar Mexico; rebellion broke out in the Yucatán and central Mexico, and from the United States were heard the ominous sounds of the mustering of private filibuster armies forming to invade northern Mexico, Cuba, and Nicaragua. With the aid of border merchants and certain influential persons in Texas and northern Mexico, a plan was developed in 1851 to separate northern Mexico from the republic to form the Republic of Sierra Madre. Two armed filibuster forays were launched into northern Mexico: the first resulting in the successful defense of Matamoros by government forces, and the second in a disastrous defeat of filibuster forces north of the little border village of Camargo. The second defeat marked the end of large-scale armed incursions into northern Mexico, but the Texas-Mexico border in southern Texas remained a volatile lawless region throughout the remainder of the nineteenth century, marked by large-scale cattle rustling and hostile Indian raids into Mexico launched from the United States.

Santa Anna assumed his fifth term as president of Mexico in 1853, but his actions to ease previous legal restrictions imposed by Liberals on the church and the military created unrest in the country. In a desperate effort to infuse funds into the cash-strapped country, Santa Anna approved the Gadsden Treaty in 1854, which ceded northern Sonora to the United States for ten million pesos. The loss of more territory to the United States enraged the citizenry of Mexico, who took to the streets in rebellion and drove the Conservative Santa Anna government from power, resulting in the reemergence of the Liberals.

A Liberal-dominated Congress approved the constitution of 1857, which superceded that of 1824, and expressed the increasingly Liberal viewpoints of its authors. The new constitution abolished clerical and military legal immunities, marked the vast tracts of church-owned lands for sale to its tenants and lessees, and no longer specified Catholicism as the state religion. The new constitution split the nation: the church, the army, and the privileged class of landowners expressed violent opposition to its liberal provisions.

In January 1858 statesman Benito Juárez assumed power as the constitutional president of Mexico, a country now sharply divided by the Conservative-Liberal struggle. In reaction, the Conservatives formed an opposition government, headed by General Miguel Miramón in Mexico City, while the Juárez constitutional government established Veracruz as its temporary capital. (Miramón would later be executed as a traitor for his part in the French intervention into Mexico.) Thus began the internecine struggle known as the War of the Reform, which continued until December 1860, when the Conservatives were driven from Mexico City by Liberal forces. Juárez held the church responsible for the war and imposed even more serious restrictions on the clergy.

By 1861 the political climate north of the Rio Grande had also radically changed: Texas had seceded from the United States and aligned its fortunes with the rebellious government of the Confederate States of America. Over the next four years the towns of Brownsville and Matamoros experienced an unparalled economic boom due to the cotton trade. With all southern ports blockaded by the Union Navy, the Confederates had only one port open for the export of their cotton, that of the little Mexican village of Bagdad, east of Matamoros. Millions of dollars in trade poured through this region during the war, creating family fortunes that continue to dominate the economics of South Texas and northern Mexico even to this day.

South of the Rio Grande, Napoleon III, the ambitious emperor of France, cast covetous eyes on Mexico. Weakened by three years of civil war that continued to sharply divide the country and deeply in debt to foreign powers, Mexico appeared to be the ideal site for an overseas empire. The

United States, now embroiled in its own civil war, was in no position to intervene on Mexico's behalf. Besides, a base of popular support for the establishment of a monarchy existed among the defeated Conservatives of Mexico. Under the pretense of debt collection, France, Great Britain, and Spain invaded Mexico in 1861, seizing the customs houses at Veracruz. Great Britain and Spain soon became aware of France's covert designs on Mexico and promptly withdrew their forces.

France proceeded to reinforce its imperial troops and, combining them with Mexican Conservative forces, put together an army that began the march inland to capture Mexico City. Despite a signal victory over French forces by the Mexican army led by Ignacio Zaragoza at Puebla on 5 May 1862, Mexican forces were forced to abandon Mexico City and began a long retreat to the north. By 1864, with the Mexican government operating in exile from the northern city of Chihuahua, occupying French forces declared Mexico to be a constitutional monarchy. Maximilian, an Austrian Hapsburg, was declared its emperor, placed on the throne of Mexico by French bayonets.

The tedious war continued. Imperial troops controlled the principal cities of Mexico, but the countryside belonged to republican troops, loyal to Juárez. A frustrated Napoleon III continued to pour money and men into Mexico without avail, and the war took on a brutal note. By 1865, Maximilian had issued an edict to the Imperial Army that all armed republican troops, when captured, were to be summarily executed. By 1866, with the U.S. Civil War at an end, the United States began to apply stiff pressure on France to withdraw its troops from Mexico. With the threats of German unification and an aggressive Austrian empire, Napoleon III, feeling uneasy about the intentions of his European neighbors, withdrew French troops from Mexico, leaving his allies, the Conservatives, to fend for themselves as best they could. By 1867, with the capture of Maximilian, the remainder of the Mexican empire crumbled. Rejecting all pleas for leniency, Juárez ordered Maximilian to be executed before a firing squad for his war crimes against the Mexican people.

Juárez died in office in 1871 and by 1877, General Porfirio Díaz assumed the presidency of Mexico, beginning a repressive thirty-year regime of relative peace and prosperity that would be shattered in 1910 by a massive revolution aimed at changing the social structure of Mexico. Under Díaz the social caste system flourished and Mexican land owner-ship fell into the hands of a wealthy few while the vast majority of peons struggled day by day to exist. Armed insurrection was the result of Díaz's arch conservatism.

In the midst of the tumultuous history of Mexico and Texas that played out during the nineteenth century, José María Carvajal was born in the Spanish municipality of San Antonio de Béxar in 1809. From his earliest interests in politics, he sided with the Liberal cause and would spend the majority of his active life battling for those rights. Although Liberal ideals were important to him, he never forgot that he was first of all, in his own words, "a true Mexican."[2] The purpose of this biography is to review the many struggles in which Carvajal participated in the name of liberalism. His life serves to document a step in the political evolution of the govern-ments of Texas and Mexico from a Spanish royal colony to that of a mod-ern representative democracy.

Carvajal entered the political arena as a legislator in the ill-fated 1835 ses-sion of the legislature of Coahuila y Tejas, held in Monclova. This session was so dominated by Liberal opposition to the tyrannical rule of Santa Anna that the Mexican army was compelled to adjourn the session indefinitely at the point of a bayonet. Carvajal fled to Texas as a fugitive; a warrant had been issued by Texas's military government for his arrest. As unrest in Texas turned to open revolution, Carvajal entered into a plot to supply arms to the Texas revolutionists and was captured in the process of delivering these armaments. In a daring escape, he was broken out of the Casamata, a prison in Matamoros, before fleeing to his home in Texas, near Victoria. There he remained in hiding from the military government but continued to urge his fellow Texans, as a member of the War Party, to take the field against Mexico's dictatorial Central government.

Carvajal hoped that revolution in Texas would be the spark that ignited the flame of a general revolution in Mexico against Santa Anna. Like many others in Texas, he wished only to restore the constitution of 1824 and return Mexico to Liberal ideals. He opposed the more radical movement for Texas independence. Although Carvajal was elected as a delegate to the convention that produced the Texas Declaration of Independence, his absence from the convention silently pointed to his opposition. Carvajal did not take up arms against the Mexican army that entered Texas in 1836, nor did he side with the invaders. His neutrality was distrusted by those who had taken up arms for independence, however, and some accused him of treason. In an act of retribution, the Texas army drove Carvajal and his relatives from their Texas homes into exile in Louisiana. Many other Hispanics in Texas had taken the same stand as Carvajal; they were now referred to by their neighbors derisively as "Mexicans"—foreigners in their own land.

Carvajal shortly returned to northern Mexico, settling in the little village of Camargo, Tamaulipas. There he met the fiery charismatic Liberal Antonio Canales Rosillo and was persuaded by his impassioned Liberal rhetoric to join in a plot against the Conservative Central government. Encouraged by the success of Texas to gain its independence, Liberal leaders in Mexico plotted to separate the northern states from the Republic to form the so-called Republic of the Rio Grande, founded on solid Liberal principles. But like so many revolutionary movements, the insurgents lacked the funds to maintain an army in the field and desperately needed foreign aid or intervention.

The revolutionaries cast eager eyes on their new neighbor to the north, claiming that both were fighting a common enemy and should unite forces. But Mirabeau B. Lamar, the president of the Republic of Texas, refused to lend aid to the Mexican revolutionaries, and the revolution soon failed as a result of attrition and a powerful Mexican Centralist army sent to the north. Carvajal emerged from this insurrection with the admiration of both Mexicans and Texans for his bravery on the battlefield and his ability to organize and lead troops. With a promise of amnesty from the Republic of Mexico for his revolutionary indiscretions, Carvajal returned to Camargo to resume his civilian pursuits.

By 1845, with war between the United States and Mexico imminent, Carvajal the Mexican Liberal was forced into another fateful decision: support the United States against his Conservative enemies who held power in Mexico City, or unite with the Conservatives to oppose the Americans. Ever true to his native country, the patriotic Carvajal opted to oppose the

Americans. During the Mexican-American War he commanded a brigade of irregulars opposing U.S. occupation forces in northern Mexico.

After the war Carvajal returned to Camargo and engaged in his civil occupation as a surveyor, but he was still chafing against the Conservative government in power. By 1850 he again succumbed to the siren call for independence and began to put in motion a second plot to separate northern Mexico from the republic, this time to form the Liberal-based Republic of the Sierra Madre. Carvajal stated to others that he wished to be remembered for his part in this revolutionary movement as the "George Washington of northern Mexico." He issued the Plan de La Loba in 1851, a liberal *pronunciamiento* (pronouncement) against the Central government, and mustered a force, the so-called Liberation Army, consisting of Mexicans and mercenary American adventurers, to support his claims.

Carvajal's pure motives soon became corrupted by reality, however: the insurrection was supported by border merchants who cared little for the ideals of liberalism. Merchants only sought an opportunity to evade the prohibitive Mexican import duties and were poised to flood northern Mexico with goods that would follow in the wake of Carvajal's army. An invading army, with the hated gringos in its ranks, led by a Protestant Hispanic who dressed and spoke like a gringo could not possibly attract Mexican support. The Liberation Army advanced into Mexico from Rio Grande City, capturing Camargo and Reynosa. After an unsuccessful ten-day siege of Matamoros, Carvajal and his men were driven off, crossing the Rio Grande into the United States to seek sanctuary. A reconstituted army, led by Carvajal, crossed the Rio Grande a second time in early 1852 and was soundly defeated by forces of the Mexican National Guard, putting an end to Carvajal's dreams for northern independence. He was charged later that year with a violation of the U.S. Federal Neutrality Act of 1818 but acquitted in a jury trial held in Galveston in 1854.

Carvajal returned to Mexico as a fugitive from justice for his part in the failed revolution but soon fell into the good graces of Juárez's Liberal government. He sided with Juárez against the Conservatives during the War of the Reform, the destructive civil war that pitted the two political parties against each other for control of the government. Carvajal was appointed military governor of Matamoros and formed a brigade of troops that battled Conservative forces near Victoria, Tamaulipas. With the defeat of the insurgent Conservative government in 1861, Juárez gained a tenuous control over the nation. But by this date Mexico faced an even more serious threat posed by French intervention.

Carvajal once again took to the field to support not only Mexican sovereignty but the ideals of liberalism. He offered his services to the government and was commissioned as a general, leading the Fieles de Tamaulipas, a battalion of infantry that would engage imperialist forces in the Huasteca region of Mexico. Carvajal employed the hit-and-run tactics against his stronger opponents that he had learned so well while opposing the American army in northern Mexico during the Mexican-American War. He was so successful in his attacks on the imperialist supply trains that radiated from the port cities of Tampico and Tuxpan that a large imperialist force was soon dispatched with orders to neutralize Carvajal.

The Carvajal battalion was surrounded in the little village of San Bartillo on 17 April 1864. After a fierce struggle their defenses were overrun, but Carvajal and some of his men were able to effect their escape. Carvajal was not downcast by the loss but soon began to reorganize his decimated forces, who were without arms, ammunition, and other supplies. His little band of patriots retreated into the wilds of the San Carlos Mountains and, as a mark of their desperate straits, Carvajal began the training of his men in the use of bows and arrows.

Juárez had not lost confidence in his lieutenant, and on 12 November 1864 he issued a commission to Carvajal to recruit a foreign army and obtain loans to support the penniless Juárez government. By March 1865, as an agent for his government, Carvajal met with General Lew Wallace concerning the issue of raising arms for the Juárez government. Both men proceeded to Washington, D.C., and from there to the financial capital of New York to raise money for the defense of Mexico. Mexican bonds were poorly subscribed to, but U.S. munitions makers, left with a large inventory at the end of the American Civil War, agreed to accept Mexican bonds in lieu of payment for arms and munitions. The arms reached Mexico and were used to defeat the French imperialists.

In 1870, feeling the weight of his sixty-one years of active campaigns in the field, Carvajal retired to his ranch just south of the Rio Grande near present-day Mission, Texas. By 1872 he was living in Soto Marina, Tamaulipas, where he died on 19 August 1874. Thus passed a distinguished Texan and a "true Mexican" who spent his life in the defense of the Liberal ideals that moved Mexico from a Spanish monarchy toward an independent state ruled by the principles of representative democracy.

ONE

The Early Life and Education of José María de Jesús Carvajal

All that our rulers want is to abolish the federal system!!
Coahuila and Texas shall never be governed by any other
form of government.

JOSÉ MARÍA DE JESÚS CARVAJAL
in a letter to Antonio Menchaca, 29 April 1835

José María de Jesús Carvajal was born in 1809, the son of José Antonio Carvajal Peña and María Gertrúdis Sánchez Soto, in the bustling village of San Antonio de Béxar, which is now known as San Antonio, Texas. At that time the village was a part of the municipality of Béxar in the province of Texas, a part of the sprawling royal empire of Spanish Mexico.

With the dawning of the nineteenth century, the quiet village of San Antonio de Béxar was to become a battleground as the winds of revolution swept time and again over Texas. Spain had failed in its efforts to colonize its wild northern province of Texas. Attempts to pacify the numerous Indian tribes residing in Texas had met with failure, and without a commitment from the Crown for the necessary resources, Texas remained in a primitive state. After three hundred years of Spanish occupation, only three villages of any size had been established. San Antonio de Béxar, the capital of Texas, described as a collection of "very indifferent houses," with a population of twenty-five hundred; to the east of San Antonio the settlement of Goliad; and to the north of San Antonio the frontier village of Nacogdoches, built to guard the ill-defined boundary between Texas and the newly acquired U.S. territory of Louisiana. The undermanned presidio at Nacogdoches attempted, without much success, to stem the flow of illegal settlers and contraband goods streaming into Spanish Texas from the United States. Connecting these three villages was a rude pathway known as the Camino Real.

The smoldering unrest in Mexico burst into the flames of revolution on 16 September 1810 with the famous *grito* of Padre Miguel Hidalgo, pronouncing the independence of Mexico from the Crown of Spain. Backed by a ragtag army of a hundred thousand Indians—armed mostly with machetes, hoes, and pitchforks—Hidalgo's rebel army achieved early victories at Guanajuato and Guadalajara. Stirred by Father Hidalgo's early successes, the republican element of the population of San Antonio mounted their own resistance to Spanish rule. The garrison of Spanish troops there, under the leadership of Juan Bautista de las Casas, switched their allegiance to the republican cause on 22 January 1811. Governor Manuel Salcedo, Simón de Herrera (the governor of Nuevo Leon), and other Spanish officials were arrested and sent under guard to Monclova, then held by rebel forces.

But the Spanish military, finally responding to the revolutionary crisis, handed Hidalgo's army a decisive defeat at Aculco, signaling the steady destruction of rebel forces. Knowing that the revolution would fail without outside help, Hidalgo dispatched rebel leader Bernardo Gutiérrez de Lara, a native of Revilla, Tamaulipas, to the United States to seek aid. News of Hidalgo's reversals filtered north into San Antonio, and many of those who had placed Casas and the republicans in power began to have second thoughts. Under the leadership of subdeacon Juan Manuel Zambrano— described by San Antonio historian and early advocate for Hispanic civil rights José Antonio Navarro as "gigantic and obese, arrogant in manner, dynamic and volatile as mercury"—a successful counterrevolution was organized. The hapless Casas, who had been motivated to seize power by selfless motives, was arrested and sent in chains to Monclova, where he was tried and executed. According to an eyewitness account by early day San Antonian Antonio Menchaca, "his [de las Casas's] head [was] severed from his body, placed in a box, sent here [San Antonio] and put in the middle of Military Plaza on a pole." Governors Salcedo and Herrera returned to San Antonio to reestablish the Crown's authority in the province of Texas.

Meanwhile, Gutiérrez de Lara, with the help of Augustus W. Magee, a

West Point graduate, had organized a filibuster army that invaded Spanish Texas in August of 1812. Under their green flag the Gutiérrez-Magee filibusters easily overpowered the small Spanish garrison at Nacogdoches, then marched on Goliad. After a short struggle Royalist troops surrendered the Mission La Bahia to their attackers. A Spanish army dispatched from San Antonio under the personal command of Salcedo laid siege to filibuster forces in La Bahia for four months, finally retreating when repeated pleas to the Spanish government for reinforcements were ignored. The Gutiérrez-Magee filibusters tracked Salcedo's Royalist forces on their return march to San Antonio, overtaking them at the Salado Creek, and defeating them decisively at the battle of Rosillo.

Governor Salcedo, with no troops or resources for further resistance, surrendered San Antonio to the filibuster army on 2 April 1813. A group of fourteen Spanish officials, including Salcedo and Herrera, were arrested and became the victims of a shocking atrocity. On the next evening a party of filibuster troops, led by one Antonio Delgado, removed the fourteen prisoners from their cells and spirited them off to a site near Salado Creek, where their throats were cut and their bodies thrown into that stream. Navarro reported the return of Delgado and his men: "I myself saw the clothing and the blood-stained adornments which those tigers carried hanging from their saddle horns, boasting publicly of their crimes and of having divided the spoils among themselves in shares." This act of cold-blooded murder recoiled upon Gutiérrez de Lara, who was replaced as civil commander and head of the filibuster army. He was met with criticism and rebuke from his partisans in San Antonio, even though he disavowed any part in the execution. The American portion of Gutiérrez's army, horrified by the barbarous act, planned to leave the army but were persuaded to stay only after the pleas of many Mexican leaders.

But peace in San Antonio was not to last for long: a large Royalist army under the command of Joaquín de Arredondo marched northward to oppose Gutiérrez de Lara's forces. The clash of arms occurred south of San Antonio on the Medina River on 18 August 1813, resulting in the rout of Gutiérrez de Lara's forces, the remnants of which fled northward for refuge in the United States along with citizens of San Antonio, such as Navarro and Menchaca who had sided with Gutiérrez de Lara's forces. The triumphant Spanish forces entered San Antonio on 18 August to initiate a reign of terror in that village. Arrendondo vowed to punish any citizens who had not actively resisted the revolutionary movement and quickly moved to achieve that goal.

On the night of 20 August three hundred citizens were imprisoned "like sheep" in a tiny cell on one of the hottest nights of the year, resulting in the suffocation of eighteen of the prisoners. On the next day one hundred sixty of the prisoners were handcuffed in pairs and set to work on the streets. Forty of the prisoners were selected for death, and on every third day three were shot in the Military Plaza, their bodies decapitated and the heads put in iron cages and left on display in the Plaza de Armas. The wives of the prisoners were themselves imprisoned in "La Quinta" and required to prepare thirty-five thousand tortillas each day for the Spanish garrison of San Antonio.

Many citizens of San Antonio fled to escape the violence, and within a few months the city bore the resemblance of a ghost town. Spanish soldiers were billeted in the many deserted homes in the city. Interestingly, a lowly young lieutenant serving in Arrendondo's royal army, one Antonio López de Santa Anna, was quartered in Navarro's home. He would return to San Antonio twenty-two years later at the head of a powerful Mexican army with the same mission: to suppress a revolutionary movement.

Young José María Carvajal would remember the horrors of Arredondo's occupation of San Antonio for the remainder of his life. Señora Gertrúdis Carvajal was one of the women placed into La Quinta to grind corn and make tortillas for the Spanish army. The citizens of San Antonio had been driven from their homes, and the children, such as five-year-old José María, were left to wander the streets, searching for a scrap of food and a warm place to sleep at night. The cries of the women in La Quinta, interspersed with the sounds of a firing squad executing the townspeople, would ever remain in his memory. But with the passing of Arredondo's army, the little village of San Antonio again assumed the quiet demeanor of a frontier settlement. The revolutionary zeal and the bloody violence of the town's former days must have played a great role in shaping the attitudes of young José María Carvajal.[1]

José Antonio Carvajal Peña, the subject's father, was a soldier who came to San Antonio de Béxar around 1785 and quite likely participated in the revolutionary unrest of the early eighteenth century. Carvajal Peña died in that village before 1821, possibly as a result of the struggle for Mexican independence there, leaving his widow Gertrúdis to raise a family of eleven children. Little is known of the eleven children save José María's two brothers, Mariano and Manuel, and one sister, Teodora Sánchez de Carvajal, who married the prominent José Luciano Navarro of San Antonio de Béxar on 11 April 1823.[2]

The Carvajal family traced their ancestry from Jerónimo Carvajal, a Canary Island settler of San António, and were distantly related to the famous Luís Carvajal, a pioneer settler of northern Mexico. The Carvajal family was related to the prominent Menchaca, Navarro, Flóres, and Pérez families of Béxar. The family name is spelled with several variants— Caravajal, Carabajal, and Carbajal—but José María signed his correspondence with a bold flourish as "Carvajal." Besides being connected to the first families of San Antonio, the Carvajal family became well acquainted with the Anglo colonists that began to appear in Texas by the mid-1820s. Stephen F. Austin, Joseph and his brother Littleberry Hawkins, Benjamin Milam, and Philip Dimitt were well acquainted with young José María and his family. While in San Antonio on business, Austin would on occasion stay overnight as a guest of the Carvajal family, who kept a boardinghouse in their residence.

Austin, deeply immersed in the business and politics of the Texas colonies, was a lifelong bachelor who professed that his responsibilities sadly left him with no time to raise a family of his own. Nevertheless, he took a special interest in children. The welfare of the widow Carvajal's family became one of Austin's many concerns, and he assumed the role of a surrogate father. Austin was especially impressed with the young José María, a precocious teenager eager to learn about the United States and Anglo culture. With the permission of Señora Carvajal, then fifteen-year-old José María accompanied Texas colonist Littleberry Hawkins on a trip to Kentucky in 1823 to seek training and a formal education.[3]

Hawkins, also impressed with young Carvajal, wrote to Austin that

"Hosa Murrah [José María] is well and going to schoole learning fast."⁴ Hawkins had apprenticed the boy to his brother-in-law, Blanchard, living in Frankfort, Kentucky, to learn the trade of saddle-making and to study the elements of English. José María remained as an apprentice for two years, then moved to Lexington, Kentucky, to work for another saddler, Peter Hedenberg. During this time he became acquainted with the noted theologian Alexander Campbell, one of the founders of the Disciples of Christ, a branch of the Church of Christ often referred to as "Campbellites."⁵ The talented Campbell had authored a translation of the English Bible, which was published in 1827. Campbell published numerous religious tracts from the printing press in his home, located in Bethany, Virginia, now in the state of West Virginia. From his home Campbell established Buffalo Seminary, for the education of the young and the training of clergy, which would become known in 1840 as Bethany College. The school survives to this day.⁶

Campbell was as impressed by young José María as Austin had been and enrolled the young man as a student in Buffalo Seminary. Carvajal lived in the Campbell home from 1826 until 1830, while attending school. Bethany College records from this early period are scant; no records have been found that indicate Carvajal graduated from the institute, but it is quite possible that the seminary issued no terminal degrees at that time.⁷ Campbell had a strong influence on José María's life, and this moral training would shape Carvajal's thinking and aid him in the many difficult decisions of his later life.

While in residence at the Campbell home, José María wrote his mother in 1826: "I have renounced the doctrines of the Church of Rome, I have not given up prayer but still find it a blessing to my soul."⁸ Young Carvajal had made the spiritual decision to become a Protestant—a disciple of Campbell. He would continue to profess his faith in God as a Protestant for the remainder of his life, even at times when it would have been more politically expedient in a Catholic Mexico dominated by the priesthood to return to the faith of his early childhood. Carvajal's political detractors in Mexico would, in later days, refer to him as an "heretico," not a "buen cristiano," to cast suspicions on his claims of being a "true Mexican." But Carvajal remained steadfast to his beliefs. During his visits to Camargo in the turbulent latter days of his life, he was observed to regularly attend religious services at a little Methodist chapel built there during the time of the American Civil War by expatriate Union sympathizers.[9]

Carvajal's concentration on English and the Anglo culture of Kentucky and Virginia had been so extensive that he confided to his mother: "I have nearly lost my language in my own tounge [*sic*] since I came here." For a brief time he signed his name in the Anglo style as "Mr. Joseph M. J. Carbajal."[10] His acquired knowledge of English and Anglo-American culture, coupled with the Hispanic language and culture of his people, would later enable him to assume a key position of leadership in the bicultural society of the peoples living along the Rio Grande.

A glimpse of Carvajal's charismatic personality can be obtained from a short note sent to Stephen F. Austin from one of Carvajal's Kentucky acquaintances, who wrote of José María: "The affectionate and praiseworthy conduct of this lad has endeared him to his acquaintances."[11] Infected with the idealism that strikes most young college students, Carvajal became concerned with the betterment of the condition of the Hispanic people in colonial Texas. With their spiritual welfare in mind, José María addressed this letter to Austin: "I have got in a box . . . , 50 copies of the Scriptures, in the Spanish Language, Translated by the Bishop of Madrid—A translation to which, no objection can be had, being made from the Latin of the Vulgate, which is universally approved by the Roman Catholics." Carvajal asked Austin to help him sell these Bibles to the Spanish-speaking peoples of Texas, hoping that the inspired word would "bring that excellent people out of this bondage and degradation both Political and Spiritual." Always the idealist, he asked that Austin sell the Bibles in a rather unique manner:

To the poor who will receive them	-00.00 —for nothing
To those able to pay	$1.50 in silver
To those better off	$2.00
To rich people	$3.00[12]

Selling Bibles in colonial Texas was a perilous enterprise, even for someone of Austin's stature. Religion was a sore point among the Texas colonists: the official state religion for the Republic of Mexico was Catholicism, and all colonists receiving land grants from Mexico had sworn to convert to that religion. But the church had not furnished Texas with any priests. With no religious instruction available, or the lack of priests to conduct marriage and funeral ceremonies, many colonists from the United States retained their Protestant religion. Unsanctioned preachers rode circuits through the wilderness servicing the spiritual needs of the people. One can only imagine the distrust and suspicion evoked among both colonists and officials of the Mexican government by someone of Austin's stature distributing Catholic Bibles among the populace. Although we do not have a copy of Austin's response to Carvajal, it is doubtful that he participated in the enterprise. Nevertheless, it is thought that Carvajal's effort represents the first attempt by anyone to bring the written Holy Word to Hispanic settlers north of the Rio Grande.

Carvajal's idealism, rather than diminishing with age, in fact became stronger and continued to focus on the welfare of his people. Before his invasion of northern Mexico in 1851, he confided to his friend John S. Ford that he wished to be remembered by his countrymen as "the George Washington of Northern Mexico."[13] This idealism could be at times his strong shield, but at other important times in his life, it would act to his detriment. His naivete, based on his assumption that other persons were motivated by the same values as he, would be manipulated on occasion by ambitious men to further their own greedy interests. Carvajal, the intellectual dreamer, envisioned a better world, but his grandiose dreams so often neglected the practical details that almost always separated success from failure.

José María returned from school in Virginia to Texas in 1830, searching for a profession whereby he could earn his daily bread. At this time in Texas probably the most lucrative opportunities for a young man seeking to acquire wealth were found in the profession of land location and surveying. Land grants received by colonists from the Republic of Mexico were often in the midst of a trackless wilderness and had to be located and surveyed to perfect the title. Surveyors were usually paid in the coin of the realm by collecting from one-third to one-half of the area of the land grant as fees for their services. But surveying was not a profession either for the faint of heart or the dull-witted. Many surveyors lost their lives in the wilds of Texas to roaming bands of hostile Indians. A surveyor needed instruments and was required to make accurate measurements and perform complex mathematical calculations.

José María opted to be a surveyor and began his course of study in early 1830. He was still a student by 31 May 1830, when Austin cautiously responded to a letter from Navarro, who was seeking to employ a surveyor, with this tentative letter of recommendation: "I do not doubt but what the commission is going to be of much advantage to you. The principal thing that it offers at present is the naming of a Surveyor. If the young man Jose Ma. Carbajal understood a little more in this science it would be well for you to name him, and I think that it would not be improper to name him, because he can do the work by subaltern practices and he would in a short time learn the theory and practice of measurements [as] he is young with very notable advancements in the sciences and has a very good English education. Also I think he can be very useful to you in many ways. —I have offered to take him to my house and instruct him in the measurement of lands. . . . I think it would be better that you send a dispatch to Milam for a surveyor and you can name Jose Ma. Carbajal when he is sufficiently advanced in that science."[14]

But by 1831, José María had mastered his chosen profession, and the bilingual surveyor rapidly obtained contracts to locate lands for the settlers. His distinctive surveying mark, an "X" with two horizontal lines above and below the mark, was soon seen hacked into the trees along the survey lines he ran. Carvajal surveyed in metes and bounds, and his knowledge of proper Spanish enabled him to navigate the intricate details required to issue a legal land title under Mexican law. His field notes often contained detailed descriptions of the terrain as well as the flora and fauna found there. In that same year he was appointed to an important commission authorized by the state government of Coahuila y Tejas to resolve several nagging questions on land ownership that had plagued Texas colonists for years.

To issue and clarify land titles to settlers living east of the San Jacinto River in Texas, the state government of Coahuila y Tejas dispatched José Francisco Madero and his surveyor and secretary, José María Carvajal, to that region in January 1831. Madero was charged by state law with issuing titles to those residents of eastern Texas who lived outside the authority of any existing empresario grants and had resided on their claims before 1828. But the national law of 6 April 1830 cancelled all pending land contracts with Anglo-Americans and forbade them from being citizens of Mexico. Further, the constitution of 1824 had barred noncitizens from settling within twenty-six miles of the Gulf of Mexico or within fifty-two miles of the Sabine River. Madero, who represented the state government, argued that most of these settlers had been living on their claims before 6 April 1830 and ex post facto were not subject to that law. Moreover, the state government had already violated the constitution by allowing the Anglos in Austin's Colony to settle along the coast, and many of the settlers wishing title to these lands had settled along the coast before 1824. But the difficulties encountered by this commission did not grow out of title to land; rather, they focused on the rising political struggle in Mexico between two factions: the Centralists and the Federalists.[15]

The Mexican Constitution of 1824, a marvelously liberal document, had been written with the intent of decentralizing political power and placing it into the hands of the state governments, thereby creating a relatively weak central government. The close resemblance of this document to that of the U.S. Constitution caused Mexican Conservative Lucas Alamán to write that the constitution of 1824 was "a monstrous graft of the constitution of the United States onto the constitution of Cádiz."[16]

However, the constitution of 1824 did not recognize the separation of church and state, rather specifying Catholicism as the state's official religion. Adherents of the constitution of 1824 became known as Federalists or Liberals, destined after almost half a century of bloody struggle to become, under Benito Juárez, the predominant political party of Mexico. Liberalism received its inspiration from the writers of the Age of Enlightenment and the success of representative democracy in the United States. They enviously eyed their neighbor to the north, which enjoyed political freedom and the benefits of laissez-faire economics. Liberals strove to modernize Mexican society by introducing representative government with political reforms that emphasized the equality of all its citizens before the law.

Those opposed to the Liberal philosophy were the Centralists or Conservatives, whose philosophy encompassed Conservative thought. Accustomed to the Royalist rule of Spain and the absolute dictates of a monarch, they preferred a strong central government that would radiate power downward to the states. Centralists thus opposed representative government and advocated a tightly controlled government economy. They believed that the defense of privilege was necessary for the protection of a well-regulated civil society, a tenet that would attract the military, the clergy, and the wealthy landowners to take up the Centralist cause. Centralists would struggle to modify the provisions of the constitution of 1824 by either opting in favor of more central control or simply abrogating its provisions entirely. Centralists would on occasion even invite European monarchy to assume the reins of power in Mexico, as in the case of Maximilian and the French intervention. The differing political philosophies of the Federalists and the Centralists would ultimately erupt into open civil disobedience and armed conflict. The Texas Revolution, the Federalist Wars of Mexico during 1839 and 1840, and nearly all of the many other violent uprisings occurring in Mexico during the nineteenth century could trace their roots to this disagreement in governmental philosophy.[17]

Juan Davis Bradburn, a Centralist who was the military governor of the district in which the questionable land titles were located, was now pitted against the two avowed Federalists, Madero and Carvajal, in a clash of political wills. Bradburn disputed the authority of the Federalist state commissioner, Madero, to issue land titles. The dispute, carried on through a lengthy correspondence between Madero and Bradburn, grew in time to be heated and personal. An angry Madero made the first overt act of disobedience by failing to make a courtesy call on Bradburn as he entered the commander's district on his surveying mission. Bradburn felt that Madero's disregard for protocol was a personal slight not only to him but to the national government. When Madero failed to respond to an ultimatum issued by Bradburn to meet with him on 13 February, Bradburn ordered the arrest of both Madero and Carvajal.

As a justification for his actions against the two Federalist surveyors, Bradburn wrote the memorandum "Memorial of Colonel Juan Davis Bradburn concerning the Events at Anahuac, 1831–1832," stating that "a meeting was set for 9 A.M. the following day, but neither he [Madero] nor his surveyor, Jose Maria Carbajal, appeared, so I considered it advisable to bring them to Anahuac. Carbajal, speaking English, promoted discord and absolute disobedience among the colonists. In my opinion, this was the only certain way to insure tranquility there, and also to protect against an attack on the small military troop under my command." Madero and Carvajal were released after ten days of incarceration and quickly moved to fulfill their commission, while Bradburn remained idle, awaiting further instructions from Mexico City on how to proceed in the dispute. Madero and Carvajal set to work feverishly to survey the lands in question. Madero finally received orders from the Central government to suspend all surveys in Bradburn's district on 12 April, but by that time he and Carvajal had filed sixty completed land titles, and the controversy had become moot. By May 1831, Madero and Carvajal had returned to the state capital in Saltillo to report the incident to state authorities.[18]

The controversy between Madero and Bradburn indicated that Carvajal had by this time cast his lot with the political doctrine of Federalism and had come of age as a surveyor. In addition to his work in East Texas, he made extensive surveys in Central Texas. In the Robertson Colony he surveyed 48,712 acres in present-day McLennan County and 27,836 acres in Robertson County.[19] The flood of surveying contracts José María received were due, in no small measure, to the Mexican government's efforts, throughout the 1820s, to attract Anglo-American settlers to Texas. Each settler with a family was allowed to purchase a league (1,428 acres) and a labor (177 acres) of choice land at a tenth of what this same land would sell for in the United States. In addition, they were exempted from the payment of customs duties for seven years and taxes for ten years in exchange for their oath of citizenship. As Mexican citizens the constitution of 1824 guaranteed most of the civil rights of a U.S. citizen to the new Texas settlers, but they were expected to adopt the Catholic faith, an issue that was never rigorously invoked by the government.

Life was pleasant for the early settlers, and empresario Stephen F. Austin would write to his sister in 1829 that "this is the most liberal and munificent Government on earth to emigrants—after being here one year you will oppose a change even to Uncle Sam."[20] And oppose change is exactly what the settlers did in 1826 when Haden Edwards proposed to carve a

"Fredonian Republic" out of Texas. More than one hundred Texas colonists united with Mexican soldiers to drive Edwards and his small filibuster army out of Texas. But by 1829, on an inspection tour of Texas, General Don Manuel Mier y Terán, reported finding a bifurcated society there, with Anglo-American cultural practices prevalent and only a small minority of Mexican settlers remaining in the country. An illegal flood of Anglo-Americans was pouring across the northern border into Texas, and General Terán warned the government that unless stern measures were taken, Texas would be forever lost to Mexico.[21]

But the Mexican government, perpetually short of funds, did not have resources to send a sufficient number of troops to either stem the tide of illegal aliens or to collect the taxes that were now coming due. Carvajal, returning from a mission for the state government of Coahuila y Tejas to inspect the northern boundary of Texas, reported his findings. From Monclova, on 18 June 1834 in a letter to the state governor, he warned that "fugitives of the north" and the "many foreigners" flooding across the northeastern border of Texas were involved in antigovernment activities and that the presidial troops on this border did not have the manpower and resources to stop these incursions.

The frontier was completely abandoned, according to Carvajal, creating a dangerous situation. In particular, he pointed to "Governor" Samuel Houston and his scheme to move a tribe of warlike Indians into Texas, referring to these Indians as "Crakes," possibly Creeks but they were most likely Cherokees. Carvajal questioned the character of the "foreigner" Houston, whom he described as an "adventurer" and "ambitious." The situation on the northeastern border had always been bad, Carvajal further reported, but now even more so because of inflammatory newspaper articles "disparaging the government." But he reminded the governor of Coahuila y Tejas that there were many good Mexican and Anglo-Americans in Texas who remained as loyal citizens. Unfortunately Carvajal's report was not acted on, and nothing was done to bolster Mexican military presence on the border between East Texas and the United States.[22]

A significant surveying contract for José María came in response to the successful application by a wealthy landowner of tracts both below and above the Rio Bravo del Norte, Martín de León, to form a colony in Texas.

Empresario de León was authorized by the Mexican government to colonize a tract of land centered on the present city of Victoria, Texas. Carvajal,
in exchange for his surveying services, became one of the forty-one original colonists to settle in the newly founded Martín de León grant. Carvajal
laid out the town site of Guadalupe Victoria, named in honor of the first
president of the Republic of Mexico.[23] In Victoria, to this day, the street
bearing the name Calle de los Diez Amigos commemorates José María
Carvajal as one of those "ten friends" who founded the city.[24]

   While completing work on the de León Colony, José María met,
courted, and won the hand of María del Refugia de León Garza, a daughter of Martín de León. But the marriage was complicated by the fact that
Refugia was a Catholic, and her mother, Patricia de la Garza de León,
powerful matriarch of the de León clan, disapproved of her daughter's
union with the Protestant Carvajal. But by the glib powers of persuasion
by which Carvajal had come to be known, he soon swayed Doña Patricia
to his side, and the marriage ceremony took place in 1832. Three sons and
possibly a daughter resulted from this union: Antonio, born in 1833, who
married Cecilia Navarro; and José María Jr., born the next year, who married Mamela Canales, a daughter of General Antonio Canales Rosillo. One
son, Cresenciano, according to the Camargo Church Baptismal Records,
died in that village on 3 January 1846. The daughter, Refugia, mentioned
by only one historian, wed Manuel Quintero, who was a captain in the
Mexican army.[25]

   José María's wedding to María del Refugia de León Garza united him
with one of the most prominent and powerful families in Texas and northern Mexico. Don Martín de León and his wife, who was of the extensive
de la Garza family of Tamaulipas, were wealthy landowners in Texas and
in northern Mexico in the area of Soto La Marina. Carvajal's brothers-in-
law included Fernando, Silvestre, Félix, and Agapito de León as well as José
Miguel Aldrete, Rafael Manchola, and the noted and respected Captain
Plácido Benavides—all prominent in the affairs of colonial Texas.[26]

   The settlers of the de León grant were principally ranchers, raising cattle, horses, and mules. In 1823, Don Martín drove a large herd of horses
and mules from his ranch, near the mouth of the Aransas River, to New
Orleans. This stock drive was arguably one of the first of any size to be

conducted north from Texas, predating the great Texas cattle drives by more than fifty years. With the proceeds of this livestock sale, de León purchased a supply of merchants goods in New Orleans and chartered a ship to return to Texas. The goods were landed near Brazos Santiago at Fronton, an official port of entry into Texas where import duties were levied. The goods were then transported back to the de León ranch, where an eager market awaited the return. The resulting transaction was immensely profitable, causing annual livestock drives that would become an economic backbone of the de León Colony.[27]

In 1832, Austin sent Carvajal as an agent to represent his interests in New Orleans, Louisiana. In a letter to his cousin living in New Orleans, Austin introduced Carvajal: "He is a sprightly, intelligent youth, and his principles are very sound and honorable. His own countrymen call him a Norte Americano. . . . Carbajal is rather enthusiastic, the fault of youth, but you can get some information from him that may amuse you."[28]

Austin had sent Carvajal to conclude some very serious business. In a letter from Nathaniel Cox in New Orleans to Austin, dated 22 March 1832, we read: "Mr. Carbajal is still here but returns in a few days with quite a small venture, having failed in making any collection from Mr. Bowie as contemplated. It affords me great pleasure to find his conduct has been such as to gain your esteem." Carvajal had attempted to collect a debt presumably owed to Austin by the Bowie family. Carvajal had met with Rezin Bowie, brother of the famous duelist. Sources report that James Bowie was away at that time in Texas, exploring the Llano and Colorado rivers.[29] That Austin would send José María on such a mission was a mark of the high esteem he felt for the young man.

Austin was instrumental in using his influence to place José María into many responsible positions of trust. With such a formidable base of support from his many important friends and kinsmen, it is not surprising that Carvajal soon entered the political arena. He gained experience in politics by serving in the civil government at San Felipe in 1831, under Austin's tutelage, and in 1832 served on the Nacogdoches town council. He served as secretary for the *ayuntamiento* (municipal government) of Béxar, selected for this post for his bilingual abilities. In 1835 the twenty-six-year-old surveyor was elected to the important post of deputy to the legislature of Coahuila y Tejas from the municipality of Béxar and was soon to receive his political baptism on the slippery slopes of Mexican national politics.

The political climate had changed in Mexico between 1833 and 1835 from liberal to conservative. During this interim Antonio López de Santa Anna, under the guise of a Liberal, had deposed the Centralist Anastasio Bustamante from power and been elected president of the republic. But fearing the effects of the Liberal reforms on the church and the army, and viewing with alarm the disintegration of Mexican authority in Texas, he moved to seize control of the government of Mexico, terminating the session of the National Congress in May 1834 and by this act renouncing the authority of the constitution of 1824. He is reported to have voiced this opinion of the efficacy of liberalism in Mexico: "It is very true that I threw up my cap for liberty with great ardor, and perfect sincerity, but very soon found the folly of it. A hundred years to come my people will not be fit for liberty. They do not know what it is, unenlightened as they are, and under the influence of a Catholic clergy, a despotism is the proper government for them, but there is no reason why it should not be a wise and virtuous one."[30]

Resistance to Santa Anna's illegal seizure of power was led in the north by the states of Zacatecas and Coahuila y Tejas. The state government of Zacatecas denounced Santa Anna's despotic government and began to raise a militia in defiance, but opposition to Santa Anna was split in Coahuila y Tejas.[31] The Federalist faction of that state had moved the state capital from Saltillo to Monclova, while the Centralist faction remained behind in opposition. The state now attempted to function with two governments and was on the brink of a civil war when President Santa Anna personally intervened to settle the squabble. He approved the relocation of the state capital to Monclova and ordered a December election for governor of the state, replacing the two governors then vying for control. But Santa Anna was suspicious of the Federalist faction in the north and ordered his brother-in-law, Martín Perfecto de Cos, to assume the post of commandant-general of the northeast at Saltillo, to monitor Federalist activities.[32]

For the March 1835 session of the legislature, held at Monclova, Texas elected these deputies to represent their interests: José María Carvajal, from the Department of Béxar; John Durst, from the Department of Nacogdoches; and Stephen F. Austin, from the Department of San Felipe. Austin was being held as a prisoner in Mexico City at this time, but it was anticipated that he would be freed to attend the opening session in Monclova.[33] But this was not to be. Austin, while having been freed from prison in early 1835, was placed on a probation that specified he could not leave Mexico City. He would be sorely missed in the upcoming session, for he was a man of mature judgment, tact, and vast experience in dealing with the government in Mexico City. His counsel would have likely led the state legislature on a more moderate course, avoiding the many clashes with the central government that were to occur during the March session.[34]

Before the session's formal opening, Carvajal was appointed secretary, again because of his proficiency in Spanish and English. One of the first decrees of the legislature authorized José María to publish the laws and decrees of the state government in both Spanish and English for the benefit of its bilingual citizenship. William Barret Travis praised this decision of the legislature to codify its laws, writing: "This Digest when published will be authentic and will have the same force as such works do in the N. States."[35]

On 14 March 1835 the legislative session began. Shortly thereafter, deputies canvassed the December gubernatorial election. The Federalist majority certified Federalists Agustín Viesca and Ramón Múzquiz as governor and vice governor, respectively. Almost immediately the three Centralist deputies from the Department of Saltillo denounced the proceedings in writing and bolted the session, returning to Saltillo.[36] The legislative session now faced its first dilemma: with the loss of the three Saltillo deputies, only seven deputies remained in attendance, fewer than the constitutionally mandated quorum of two-thirds of the body. A motion was then proposed to suspend the rules and continue the legislative session. Deputy Carvajal and two other legislators urged the adoption of the motion, which after much discussion was approved. But the proceedings of the session had already been rendered moot by the departure of the Saltillo delegation, and none of the subsequent legislation enacted during this session was legally binding. Perhaps it would have been wiser to adjourn the session, but several powerful lobbyists had journeyed to

Monclova and were strongly pressuring the deputies to act on their proposals concerning land-speculation ventures. The most prominent lobbyist attending was the Texas land speculator Samuel May Williams, carrying with him a large agenda of business matters to bring before the deputies.[37]

Probably the most disastrous action of this "rump" legislature was passage of the so-called Four Hundred League Law. This act authorized the governor, in order to meet "the present exigencies of the state," to sell up to four hundred leagues (more than 1.5 million acres) of the state's public lands. Article 2 of the act further authorized the governor to regulate the colonization of this land as he thought proper, "without subjection to the provision of the law of the 26th of March of year last past," a provision clearly in violation of the existing national laws on colonization.[38]

The original intent of this law, first proposed by the legislature in the 1834 session, was to place money in the empty state treasury for the creation of a state militia. The militia was critically needed to restrain the many destructive Indian raids then occurring throughout the state at that time. After the seizure of the government by Santa Anna in 1835, a strong state militia might have other uses. The Central government was adamantly opposed to this law, fearing that a standing state militia would be used to oppose the dictatorship of Santa Anna.

The lands offered for sale by the legislature were located in Texas, not Coahuila, a provision of the law that was irately opposed by Texans. But even more infuriating was the manner in which these land sales were consummated. The general public was not given the opportunity to bid on these parcels of public land, and it appeared to Texans that the land sale was the action of legislative "insiders." The swarms of land speculators in attendance at the legislative session descended on the governor with money in hand to purchase portions of this immense tract. Samuel May Williams and Deputy John Durst alone snapped up 124 leagues of the public land, never mind that Durst had acted in a clear conflict of interest, while other speculators bought up the remainder of the 400 leagues.[39]

From Mexico City, Stephen F. Austin wrote, on 15 April 1835, his reaction to the actions of the legislature: "The legislature of Monclova has involved matters in a beautiful tangle by the cursed law authorizing the Govr. to dispose of 400 leagues of land as he pleases. I fear this law will

[cre]ate much more discontent in Texas—nothing could have been more imprudent. . . . If Durst and Carbajal voted for the 400 league law—tell them to remember what kind of constituents they have and be more cautious in the future."[40] Austin later remarked that "the 400 le[ague] law has totally destroyed the moral standing of that legislature with all parties—and the Commandant Genl. [Cos] has gained credit."[41]

Carvajal, writing from Monclova to his cousin Antonio Menchaca in Nacogdoches on 29 April 1835, expressed the frenetic tone of the legislature: "How can you think, that it is possible for me to keep my head straight amid the Babylon of Business. . . . The General Government is fast going to ruin. The Congress has made Santa Anna a dictator, or something like it. Santa Anna is marching against Zacatecas and Zacatecas will defend itself to the last. All that our rulers want is *to abolish the federal system!!* Coahuila and Texas shall never be governed by any other form of government."[42]

Back in Texas, Thomas Jefferson Chambers voiced the opinion of many Texas settlers concerning the sale of the public lands: "I understand that copies of a letter written by Carabajal are circulating . . . in which he states, among other things, that the general government has decreed the confiscation of the lands of the colonists, and their expulsion from the Country, with a view to alarm and excite them to rise against the general government. . . . such statements are utterly groundless and false. . . . The simple facts are these: the administration of the government of this state during the present year, has been of the most shameful character. Poor Viesca was completely hoodwinked and deceived by a few *** whose only object was to use the government for their own private use. A law was obtained for the sale of Four Hundred Leagues of vacant land, and the most shameless acts of speculation were committed against the state and the interests of Texas."[43]

Within two days of the passage of this act, General Cos wrote an angry response, declaring the act to be illegal, for it clearly violated the provisions of the Federal Colonization Law. General Cos then contacted the municipalities in Texas with orders to forbid the location or survey of any of the newly purchased lands.[44] The Central government quickly responded by passage of the Federal Militia Reduction Act of 31 March 1835. The law required that "the local militia in the States, Districts, and Territories shall be reduced to a ratio of one militiaman for each five hundred inhabitants, organized according to the laws governing the matter, distributed for the service at the will of the said states and General Government."[45]

Quickly on the heels of this action came the federal law of 25 April 1835, which invalidated the Four Hundred League Law, arguing that this state act violated the federal law of 18 August 1824. But the state legislature refused to obey the order, claiming that they had already sold the land and received the money. To nullify the contracts would "destroy the public faith" and would be an ex post facto decision.[46] Legal sparring between the Central government and the state of Coahuila y Tejas continued until 20 May 1835, when General Cos lost patience with the legislature. He dispatched troops from Saltillo to Monclova to close the session and put an end to the "squandering" of public lands by a legislature "pandering" to the Anglo-American speculators.[47] With word that troops were approaching, the session was quickly terminated, and the deputies, governor, and speculators fled Monclova as fugitives to avoid arrest.

Simultaneous to the actions of General Cos, Mexican troops entered the state of Zacatecas under the personal command of General Santa Anna to put down the state of open revolt that then existed. After defeating an army of five thousand poorly armed state militia at the battle of Guadalupe on 11 May 1835, the victorious Centralist army was turned loose in the capital city to commit shameful acts of rape, pillage, and slaughter against the civilian population. Monclova did not fare as badly as did the city of Zacatecas, but the state legislature now stood in adjournment, at the point of a bayonet.[48] By the end of June 1835, José María was seen riding into the Texas town of San Felipe de Austin, as a fugitive, "offering land to the dispersed Anglo-American in exchange for military support."[49]

General Cos had issued orders for the arrest of all Federalist legislators that had voted for the four hundred league land sale. But Colonel Domingo de Ugartechea, principal commandant of Coahuila y Tejas, had ordered that José María be released after the fleeing legislator had been detained in Guerrero on 3 June 1835 while en route to Texas. Colonel Ugartechea reversed his decision after a personal interview with Carvajal in San Antonio on 20 June 1835 and issued secret orders to his troops for the arrest of José

María. In a message of 8 August 1835 addressed to the "Chief of the Brazos," Ugartechea ordered "the apprehension of Traves Barret [William Barret Travis] . . . as I have likewise done before about Lorenzo Zavala and other strangers." In an afterthought at the bottom of the order this addendum was scrawled: "You will be pleased to execute it likewise on the persons of Deputy Jose Maria Carvajal and Don Juan Zambrano." Ugartechea dispatched a force of six soldiers to apprehend Carvajal at his home in Guadalupe Victoria. The soldiers soon returned to report that José María was not there but had departed three days earlier with James Bowie.[50]

Another version of this story exists, however, as told by John J. Linn, who related that the Mexican soldiers who came to arrest José María were driven away. The citizens of Guadalupe Victoria had been warned of their approach, and a party of thirty armed men assembled in the four corners of the public square to surround the party of Mexican soldiers. The alcalde of Victoria, Captain Plácido Benavides, José María's brother-in-law, was handed an order from the military to deliver up the body of one José María Carvajal. According to Linn, a resident of a nearby settlement and probably one of the armed citizens, Benavides replied coolly to the Mexican officer that "he could inform Colonel Urgartechea that the body of Carbajal nor the body of any other citizen of Victoria would be delivered into the hands of the military, as he was a constitutional officer, and not at all amenable to the military." The citizens stationed in the corners of the main square then menacingly converged on the Mexican soldiers standing in the center of the plaza, and not wishing to pursue the matter further, the soldiers fled from whence they came without José María.[51]

Through his radical comments and actions against the dictatorial government of General Santa Anna, José María had become associated in the minds of many Texans with the so-called War Party, men who advocated open conflict with Mexico. In a letter of 5 July 1835 from James Kerr to Thomas Jefferson Chambers, some of the leaders of this party in Texas were identified: "[Samuel May] Williams, [Frank W.] Johnson, [José María de Jesús] Carbajal, [James] Bowie, and others are shouting: 'Wolf! Wolf!!, Condemnation!!! Destruction—War,— To Arms!!' . . . [their true aim being] to deceive many persons and make them believe that an army is coming to destroy their property and annul their rights in Texas. Carvajal has fled, headed for San Felipe. When he passed through my neighborhood he was talking very high sounding words of alarm."[52]

An 18 July 1835 letter written by Carvajal, now a fugitive in hiding, was titled "A True Mexican to Johnson, et al." and was addressed to Frank W. Johnson, Moseley Baker, and [name illegible] Givins (possibly Edward Gritten). The letter, which was written in a location characterized by Carvajal as "40 miles from no where," gives insight into the reaction of a Texas Federalist to Santa Anna's dictatorial government: "Every day my hopes for my Country's cause brightens, because the tyrant evinces uniquivocal [sic] evidence of his being intoxicated with his apparent success. . . . The evils he has caused his indulgent country are incalculable, and the Sons of free will have redress—they will be free and 'tis not in the power of man to enslave them . . . 250 men the Battallion [sic] Morelos landed at Copano some days since—they may be in Goliad now—were at the mission some four or 5 days ago. S[an]ta Anna is afraid of Urgartechea because he has always been of the liberal [Federalist] party. Col. Cariaga [Colonel Nicolás Condelle] Comt. of the Morelos is sent to take the Command from him, who with his Battallion [sic] is a blood thirsty black son of a whore!"

Carvajal's letter documents the steps that were being taken by the Central government to reinforce the Mexican military presence in Texas. Colonel Nicolás Condelle, commanding the Morelos Battalion, had just arrived in Texas with additional troops in response to an urgent appeal from Colonel Ugartechea for reinforcements. In a May 1835 report to his superior, General Cos, Colonel Ugartechea stated that he had "scarcely more than a hundred available men" with which to garrison Texas, and he estimated that the Texans could "place a thousand men under arms." These troops were ordered to reinforce the garrison at San Antonio de Béxar. That village would fall on 11 December 1835 to the Texas Colonial Army, but Colonel Condelle, according to Texas historian Alwyn Barr, "led a tenacious defense, arguing against surrender even when there seemed little choice."[53]

Carvajal continued his letter by observing that "we cannot hear a word from Bejar. I cannot understand it. Certainly they intercept everything. Yet we have some hopes that Ugartechea may pronounce with about 100 regulars. . . . Cant [*sic*] hear of the result of your last meeting—hope the people have behaved worthy of themselves. One thing is certain—they may chuse [*sic*] which they have to fight the usurper of his Country's rights, or the Govt they have sworn to obey! If they do not join now in defense of the Constitution and laws, the nation will have ample right to accuse them of the blackest ingratitude, want of principle, and as traitors to the Country of their adoption, and the time has now arrived or soon will when those who are not true and faithful should be well punished. The very existence of the Govt and the dignity of the nation requires it." José María closed the letter with the significant signature "a true Mexican."[54]

He had, by this letter, announced that he did not oppose the true government of Mexico as delineated by the constitution of 1824; rather, he opposed the dictatorial regime of Santa Anna. This feeling was shared by a large portion of the Texan population at this time, as there was little sentiment for independence. The very army of Texan settlers who were to drive General Cos from San Antonio de Béxar referred to themselves simply as "the Colonial Army of Texas" as late as December 1835. Carvajal, like so many other settlers, simply wanted to remain a Mexican citizen, but governed by the principles of the constitution of 1824, not the dictatorial whims of Santa Anna. He, as well as many other Tejanos (Texas Hispanics), would not strongly support the movement for Texas independence declared in the next year.

The issue of independence was divisive in the Hispanic community of Texas, with differences of opinion extending even to members of the same family. This difficult issue divided many political groups in Mexico, even including officers on Santa Anna's staff, such as General José Urrea, a Liberal who would later be one of the leaders of the Federalist revolt in northern Mexico in 1837. But Urrea, as so many others, could not stand by idly and allow his beloved country to be dismembered; he was a Mexican first and a republican reformer second.[55]

By their inaction Carvajal and many other Tejanos would be wrongly accused by many as being enemies of the new Republic of Texas after the culmination of the successful revolution. Independence in Texas marked the onset of acts of discrimination against Texas Hispanics that continue to this day. Carvajal remained active in his protest against the Mexican government. In July 1835 he reportedly captured a courier, bearing letters from General Cos and Colonel Ugartechea. José María then read their inflammatory contents aloud to an excited crowd of Texans at San Felipe.[56] By 1 August 1835 the military district of Coahuila y Tejas had issued arrest warrants for William B. Travis, Samuel M. Williams, R. M. Williamson, Frank W. Johnson, Moseley Baker, and Lorenzo de Zavala. On September 1835, Colonel Ugartechea expanded the list to include John H. Moore, José María Carvajal, Juan Zambrano, and the person or persons "who opened the official correspondence of the Commandancy General and his command." But such local civil political chiefs as Plácido Benavides refused to honor any military warrants.[57]

Before the capture of San Antonio by rebellious Texans in December 1835, Santa Anna had several excuses for sending a larger military force into Texas. He planned to search for and arrest the deputies and land speculators responsible for the Four Hundred League Law and the subsequent land sales and to arrest the citizens listed in the August and September arrest warrants. More important, Santa Anna wanted to collect the "excess" arms that would be available due to the newly passed Militia Reduction Act, a law that served as an excuse for disarming the rebellious Texans.[58]

But after December 1835, with an openly rebellious Texan army in the field, Santa Anna needed no such excuses for military action. He set about preparing an army to enter the rebellious state and drive the traitors from Texas soil. Tumultuous events were now unfolding, and their influence on the life of Carvajal would be profound. As a leader of the revolt against Santa Anna and his Centralist government, Carvajal was poised to offer great services to Texas. His knowledge of the cultures of both the Anglo-American and the Mexican settlers foretold of a major role for him in Texas history. Yet at this point Carvajal appeared to be unable to predict that the revolt was to culminate in a struggle for the separation of Texas from the Republic of Mexico. But neither could the vast majority of other Texans who would soon be engaging Santa Anna's army. Carvajal's decision of where to cast his support would remove him from a possible leadership role in the struggle and relegate him to that of a minor figure, often only a footnote in the pages of history.

TWO

Revolution Comes to Texas

He who claims a home and a habitation in Texas—
must now fight for it, or abandon it, to one who will.

THOMAS JEFFERSON RUSK,
commander of the Republic of Texas Army,
27 June 1836

By October 1835 open revolt had begun in Texas against the government of Antonio López de Santa Anna. Even at this date there was no talk of independence, only the hope by many that Mexican troops sent to Texas would be withdrawn. But to José María Carvajal and the other members of the so-called War Party, this confrontation was the culmination of their plans. They felt that revolution in Texas would be the harbinger of a general uprising in Mexico that would replace Santa Anna with a Liberal government and restore the country's 1824 constitution. At this time not even Carvajal could assess the extent to which Texas settlers, nurtured in the civil freedoms guaranteed by the U.S. Constitution, would react to the despotic measures of Santa Anna. Even the diplomatic senior statesman of Texas, Stephen F. Austin, the perpetual balance wheel in relations between the Texas colonists and the Mexican government, had become embittered by his unjust imprisonment in Mexico City. He could foresee that no further compromise with the Centralist government was possible. Writing to the Committee of Safety in Nacogdoches on 4 October 1835, Austin declared: "War is declared against military despotism. . . . Arms and ammunition are needed; we have more men than guns. Could not some musket be procured from the other side of the Sabine?"[1]

In response to this appeal from his mentor and benefactor, José María became an accomplice in a plot to supply arms for the Texas Colonial Army, soon to take the field against the forces of Santa Anna. Carvajal, his brother-in-law Fernando de León, and the merchant Peter Kerr put into action the time-honored means for raising capital first devised by Don Martín de León. The three men rounded up a herd of horses and mules destined for the New Orleans market. After an overland drive from the De León Colony, the herd reached New Orleans and was sold. Kerr purchased trade goods for the Texas market with his share, but Carvajal and de León bought arms and ammunition with their portion of the profits. Among the arms purchased was a six-pounder and two four-pounder cannons, eighteen kegs of powder, and a variety of small arms and ammunition. Texas historian Victor M. Rose claimed that their purchases included "500 muskets, two pieces of artillery, with a full equipment of ammunition valued at $35,000." The schooner *Hannah Elizabeth* was chartered to smuggle the arms to a clandestine location at the mouth of Garcítas Creek, below Guadalupe Victoria.

In a letter of 4 November 1835, George Fisher, newspaper editor and onetime operator of the custom house at Anahuac, wrote to Stephen F. Austin from New Orleans concerning preparations for war but concluded with a postscript to alert Austin to ongoing events: "P.S. Carbajal, Fernando de Leon and Peter Oar [*sic*], have chartered a vessel, to leave here in a few days for the 'Garcitas' with provisions and merchandize [*sic*], for family use, as they say."[2] On or about 19 November the Mexican warship *Bravo* caught sight of the *Hannah Elizabeth* in Lavaca Bay and, suspecting that the schooner was smuggling goods, set out in pursuit. The *Hannah* was overtaken when it ran aground in the shallow waters near Passo Cavallo, but not before the crew had thrown overboard the entire supply of arms and ammunition. Such actions were justified, as the ship could have been confiscated for transporting the contraband of war and the captain and crew could have been sentenced to death or long terms of incarceration.

The *Bravo* sent a boarding party of twelve men commanded by a Lieutenant Mateo to take control of the prize. They left shortly after boarding, taking several prisoners from the *Hannah*. The next day the Texan privateer *William Robbins* approached and recaptured the remains of the *Hannah*, forcing the remaining members of the *Bravo*'s boarding party to surrender. The *Hannah* had broken up during the night, rolling out its masts from the pounding of the breakers, which had ripped up the deck. Mateo reported to his captors that the *Hannah Elizabeth* had on board fifteen Americans, five Mexicans, and one female passenger.

Among those returned as prisoners to the *Bravo* were Carvajal and de León. Kerr had successfully managed to plead his innocence and had not been arrested by the Mexican boarding party. The arms investment of Carvajal and de León was a total loss for which they were never recompensed by the Republic of Texas. Both men were taken to Brazos Santiago, where they were imprisoned, awaiting a hearing. De León, who was not considered an important prisoner, bribed his guards and made a quick escape. But a prisoner as valuable as Carvajal, with several outstanding warrants, could not purchase his freedom that easily. He was taken from Brazos Santiago to a more secure prison in Matamoros, known as the Casamata.

From there it was decided that Carvajal was to be transported to the castle of San Juan de Ullóa near Veracruz. Realizing that his fate was sealed when he arrived there, Carvajal set out to discover means of escape. On the day of his scheduled transfer to a ship bound for Veracruz, and his likely death by firing squad, José María managed with the help of friends to slip out of the prison. The escape plan was engineered by Carvajal's brother-in-law, Captain Plácido Benavides. In early February, Benavides and a group of volunteers entered Matamoros undetected and made their way to the Casamata. Using de Leòn family gold, Benavides bribed the guards, who released Carvajal. But the escape was soon reported, and a wild chase ensued in which twenty-two of Benavides's men were captured. But the captain and his brother-in-law made good in their escape from Matamoros, returning to Victoria.

Interestingly, the U.S. government claimed credit for the release of all prisoners taken on board the *Bravo*, except for the captain of the *Hannah Elizabeth*, through the efforts of the American consul at Matamoros. This account is unlikely, however, because the Mexican government would not have released as important a prisoner as Carvajal simply as a gesture of goodwill. It was probably a face-saving announcement authored by the Mexican government.[3]

Carvajal returned to his home near Guadalupe Victoria, where by 20 December 1835 some historians claim that he signed the famous Goliad Declaration of Independence. But based on his stated political philosophy, this claim is doubtful. Texas historian Hobart Huson lists the signature as "M. Carbajal," which is likely the signature of Mariano Carvajal, José María's brother. Be that as it may, however, the Goliad Declaration of Independence was a remarkable document predating the Texas Declaration of Independence by several months. Its signers stated that Texas should be a "free, sovereign, and independent State." To those ends, the ninety-one signers, the leading Anglo and Hispanic settlers of the Goliad area, pledged their lives, fortunes, and honor.[4]

It was not long until M. Carvajal's pledge was redeemed with his blood for the cause of Texas independence. He had enlisted as a volunteer in James W. Fannin's command, a member of Captain Samuel Overton Pettus's company, the San Antonio Grays. Mariano's rank as second lieutenant was confirmed by the Washington Convention on 10 March 1836.[5] Texas soldier Philip Dimitt wrote on 15 April 1836 that "the Mexican, Mariano Carbajal, brother-in-law to Edward Gritten, was with my company at the taking of La Bahia on the 9th October last, when he fought with the greatest gallantry and enthusiasm, and has since perished in Col. Fannin's division, having behaved on all occasions like a true soldier in the cause of Texas, and manifested the most sincere and ardent devotion to that of independence." Dimitt's account of Mariano Carvajal was seconded by the eyewitness statements of soldiers Benjamin H. Holland and William Brenan of Fannin's command, who had managed to escape from the Mexican firing squads at Goliad, as well as that of Captain Jack Shackelford, who was spared from the slaughter. They wrote: "This is to certify that the above mentioned Carbajal served with Col. Fannin, and gallantly fought at the battle of Coleto, and was afterward inhumanely and traitorously butchered at Goliad."[6] The debate between those Hispanics advocating independence for Texas and those wishing only to overthrow Santa Anna's illegal government had split even the Carvajal family.

In early 1836, John J. Linn and José Carvajal were elected delegates from Guadalupe Victoria to the convention held at Washington-on-the-Brazos that would ultimately declare Texas to be independent from Mexico. While en route from Victoria to the conference site, Linn and Carvajal received word that a large force of Mexican soldiers were advancing on their homes. They halted in their journey, returning home to evacuate their families. Fresh in their minds must have been the barbaric treatment of women and children by Mexican troops at the city of Zacatecas in the previous year, troops under the direct command of General Santa Anna. Word of Santa Anna's actions at Zacatecas had spread panic in the ranks of civilians throughout Texas. Women and children in the direct path of Santa Anna's army panicked at its approach and crowded the roads leading north, creating an incident in Texas history known as the "runaway scrape."

Neither delegate attended the convention, but it would have been interesting to see how Carvajal would have voted on the resolution for independence, and whether he would have attached his signature to the Declaration of Independence. But such was not to be. Many settlers in Texas began to sense by late 1835 that the uprising then sweeping Texas was not merely a clash between the Centralists and the Federalists; rather, it was a deeper movement for Texas independence from Mexico. Carvajal was a strong Federalist but was also strongly in favor of preserving his native country, Mexico, from partition. He had two options: join the forces of General Santa Anna to quell the Texas Revolution, or remain neutral and not endorse either side. He, as well as many other Hispanics, chose the latter option.[7]

With Texas independence vindicated by the battle of San Jacinto, there began a black period in Texas history during which Hispanics who had remained neutral in the struggle against Mexico were the subject of oppression and discrimination. The instigators of this behavior were Texans who had fought for independence as well as other speculators and opportunists who had flooded into Texas after independence had been won. The de León colonists were no exception: the Benavides, Carvajal, and de León families were soon driven off their lands.

In May 1836 the Republic of Texas Army, commanded by Brigadier General Thomas Jefferson Rusk, was ordered by Secretary of War Mirabeau B. Lamar to "keep your troops in motion, moving in the rear of the enemy, but not approaching near enough to create any collision between the armies." The Texan army shadowed the defeated Mexican army, now commanded by General José Urrea, as it retreated out of Texas under the orders of Santa Anna, who had been captured by the Texans at San Jacinto. The Republic of Texas Army, then at a strength of 350 men, halted its advance to the south at Guadalupe Victoria on 17 June 1836. At this village Rusk received the disturbing word that the Mexican Congress had decided to continue the war against Texas, and General Urrea, chosen to lead the next expedition into Texas, was at Matamoros with the Mexican army. From Victoria, Rusk expressed the plight of the infant republic by writing to his fellow citizens on 27 June 1836: "He who claims a home and a habitation in Texas—must now fight for it, or abandon it, to one who will."[8]

It was at the height of this war hysteria that Rusk wrote from Victoria to Captain Dimitt on 22 June 1836: "I understand that some of the Mexican families near the point are pretending that they have no order to remove. A special order was issued to the Citizens of this place and a general order to all the Citizens to remove east instantly. I have sent down the De Leon [and] Carabajal familys and have sent men with them to see that they meet on Board the vessels. I shall detach more to day and send at least the men on board with directions to report themselves to the Cabinet for their dispositions. I shall leave Cavalry here and in advance and have directed them expressly to see my order as to the removal of the families and such Strictly complied with as you will be near the vessels and the Steam Boat when they arrive I will thank you to render what assistance may be in your power in getting them all on board & off."[9]

The Mexican threat of invasion never materialized, but great harm had been done. The Carvajal, Benavides, and de León families had been driven from their lands, and squatters soon descended on the de León grant to occupy their vacated lands. These proud people no longer had a home in their native country, Mexico, and were treated as aliens in the newly formed Republic of Texas. The only reason found for driving these families from their homes was offered on 20 July 1836, written in Velasco: "Gen. Rusk has ordered the Mexican families on the Guadalupe, and La Baca, and those who were likely to afford information to the enemy to retire upon the Rio Grande, or take themselves off to the Colorado. Carbajal De Leon and some others, intend making a summer sojourn in

New-Orleans. Health to them!"[10] It is of interest to note that by this date the de León and Carvajal families were referred to as "Mexicans," whose loyalty to the Republic of Texas was suspect.

Historian Anna C. Castillo Crimm reported that the de León family departed from their homes with fifteen mule loads of goods bound for Matagorda. At this village they embarked for New Orleans aboard the *C. P. Williams* in June 1836. The ship's manifest listed seventy passengers, including Patricia De León and the remainder of her children and their families. Also included were José María Carvajal and his family, the three brothers of Plácido Benavides and their families, as well as nine other families.[11]

The stay in Louisiana was grim for this group of penniless expatriates. Their only means of income was fine sewing by the women of the group and manual labor by the men. In 1837, Plácido Benavides died in the village of Opelousas, Louisiana, of unknown causes. On 17 February 1838 one Joseph M. Carvajal appeared before the court at Opelousas, St. Landry Parish, to issue a power of attorney to his old friend and mentor, Littleberry Hawkins, an attorney residing in the Austin Colony. He specifically charged Hawkins with collecting "all sums of money debts demands and papers belonging to me" from the persons of James M. Morris and Thomas W. Mather, both of Austin's Colony. The state of poverty of the Carvajal family had no doubt triggered this action. Carvajal's success in collecting these debts is unknown.[12]

The Carvajal, de León, and Benavides families remained in Louisiana for about three years, then took up residence in Soto la Marina, Tamaulipas, the childhood home of Patricia de la Garza de León, the widow of Martin de León. An embittered José María renounced any claim to citizenship in the Republic of Texas and steadfastly pronounced himself thereafter to be only "a true Mexican."[13]

In 1843, Silvestre de León returned to his ranch near Victoria to begin the long battle to reclaim his family's lands. The populace around Victoria had changed drastically during his enforced absence. Men of desperate character roamed the country, and squatters occupied the de León properties. This peaceful land had been turned over to the outlaws, claim jumpers, and rustlers. Silvestre de León was murdered this same year by the infamous Mabry B. "Mustang" Gray, when he attempted to halt Gray and his gang in the act of rustling de León cattle. Mustang Gray was never punished for these crimes and many others that he committed against the peoples of northern Mexico and South Texas.[14] Yet de León's death did not halt the family's struggle to regain their lands. The details of their many court battles to evict those unrightfully possessing their lands are found in an interesting account by Castillo Crimm.

THREE

The Federalist Wars of Northern Mexico, 1839–1840

This day about 18 or 20 were killed—no Mexicans being injured, none having joined in the fight except Zapata and Carbahal [sic], who both behaved exceedingly well, the latter having an arm broken in the charge.

MAJOR RICHARD ROMAN,
describing the battle of Alcantro, 3 October 1839

The disastrous loss of Texas had driven Antonio López de Santa Anna into retirement at his hacienda Manga de Clavo, but the Centralist regime he had earlier placed in power continued to rule. Discontent swept Mexico; Mexicans blamed the Centralists for policies that contributed to the loss of Texas and distrusted the government of Anastasio Bustamante, Santa Anna's surrogate. Their major desire was for a return to the Federalist system of representative government and the constitution of 1824. Unrest became revolution and uncoordinated revolts broke out in the Yucatán and the southern states that spread throughout Mexico to the northern states, finally resulting in a general civil war. The northern states of Tamaulipas, Nuevo León, and Coahuila, far away from the seat of government in Mexico City, had received little support or sympathy from the Central government on how to control the devastating Indian raids that plagued their region. Requests for more soldiers to guard the frontier were unanswered, and when troops were sent, they were of the presidial variety, content to assume defensive positions behind the walls of villages but unaccustomed to offensive action and the fatigue of long and dusty cavalry patrols. The people of the north (*norteños*), weary of the government's unfulfilled promises, vied to emulate the successful struggle of their Texan neighbors and took up arms to oppose their government. Some norteños even went so far as to express the desire that some day their region of Mexico might be united with Texas in a North Mexico Republic.

The Federalist Revolution, also known as the Federalist Wars in northern Mexico, commenced in 1837 and represents a complex piece in the pattern that formed the broad history of the Federalist uprisings in Mexico from 1837 to 1841. I shall remain within the scope of this book, however, and confine the discussion only to that part of the revolt in northern Mexico associated with José María Carvajal. The leader of this revolt was the charismatic Antonio Canales Rosillo, an attorney from Monterey.[1] The Federalist Wars marked the beginning of a stormy relationship between Antonio Canales Rosillo and José Carvajal that would end only with the death of Canales Rosillo around 1852.

The Carvajal and Canales families were closely intertwined. José María named one of his sons Antonio, in honor of the Federalist leader, and upon the death of Canales Rosillo, Carvajal took one of Canales Rosillo's sons, Servando, to be raised as a member of his own family. Servando warmly respected his surrogate father and would later risk his own political future to save José María's life during a coup. José María Carvajal Jr. was to wed Mamela Canales, a daughter of Canales Rosillo. But the two powerful border leaders and friends were not to remain as political allies. By 1852 they would be leading armies against each other in a battle outside the village of Camargo, just south of the Rio Grande. Angry that Canales Rosillo would oppose him and the ideals for which he was fighting, José María would later refer to Antonio Canales in a speech as that "faithless traitor."[2] The possible causes of the split between these two powerful northern Mexico *caudillos* (leaders or chiefs) is detailed in a later chapter.

On 5 November 1838, Antonio Canales Rosillo, issued a *pronunciamiento* (pronouncement) in Guerrero, Tamaulipas, against the Centralist puppet government of Bustamante, controlled by Santa Anna. In his statement of defiance against the government Canales Rosillo raised the familiar cry for the restoration of the constitution of 1824. By the end of that same month the states of northern Mexico were in revolt, and José María Carvajal was one of the many Mexicans who took up arms for Canales Rosillo and the

Federalist cause. By virtue of his bilingual and bicultural background, Carvajal was appointed chief of staff of the Federalist army, at the rank of lieutenant colonel. Fluency in both English and Spanish was a critical necessity for the cause. Diplomatic correspondence and good public relations with the Republic of Texas government were of primary importance, as the northern Federalists hoped to lure Texans into the conflict on their side. Carvajal had a wide circle of friends and acquaintances among Texas leaders and could correspond with many on a first-name basis. Many Anglo-Americans filled the ranks of the Federalist army, and the necessity of issuing cogent orders in both languages was critical for the proper execution of marching and battle orders. Carvajal was the obvious choice for this assignment.

Commanding the cavalry of Canales Rosillo's Federalist army was that noble horseman of southern Texas and northern Mexico, Antonio Zapata. Zapata resided in Revilla, now the ghost town of Guerrero Viejo, partly covered by the waters of Falcon Lake. In a time of peace Zapata was respected by all as an honest businessman in his dealings as a stockman and rancher. In times of unrest Zapata, proclaimed as one of the greatest horsemen of the border, was truly fearless in the defense of his region against marauding bands of Indians and outlaws. Simply said, Antonio Zapata was a man who never turned his back on either a friend or an enemy. His betrayal and death was one of the tragic losses to northern Mexico from the Federalist Wars.[3]

Fighting soon began, and the Centralist troops that garrisoned the principal Mexican towns along the Rio Grande were, by a series of military actions, driven from their posts. This disorganized remnant of Centralist troops was ordered to concentrate at Matamoros for the defense of that city. Federalist troops moved eastward along the Rio Grande in pursuit of the fleeing Centralists, eventually moving into positions surrounding Matamoros. But the Federalist army lacked the sinews of war, food, ammunition, and, most important, cannons needed to force their way past the barricades blocking the streets of Matamoros. Because of the army's weakened condition, Canales Rosillo could do no more than ring the city with his troops and lay siege, hoping to starve out the defenders. The Centralist defenders of Matamoros were also plagued by shortages, as the eastern coast of Mexico was blockaded at this time by the French naval fleet. France had declared war on Mexico for its failure to pay debts owed to French citizens in a comic-opera affair that came to be known as the Pastry War. The Central government of Mexico could do little to relieve the siege surrounding Matamoros or to supply its defenders, as they momentarily expected a French land invasion aimed at Mexico City.

While the siege of Matamoros continued, Canales Rosillo wrote to Mirabeau B. Lamar, now president of the Republic of Texas, requesting aid for his cause from Texas. But Lamar wisely refused to commit Texas resources and enforced a policy of neutrality for the republic. The cessation of hostilities between Mexico and France occurred on 7 April 1839 with a peace treaty that guaranteed an accelerated repayment of Mexican debts. Ultimately, the Pastry War had no lasting effects either on France or Mexico, with one possible exception: the political rebirth of Santa Anna. Eager to return to the forefront of Mexican politics, Santa Anna saw an opportunity in this latest Mexican struggle. He emerged from retirement and organized a Mexican army that he led against the French at Veracruz. During a brief clash there Santa Anna lost a leg to a French cannonball but partially restored his military reputation with the Mexican people to its pre–San Jacinto luster as a military hero.

Centralist armies, now freed from the need to protect Mexico City from the French, marched north to relieve the encirclement of Matamoros. General Canales Rosillo, despite the protests of his officers and men, ordered the Federalist army into retreat. The timorous behavior of Canales Rosillo, which some observers characterized as outright cowardice, had created a rift in the Federalist forces. With dissention among the ranks, low morale, and a lack of supplies and arms, the rebellion in the north began to crumble by fall of 1839.[4] The remnants of a disorganized and dispirited Federalist army were driven northward across the Rio Grande and set up headquarters at Lipantitlán, on the Nueces River, then claimed by Mexico as their northern boundary. From there General Canales Rosillo, Carvajal, and northern Mexican Federalist Carlos Lazo set out on a diplomatic mission to obtain aid for their cause from the Republic of Texas. Accompanied by an armed guard, these three men visited San Antonio in August 1839.

Officials of the Republic of Texas, anxious not to become involved in the hostilities, granted the party "personal protection" but offered no diplomatic status. Carvajal, a well-known figure in San Antonio, persuaded Luciano Navarro, his brother-in-law, to write a letter of introduction to President Lamar, and the party journeyed to Austin for an interview with the president. Lamar remained adamant in his refusal to commit any resources to the rebellion, offering only political asylum and an open policy of trade with the Federalists, but no efforts were made to restrict the recruitment of volunteers from Texas for the Federalist army. Emotional speeches by Canales Rosillo, ably translated into English by Carvajal, and like efforts by the many Federalist sympathizers in Texas soon caused Texans to volunteer for service in the Federalist army. Recruitment was aided by an economic stagnation created in Texas as a consequence of the Panic of 1837 in the United States. Promises of money and land persuaded many penurious young Texans to enter into the ranks of the Federalist army.

The new Federalist army assembled on the Nueces River in August 1839 and organized into two divisions, under the overall command of Canales Rosillo. One division consisted of Mexicans and the other was manned by 226 Texans, under the command of Reuben Ross and Richard Roman. This latter division was staffed by such prominent Texas fighting men as John T. Price, Henry Ryals, and Ewen Cameron. The Mexican division, totaling 900 men, contained a regiment of infantry under Colonel Luís Lopez and two cavalry units commanded by Colonels José María Gonzáles and Antonio Zapata. Colonel José María Carvajal remained as chief of staff.[5]

The new Federalist army crossed the Rio Grande below Guerrero on 30 September 1839 and by 3 October had clashed with the Centralist army, led by Colonel Francisco Gonzáles Pavón. The battle—known as the battle of the Álamo, or the battle of the Alcantro (el Cántaro)—was fought about twelve miles southwest of Mier, in a rough hilly country. Pavón had posted his soldiers on the crown of a hill, while the Texan division had been ordered to occupy a ravine known locally as Alto Limpio at the base of this hill. From the heights Pavón pounded the Texans with his artillery, which consisted of one long nine-pounder, two six-pounders, and a seven-inch howitzer. The bombardment continued for four hours while Canales

Rosillo and the inactive Mexican division stood by idly, out of range of Pavón's cannons. As no fire was returned from the chaparral-covered ravine, Pavón unwisely assumed that most of the Texans had been slain by his artillery barrage. He ordered the Centralist infantry to advance down the hill and attack the Texans hiding in the ravine.

Centralist soldiers were well within rifle range when they discovered that the Texans had placed themselves behind the many boulders dotting the ravine and had taken no casualties from the many cannon balls and shells that had whizzed through their ranks. But it was too late for the Centralists to profit from this knowledge; at a prearranged signal, Cameron rose up from behind a boulder and shot the Mexican Centralist drummer leading the advance. Texans poured a murderous fire into the ranks of the Centralists, and the Federalist Mexican division was then ordered to attack Pavón's exposed right flank. The attack was a half-hearted affair, "without making an impression," seeking a position of safety behind the Texas division.[6]

The Centralists fell back to regroup and charged a second time with equally unfavorable results. Pavón recalled his troops back a second time to the safety of his artillery and renewed the bombardment of the Texas division, which had been ordered to retain its former position in the ravine. Colonel Ross then informed General Canales Rosillo that he could not hold this position much longer, as Pavón's artillery had now accurately targeted the Texans, and requested some diversionary movement to reduce the pressure. But the Mexican division remained inactive and did not respond to Ross's request. The Centralist army, sensing a victory, launched a third all-out attack to overrun the Texas positions. Even at this critical time Canales Rosillo refused to order up the Mexican division, which stood idly by as "Canales sounded his horn and galloped about in the chaparals about ½ mile from the enemy."[7]

Carvajal and Zapata, angered and humiliated by the cowardice of their leader, organized about twenty-five men to advance to the Texans' aid. In this resulting action, José María was severely wounded by a musket ball that broke his left arm and resulted in its permanent paralysis. For the remainder of his life, he would suspend his left arm from a colorful sling made from a silk cloth bandana that encircled his neck. A participant in the battle, Major Richard Roman, wrote this report: "Antonio Canales force consisted of 300 men, ¾ of which were Carese [Carrizo] Indians, armed with Lances badly constructed—Jos M. Carabajal was with him as counselor &C, having no command. . . . This day about 18 or 20 were killed—no Mexicans being injured, none having joined in the fight except Zapata and Carbahal, who both behaved exceedingly well, the latter having an arm broken in the charge."[8]

The Centralist attack failed: a well-aimed Texan musket ball killed the officer leading the attack, throwing the Centralist forces into confusion. The Texans then poured out of the ravine in a daring counterattack on the Centralists and were there joined by Canales Rosillo and the Mexican division. By nightfall the two armies disengaged, but by the next morning Pavón's forces, surrounded and suffering from lack of water, surrendered to the Federalists. Despite this signal victory, the small Federalist army, low on ammunition and supplies and lacking cannons, were no match for the more massive Centralist forces closing in on them from the south. After a failure again to capture Matamoros on December 1839, coupled with their defeat north of Monterey in early January 1840, the remains of a disheartened Federalist army were driven across the Rio Grande a second time on 7 January 1840.

Shortly thereafter, Canales Rosillo, unable to gain military supremacy on the Centralists, opened a political struggle to separate the states of northern Mexico from the Central government. He organized a meeting in Laredo, Texas, with delegates from the northern states with the intent to form the so-called Republic of the Rio Grande. The republic was to consist of the Mexican states of Tamaulipas, Nuevo León, Coahuila, and that disputed portion of territory north of the Rio Grande, south of the Nueces River, and east of the Medina River known as the Nueces Strip.

Delegates from these states selected northern Mexican Federalist Jesús Cárdenas as president, Francisco Vidaurri y Villasenor as vice president, and Antonio Canales Rosillo as commander in chief of the army. A general council was constituted, consisting of representatives from each state, with Canales, Carvajal, and Juan Pablo Anaya designated as supplementary members; José María was designated as secretary.[9] The capital of the new republic was located at Guerrero, Tamaulipas, (present-day Guerrero Viejo is now a deserted town partly covered by the waters of Falcon Lake), where the new administration and its army relocated. But the government of the new republic and its small army were soon driven from Guerrero by a Centralist army, commanded by Mariano Arista, and by March 1840 had returned to their former camp on the Nueces River.

On 8 April 1840, President Cárdenas appointed Carvajal to represent the Republic of the Rio Grande in Austin. A delegation led by Cárdenas, Canales Rosillo, and Carvajal then commenced a second visit to Texas, in a fresh attempt to solicit diplomatic recognition from the Republic of Texas and recruit supplies and volunteers for the impoverished Federalist army.[10] Canales visited Austin and had an interview with the president of the Republic of Texas, but a cordial Lamar again refused to intervene in a struggle he rightly considered to be a Mexican civil war.

In a letter of 27 July 1840, Carvajal expressed his own cordial feelings to President Lamar: "Your [Lamar's] talents and good fortune permit me to say, Sir, have now placed you in a situation to immortalize your name beyond the reach of envious and vindicative [*sic*] enemies, of ensuring at little cost the prosperity and happiness of the Country over which you preside, and of making to yourself millions of admiring and grateful friends in Mexico and all over [the] country at least as many friends as in Texas."[11] The diplomatic and flattering tone of this letter indicates that Carvajal had by now developed the ambassadorial skills worthy of a government leader.

Cárdenas was warmly received at Victoria, Texas, but some Texans remained suspicious of Federalist motives. George W. Hockley, who had served as chief of staff of the Texas army during the Texas Revolution, wrote a word of warning about the visit: "Genls Canales & Carbajal have been and still are a curse to our country. They are a primary cause of our late mutinies at Béxar, now fortunately quelled and their agents doubtless still at work. They should have been allowed time to recruit their horses, and leave the Republic. They are Mexicans and they are enemies. Time will show that I am right. The fact is now being developed."[12]

A delegation led by Canales and Carvajal left Austin on 2 May 1840 and stopped en route to Houston at Bastrop, Texas. A ball was given there to honor the occasion, and Canales Rosillo addressed the crowd in Spanish. He expressed appreciation to the people of Texas for their hospitality and further stated: "We are fighting for liberty, both civil and religious, the principles of which are the same everywhere; we are now following the footsteps of Texas, and wish to establish a government of our own independent of Mexico, and modeled after your own." His remarks were translated by José María, whose English was characterized by a spectator as "fluent and being free from any offensive idiom or provincialism in accent or expression."[13]

The recruiting efforts of Cárdenas, Canales Rosillo, and Carvajal in Texas were very effective. Men abandoned their civil pursuits, and even the soldiers of the Texas army began to desert their posts to take up arms for the Republic of the Rio Grande in response to the Federalist promise of money and land. President Lamar, on 14 March 1840, issued a stern proclamation warning of the penalty for desertion from the army but otherwise took no further steps to curb recruiting efforts. A newspaper editor, skeptical of the motives of Canales Rosillo and his cohorts, wrote: "Many young men are leaving Houston and Galveston for the Federal Army, they had better stay at home. It is a humbug—To call the Federalists patriots and maintain that they are fighting in a holy cause."[14]

By early 1840 a new Federalist army had assembled at Lipantitlán, near the Nueces River, to advance again on northern Mexico. The army consisted of about two hundred Texans commanded by Juan N. Seguin and Samuel W. Jordan, about three hundred Mexican rancheros, and about eighty Carrizo Indians. Whether Carvajal was with the Federalist army at this time is unknown; the wounded veteran of the earlier Federalist Wars could have been serving in Texas in some diplomatic capacity.

At this time Antonio Zapata was betrayed and murdered. The Federalist army had moved up the Rio Grande above Laredo and was then camped at San Fernando de las Rosas. The leader of the Centralist army in the north, General Mariano Arista, had received word of the Federalist presence in that region and had put his army on the road, bearing down on the unwary Federalists. To obtain some knowledge of Centralist troop movements, Canales Rosillo had ordered Zapata on a scout to the little town of Morelos, west of San Fernando. Zapata reached Morelos on the evening of 13 March 1840 with a company of about twenty-five men. The town was sympathetic to the Centralist cause, however, and immediately dispatched a messenger to General Arista, notifying him of Zapata's presence. By return message Arista requested that town officials attempt to detain Zapata and his men until Arista could dispatch his cavalry to Morelos.

The next morning, as Zapata was making preparation to return to San Fernando, town officials approached him with overtures of friendship, asking that he remain for a day with them, as they were about to kill a beef for a celebration in his honor. Zapata, unsuspecting of treachery, agreed to spend the day, allowing his mounts to be cared for by the citizens. The Centralist cavalry, under Colonel Reyes, soon reached Morelos and joined up with the citizens to attack Zapata and his men, who were now afoot. Zapata and his men rushed into a building, where they were surrounded. They fought against the unequal odds until their ammunition was exhausted and they were forced to surrender. Zapata stepped from the building and surrendered, breaking his sword over his knee. Zapata's command had suffered seven dead, including young Bud Edmondson, who was engaged to Zapata's daughter.

Arista arrived in Morelos the next day and offered Zapata his life if he would lay down his arms and refuse to cooperate any further with the Federalists. Zapata refused the offer and is reported to have said: "Shoot me, then, for I will never lay down my arms until the rights of my people are redressed." The noble Zapata was marched before a firing squad, and one of his men imprisoned nearby reported: "We could hear the roar of the guns that ended the life of one of the bravest of Mexico's soldiers." Arista then ordered Zapata's body decapitated. The head was placed in a cask of brandy and taken by armed guard to the towns along the Rio Grande and exhibited as an example of what revolutionaries should expect from the Central government. The head was publicly exhibited in Laredo and other towns, finally ending up in the town he had lived in: Guerrero. There the gruesome sight was mounted on a pole and remained for viewing near his home, in sight of Zapata's wife and children, for three days.[15]

The full story of the last disastrous campaign of the Federalists in northern Mexico can be found, for example, in *After San Jacinto: The Texas-Mexican Frontier, 1836–1841,* by historian John Milton Nance. It is also important to mention the betrayal of the Texan Auxiliary Division at

Saltillo by Federalists Juan Molano, General Canales Rosillo's brother-in-law, and Luis López. Those Texans that survived the disastrous trap at Saltillo hated Canales Rosillo and swore vengeance for the death of their comrades, threatening to kill Canales Rosillo on sight.[16] A strong Centralist army had driven the Federalists from northern Mexico for a third time, and the dispirited commander of the Federalist army, Canales Rosillo, abandoned the dreams of many for an independent republic in northern Mexico as well as the dreams of his struggling army to make an accommodation with the Centralists. He signed an armistice and amnesty agreement with General Mariano Arista commanding the Centralist Army of the North on 7 November 1840, and with that the Republic of the Rio Grande passed into oblivion.[17]

FOUR

The Mexican-American War in Northern Mexico

Oh! General! Must we after so many sacrifices for the honor of our country, suffer such outrages from vile and infamous cowards? I therefore ask you to certify publicly, if I and my squadron act under your orders and instructions.

COLONEL JOSÉ MARÍA CARVAJAL,
commanding a brigade of irregulars, to General José Urrea,
Independente, San Luis Potosí, 31 July 1847

With the collapse of the dream for an independent northern Mexico, José María Carvajal availed himself of the amnesty agreement to return to peaceful pursuits. But he still considered himself a strong Federalist and bided his time for the next opportunity to pronounce against the Centralists governing Mexico. He settled in Camargo, Tamaulipas, returning to his civilian trade of surveying and the teaching of literature in the local school "to survive."[1] For the next four or five years of his turbulent life, Carvajal seemed to find some peace and domestic tranquility. But by 1845 another dark cloud loomed on the horizon that would affect the future of Mexico: the prospect for annexation of the Republic of Texas to the United States.

Since the formation of the republic in 1836, Mexicans retained the hope that some day Texas would be returned to Mexico, either by force or diplomacy. To Mexicans, seething with anger over the dispossession of their northern territory, the Republic of Texas was an illegitimate government without even a well-defined boundary. The State of Tamaulipas, south of Texas, claimed the Nueces River as its northern boundary, while the Republic of Texas claimed the Rio Grande as its southern limit, leaving the strip of land between these two rivers, known as the Nueces Strip, in disputed ownership. In the decade between the battles of San Jacinto and Palo Alto, the opening shots of the Mexican-American War, this territory became a no-man's-land that saw armies from Mexico and the Republic of Texas cross and recross in what historian John Milton Nance has referred to as a period of attack and counterattack.

With no established governing authority, the Nueces Strip became the home for the dregs of both societies: murderers, thieves, rustlers, and freebooters who had escaped there to avoid the strictures of a civilized society. Meanwhile, the United States avidly eyed Texas as another in its series of land acquisitions that would define its modern-day boundaries and fulfill the prophesy of Manifest Destiny. After a hard-fought battle in the U.S. Congress, President John Tyler, in his waning days in office in 1845, signed a bill to annex Texas to the United States. The reaction in Mexico was swift: diplomatic relations with the United States were severed and the Mexican government angrily pronounced the annexation of Texas as an act of war. Annexation had served final notice on Mexico that the country had forever lost its Texas lands. Tyler's successor, James K. Polk, adamantly supported the addition of Texas to the Union, and has been viewed by many historians as eager to use the conflicting claims over the ownership of the Nueces Strip as an excuse to provoke Mexico into war.

The actions of the United States presented several troubling aspects to José María. In a 20 April 1845 letter to Valentín Gómez Farías, the former president of Mexico, Carvajal expressed these concerns:

> Permit me to express my opinion about the addition of Texas to the United States. . . . I have listened to a Mexican that expresses the opinion that since the states of Texas and Coahuila were originally confederated as one, that this territory by law was added to our neighbors to the North; grand mistake! The original boundaries for Texas to the south were the Nueces and Medina Rivers, by the west the meridian of Mexico a little more, 99 longitude west of London or 22 degrees of Washington, through the North with the Red river and through the East to the Louisiana gulf. This will only give them up to 34 degrees 20 minutes North latitude, up to the Arkansas river.

But Carvajal knew that a precise boundary of Texas did not exist at that time and thought the United States might take advantage of the ambiguity: "Even if we give a literal meaning, they [the United States] wish to usurp double or quadruple the territory of Texas. You know by the Texas Constitution, the line of the South extends a mile to the South of the Rio Grande and by the West there is no limit." He felt that the true motive of the United States was to claim that "the Texas boundaries would run from the South on a line parallel to the Rio Grande till 29 degrees North latitude extending West till the Pacific Ocean. This Ocean is the Occidental boundary, and through the east is the Mexican Gulf."

José María predicted a war between the United States and Mexico over the boundaries of Texas, prophesying many of the actual tactics that would later be used:

> The American primary plans were already exposed up to now, and the second one [plan] was the following: take on positions immediately and if Mexico is against it, which it is natural and just, to send an army of 60000 men for that line, In the West they will fortify on those towns and the army will depend on them taking gold and silver from the churches and national facilities for their subsistence. The [U.S.] army will fortify all the ports from both sides from East to the West coast. For this purpose, competent armies will be sent. The army who arrives first in this invasion of Veracruz will have the objective to capture Mexico City. Then, they will force the Mexicans to sign an agreement and give up everything.

Finally, Carvajal predicted that Mexico would vigorously defend its territory and would hope to secure the aid of Great Britain in a possible blockade of U.S. ports.[2]

Would Carvajal and the Federalists of northern Mexico now support the official government of Mexico in their struggle against the United States? The answer depended on whether the United States would recognize the Federalist Party, now dormant, and give them some control over northern Mexico. By fall 1845 the American Army of Occupation had been ordered to establish a base of operations near Corpus Christi, Texas, to assert U.S. claims to the Nueces Strip. Late 1845 found the government of Mexico in its chronic state of instability. In early January 1845 the

Mexican Congress deposed Santa Anna from the presidency of the republic, and his legal successor, José Joaquín de Herrera, assumed the vacant office. Although initially popular with the people, Herrera attempted unsuccessfully to walk the tightrope between his Liberal and Conservative constituencies. On 29 December 1845, Herrera was deposed in a coup led by General Mariano Paredes y Arrillaga, who represented a coalition of the clergy, the military, and the Conservative factions. Paredes represented everything the Federalists were opposed to; an environment grew in Mexico that was ripe for revolution by the Liberals.

On 29 January 1846, General Zachary Taylor, commanding the Army of Occupation, then camped near Corpus Christi, received a remarkable communication from the Federalist leader, General Antonio Canales Rosillo, who styled himself as "military commandant of the frontier": "You will doubtless have heard of the Conspiracy of General Paredes and his Army, against the constituted authorities and laws of his Country: and that he has so far consummated his criminal plans, as to enter the City of Mexico by means of Treachery, dissolving our National Congress & deposing the President Herrera: while by a Court Martial he constitutes himself President of our Republic, and daringly and falsely he pretends to act for & with the consent of the nation." Canales stated his determination either to overthrow the unconstitutional government of General Paredes, or "these Northern States will separate forever from Mexico." Canales then asked Taylor for a meeting between them "or my agent, Mr. J.M.J. Carvajal." According to Canales, "Northern States generally are so wearied of the eternal commotions of the Interior, that it is not difficult to foresee the division of our Country into two or three Republics, provided a foreign invasion do not prevent it." So that Taylor would recognize Canales's military power, the latter general closed his communication by assuring the American leader that "I am in command of all the really fighting men among the citizens and Militia, and some few regulars."[3]

José María Carvajal had included with the letter orders to open verbal negotiations immediately with General Taylor. The discussions appeared to have been amicable, but Taylor requested that Carvajal submit a written memorandum of his "views and suggestions in relation to the matters with which he was charged by Genl. Canales." Carvajal produced a lengthy memorandum whose purpose was to prevent the interruption of "friendly relations" that had existed in the past between the two countries. From the context of this and the previous message from Canales, it is not clear which country Carvajal represented in these meetings. The Mexican army, which Carvajal identified as the army of General Paredes, might "commit hostilities" on the U.S. Army, but this Mexican army did not represent the people of Mexico and its actions were not sanctioned.

To prevent any such attack, Carvajal requested that the United States aid the forces of General Canales with the arms and supplies necessary to outfit three thousand men "until Paredes' force be put down." In particular, Carvajal requested "five thousand Harpers Ferry Yagers, old Fabric: one thousand pairs Pistols of same, large Belt: ten thousand U. States muskets accutered [sic], and a sufficient supply of ammunition. We also want money to support our forces without oppressing the people, so as to make them feel the advantage of our Policy over that of Paredes." In return, Carvajal pledged the Canales government to sustain U.S. claims to Texas, leaving the settlement of the boundary question as an item for negotiation with the newly formed government. Repayment of the proposed military loan could be funded by the proceeds of the customs houses or by an adjustment of the boundary between the two countries.

In the event of some unforeseen military crisis, Carvajal asked for the right to recruit "one or two thousand volunteers" from the United States but discouraged the establishment of any permanent U.S. Army military bases on the "Rio Bravo del Norte." Carvajal felt that a permanent presence by the U.S. Army, "without some previous understanding, may produce unhappy results, which would defeat entirely the philanthropic [sic] and Patriotic views that induced him [Carvajal] to undertake the present Agency. Should the Rio Nueces be now Provisionally adopted as the Boundary, or the present station continued if desired, (without permitting these lands to the south to be surveyed or located); and should the U.S. be determined not to give up her claim to the Del Norte, Mr. Carvajal believes the line might be extended so far in future (without forcing matters) in an amicable way, provided some patience is exercised, and after our People become better acquainted with the Laws and Govt of the U. States. An immediate contact without some understanding, might be ruinous to our hopes."[4]

Canales Rosillo and Carvajal had attempted to take advantage of the hostile environment that now existed between the United States and Mexico to push for the Federalist agenda: the creation of an independent Federalist state in northern Mexico, a resurrection of the old dream of the Republic of the Rio Grande. A careful analysis of the wording indicates that in exchange for armaments, supplies, money, and the opportunity to recruit volunteers in the United States for the Federalist army, the two credential-less diplomats had offered nothing in return but a tenuous promise of "friendship" with the United States and further asked that the status quo remain in effect between the United States and Mexico: no U.S. Army troops in the Nueces Strip. But what diplomatic credentials did Carvajal carry, other than the authorization of the leaders of a defeated Federalist rebellion? Any agreement he might sign with the United States would have no backing from any recognized government in Mexico, be it Federalist or Centralist.

With the unpredictable and volatile nature of Mexican politics, it was quite likely that if the United States furnished aid to the Federalists in northern Mexico, these guns might later be turned on Taylor's forces in an attempt to establish Federalist control over the Nueces Strip. The Canales / Carvajal correspondence must have appeared as treasonous to the Polk administration in Washington, D.C., which was unfamiliar with the convoluted nature of Mexican politics.

Taylor, a bit puzzled by these extraordinary communications from Canales and Carvajal, bundled up both letters and sent them off to Washington, D.C., for instructions on how to further proceed. A reply was received, dated 2 March 1846, from Secretary of War William L. Marcy: "In case of war between this country and Mexico we should be ready to avail ourselves of all the advantages which could be fairly derived from Mexicans disaffected to their rulers—and considering the manner in which these rulers have risen to power, it would not be a matter of surprise [*sic*] if this disaffection should be extensive and of a character to embarrass the Mexican Government in carrying on hostilies [*sic*] with the United States." Marcy was puzzled that Taylor had offered no assessment as to the character or position of Canales but in any event concluded that the government could not furnish any aid to Mexican Federalists: "It is not authorized to furnish arms or money to those Mexicans who may be disposed to resist the domination of Paredes." However, Marcy told Taylor, that in the event that "any considerable number of Mexicans should retire across that river [the Rio Grande] and be willing to enter into the service of the United States, you are authorized to receive them as volunteers."[5]

By the date this letter was received, however, the matter was moot. Taylor's forces had already advanced south of the Nueces River, the southern boundary of Texas as stipulated by Federalists, to the Rio Grande and were preparing fortifications opposite Matamoros. With the eve of the opening battles of the Mexican-American War at hand, Carvajal and the Federalist forces were presented with unpalatable alternatives as to whom their loyalties were due. To align themselves with the hated *norteamericanos,* whose goal was to dismember Mexico anew, would be an unforgivable act of treason against their native land. Their other alternative was to support the despised Centralist government, and after the termination of hostilities with the United States, the internecine struggle between the Federalists and the Centralists as to who would rule Mexico could be resumed. Thus it was, against his own best political instincts, that Carvajal aligned himself with the Centralist government in Mexico City to oppose U.S. forces.

During the Mexican War, from 1846 to 1848, José María Carvajal was reported to have commanded a brigade of irregular troops in northeastern Mexico, probably centered around the area of Soto La Marina, his earlier residence. Carvajal's troops carried on a guerrilla war against General Taylor's forces, which had captured and occupied the major cities and villages of this region. But try as they may, American forces could not pacify the countryside where the irregulars commanded by Canales and Carvajal repeatedly attacked small outposts and harassed American supply columns.

Carvajal's home by this time was located near Camargo at the little village of Villanueva, now an interesting ghost town. In 1846 the Rio San Juan had flooded the village of Camargo, located near the confluence of that river and the Rio Grande, destroying most of the adobe buildings. Many of the villagers relocated to a higher elevation, southwest of Camargo on the left bank of the Rio San Juan. José María, using his skills as a surveyor, laid out the site of "New Camargo," locating it on a prominence about three miles from the present town. For laying out the site, Carvajal was given seven choice lots in the town site for the construction of his palatial home, which is discussed in more detail later in this chapter.

The occupation of Camargo by rowdy American troops in July 1846 hastened the relocation of many Camargoites to the new town site. One American officer visiting Villanueva on 28 August 1846 wrote that "I entered a house in which there were a man and a woman. I noticed that they were unusually reserved, particularly as it appeared to be the house of an American, for in one corner was a surveyor's compass, and on the table a case of surveyor's instruments and several English books. There were also two or three very white and intelligent looking children in the house. I asked the boy his name and he said it was 'Antonio Carbajal.' He was the son of the notorious Carbajal."[6]

The Camargo Church Baptism Records lists the death of the child Cresenciano Caravajal on 3 January 1846, "the son of Jose Maria Caravajal." But Carvajal spent little time in Camargo, then occupied by American forces, during the war years. As a Federalist, he had correctly offered his services to the Tamaulipas state government rather than the national government, becoming an officer in the Tamaulipas state militia at the rank of colonel, serving again under the command of his old friend and comrade-in-arms, General Antonio Canales Rosillo.

As a member of Canales's irregular state forces, it is possible that Carvajal participated in the battle of Palo Alto, on 8 May 1846, but no documentation exists to support this claim. In fact, little documentation at all now exists of Carvajal's military career during the Mexican-American War. Constantly on the run to escape pursuing American forces in a covert hit-and-run guerrilla campaign, Carvajal could little afford to have his communications intercepted. Basically, Carvajal led a group of partisans who controlled the roads of northeastern Mexico. Their primary function was to attack small groups of military forces, supply trains, and merchants traveling the roads. Wagon and pack mule trains laden with military supplies for the American forces stationed at Monterey and Saltillo were captured by Carvajal's forces, and these supplies became the staples used to sustain the guerrilla army. The surplus supplies, as well as the mules and burros, were sold to the Mexican civilian population, and the wagons burned.

Merchant caravans from American-occupied Matamoros laden with such commercial goods as calico cloth and tobacco were also seized by Carvajal, and the merchants were required to pay a "Mexican tariff"—a euphemism for tribute. If the merchant could not produce the often exorbitant asking prices, Carvajal's forces simply kept the goods for resale to a Mexican population eager for foreign merchandise. By these means, funds were raised to underwrite the Mexican war effort.

American military patrols scoured the countryside searching for the guerrilla forces of Canales and Carvajal, forcing these Mexican irregulars to be eternally on the move. Their constant movement and the requirement of absolute secrecy for their plans made it difficult to document their activities. Reports on Carvajal's irregulars were limited to the often biased newspaper articles written by American reporters, appearing principally in the *American Flag* of Matamoros, Mexico, the organ of U.S. merchants living in occupied Matamoros, or reports by correspondents writing from northern Mexico to the *New Orleans Picayune*. These reports give us some idea about Carvajal's efforts to oppose the American army during the Mexican-American War.

An item of 4 July 1846 indicated that a Mr. De Gray, an American merchant traveling from Chihuahua to San Antonio, Texas, was given a passport by Carvajal to travel the roads of northern Mexico without molestation.[7] A typical passport issued by Carvajal to an American traveler in northern Mexico was found in the *American Flag* of 24 July 1846: "The bearer of this is Mr. Rodgers of this place, a highly respectable man, as I am informed— going on to the Rio Grande, with his two sons, for commercial purposes. As you are not at war with private individuals who have no connection with the U. States Army, I trust should you meet him, in consideration of the kindness and protection which my friends and yours have always shown your countrymen here, you will permit him to pass freely without hinderance [sic] or molestation." *American Flag* editor I. N. Fleeson complimented Carvajal by noting that "there is no doubt, had he [Rodgers] fallen in with any of Canales' party this would have been a sufficient passport for him, as Carvajal is known to possess great control over these troops, besides being a gentleman who would pay every respect to the requests of this letter."[8]

In early February 1847 an American correspondent to the *Picayune* reported on an encounter with Carvajal's forces. A mule train of about five hundred animals, laden with supplies for the American army garrison at Monterey, was stampeded during the night by a guerrilla force. Guerrilla forces captured eighty-two mules but were pursued by American military forces, which tracked the stolen animals to the village of China. Americans entered the town from two directions to trap any guerrillas lingering there. The correspondent reported: "In China they came near grabbing the famous Carvajal, one of the moving spirits of all these depredations. He was sitting in the house with the priest—they had just returned from mass—when Morgan and his party came into sight, and the sentinel on the tower no doubt communicated the fact to him, and he vamo[o]sed."[9]

By 1847 the guerrilla war in northern Mexico had turned into a series of violent raids by both sides with no one considered as a neutral and in which no quarter was neither asked for nor given. On 24 February a combined force of Mexican cavalry and guerrillas attacked a U.S. Army wagon train moving southward from Cerralvo, burned the wagons, and massacred forty to fifty U.S. teamsters. Revenge was soon in coming. Leading a mob of "Texas rangers, teamsters, and other persons," the infamous Mabry B. "Mustang" Gray attacked the Rancho Guadalupe, near Ramos, in early March 1847, murdering twenty-four unarmed civilians. A shocked General Taylor attempted to determine the perpetrators of the crime but was met by a wall of silence from his soldiers. "I could not possibly ascertain what individuals were concerned in this atrocious massacre," Taylor wrote, yet the identities of the culprits were common knowledge to all the men in the ranks.[10]

A communication from General Canales to his adjutant expressed anger for this wanton act as well as a guarantee of reprisals to be subsequently taken against all Americans found in northern Mexico: "I learn, with the greatest indignation, that the Americans have committed a most horrible massacre at the rancho of the Guadalupe. They made prisoners, in their own houses and by the side of their families, twenty-five peaceable men and immediately shot them . . . there is no other course left us than retaliation. . . . you will immediately declare martial law, with the understanding that eight days after the publication of the same every individual who has not taken up arms (being capable of so doing) shall be considered a traitor and instantly shot. Martial law being in force, you are bound to give no quarters to any American whom you may meet or who may present himself to you, even though he be without arms."[11]

By 19 May 1847 the war in northern Mexico had created an environment in which there were no civilians. Fleeson reported in the *American Flag* that the roads out of Matamoros were blocked by Carvajal's guerrilla band: "Carabajal [*sic*] still keeps himself in our vicinity—his camp is about sixty miles from here, on the San Fernando road. The force under his command is small—not exceeding fifty men—but sufficient to plunder all trading parties coming in or out from Matamoros. We once thought Carabajal a gentleman and above such petty plundering, and right sorry are we to find him at the head of a dastardly band of robbers. His education and talents fit him for a higher station, and (knowing that he reads the *Flag*) we appeal to him to cast himself loose from his present evil associates and seek a more elevated position. If he does not, we expect to hear of his being elevated to the topmost branch of the tallest tree between here and San Fernando."[12]

Newspapers reported Carvajal's irregulars to be at many different locations in northern Mexico, often at the same time, no doubt a credit to the mobility of his band and the fog created by the secret nature of his movements. At about the same time as he was reported near San Fernando, the *Monterey Pioneer*, a newspaper published in that city, reported Carvajal's forces as "still lurking" about the city of Cadereyta, near Monterey, at the head of a hundred men. The guerrilla force was robbing travelers and traveling merchants on the road and selling the plunder at a store in the vicinity.[13]

But the old dream of an independent republic comprising the northern states of the Republic of Mexico still fired the imagination of some Mexican leaders. Rumors were being circulated along the border that influential Mexicans were at this time engaged in a project to proclaim the independence of Tamaulipas. Some sources reported that an influential Mexican from that state had arrived in Matamoros to confer with the American commandant of that garrison to learn what cooperation could be garnered from American forces for the movement. It is probable that this "influential Mexican" was none other than José María Carvajal.

The rumors of Mexican citizens seeking independence had some factual basis, however. On 28 November 1846, President James K. Polk reported in his diary the reception of a letter of 23 November authored by one Aelaria [*sic*] de Masa, M.D., a Mexican citizen residing in Tamaulipas, who stated that the inhabitants of the "Northern Provinces" of Mexico wished to establish an independent republic. De Masa asked President Polk to guarantee that the United States would not annex this region of northern Mexico, and that the contemplated republic would be protected and defended by the United States as long as the war continued. Polk found the guarantee too binding on the part of the United States, which might receive this territory as a part of the indemnities of a peace settlement, and further questioned de Masa's authority to negotiate such a plan without any credentials or letters of introduction from his countrymen.[14]

By 26 June 1847, Fleeson added fuel to the fire by reporting "positive information" in the *American Flag* that eight days earlier Carvajal had been in Ciudad Victoria, Tamaulipas, conferring with influential men of that city to determine the destiny of several states of northern Mexico. Fleeson reported that the conference was "no more nor less, than a separation from the Mexican confederacy and the establishment of an independent government. Carrabajal [*sic*] has been alive to this subject for years, and will let pass no opportunity to accomplish his cherished purpose—now, he thinks, is the proper time, and as we know him to be a man of enlarged views, talent and energy, there is great prospect of his success."[15] Reports of plots for independence among Mexican leaders would surface on several occasions during the course of the war. More details on these movements and the covert support they received from American adventurers is found in Chapter 5.

But Carvajal remained careful not to relax his struggle against the American occupation of northern Mexico. On 10 July 1847 the *American Flag* reported a "rumor that had been afloat" that Carvajal's forces had or were about to sack the village of San Fernando, Tamaulipas. The city's inhabitants were reported to have been "too friendly to the Americans," and Carvajal's punitive actions were to be taken to correct this policy.[16]

By July 1847 the war had begun to wreak havoc on the weak economy of the Republic of Mexico. Each state was required to generate funds for the continued war effort, and a large contribution was assessed to Tamaulipas. General José Urrea and a force of Mexican regulars were sent to Victoria, the state capital, to collect funds at the point of a bayonet, if necessary. In turn, Carvajal was pressured to increase the revenues taken from travelers on state roads; he was reported moving all over the country, "here one day, there the next," fleecing the travelers on the roads, "even to their shirts."[17]

A party of travelers captured by Carvajal's forces near San Carlos, Tamaulipas, on 3 July 1847, included Ernest Montilly, a Frenchman, and American Elias B. Lundy. The Frenchman was robbed but was reported to have been treated well by the guerrillas. But Lundy, who was also robbed, was said to have been treated harshly because he was an American.[18] The report proved to be false, however, and in a letter sent from Soto La Marina on 4 July by Montilly and Lundy, they stated that they had been captured by Carvajal, "who had treated them with great kindness, and assured them they would be released upon proper evidence being furnished that they were not in the employ of the United States government." The two travelers were to be held until an order was received from General Urrea, then at Tula, for their release.[19]

Carvajal continued to prosecute the guerrilla war in northern Mexico. By 28 July 1847 the *American Flag* reported Carvajal's force, now consisting of about 250 men, were located at Rancho La Vacaria some twenty-five leagues from Matamoros on the road to Linares. At this site they are said to have captured trains of pack mules laden with corn, soap, sugar, and other products destined for Matamoros. The guerrillas had likewise captured a hundred *cargas* of goods (a *carga* is about 5.15 bushels) destined for Monterey from that city. "They [Carvajal's forces] appear determined to spare neither friends or foes, but confiscate all they can intercept as fair booty."[20] The captured booty, belonging to a Mr. Tarniver of Matamoros, was principally tobacco valued at twenty-five thousand dollars.[21]

At the village of China, located in the center of Carvajal's territory, a sign boasting of defiance to American occupation was found posted on a local door:

BUSTS MADE HERE

The proprietors recently were on a Bust and busted up a whole group near Papagallos. This placed them in possession of a fresh stock and latest fashions from Paris. All orders thankfully received, promptly attended to, neatly executed and cash taken for work done at this office. The unfinished mouth and nose of Gen. Taylor compose part of our present stock. God and Liberty.

Conales [sic], Caravahal [sic] & Co.[22]

Carvajal continued his secret movements throughout northern Mexico and was reported on 4 September 1847 to be near Soto La Marina.[23] Attacks on Mexican merchant trains in Tamaulipas by Canales and Carvajal attracted the attention of the state government, which published a proclamation denouncing the two guerrilla chieftains. Again, editor Fleeson: "The acting Governor of Tamaulipas had issued a Bando [edict] denouncing Carbajal, Canales . . . as a set of highway robbers, who, in collecting duties and confiscating the property of Mexican citizens engaged in traffic with the Americans, were acting without authority from either the General or State Governments. . . . The Governor . . . called upon all good citizens of the State to resist their illegal demands and assist in breaking up the robber gangs. Thus authorized by the Governor, the Traders have armed themselves, bid defiance . . . and are now bringing their produce to market and returning with their purchases without fear of molestation."[24]

An angry Carvajal responded in the 18 August 1847 issue of the *Independente* of San Luis Potosí with an open letter to the State Congress questioning the legitimacy of two members of the Tamaulipas state government: "Jose Maria J. Carbajal, a citizen of Tamaulipas respectively [sic] asks for the correction of a grave infraction of the fundamental code, as it involves the nullity of all acts of the executive power now wielded by incompetent persons. I refer to Francisco Vital Fernandez, and Jose Ildefonso Castillo, the present Governor and Secretary of State of Tamaulipas." Carvajal pointed out an article of the State Constitution of Tamaulipas forbidding anyone serving in the military from being governor of the state, and a second article requiring a minimum residency in the state of three years for any office holder. These articles needed to apply to the current incumbents, in particular: "Sr. Fernandez is in the military service of the government, and since the 11th or 12th of November, 1846. Sr. Castillo is a foreigner, and has resided in Tamaulipas, only since September, 1845. . . . This state of things ought not to exist, and you will please to declare the nullity of the nominations, and of the acts of Srs. Fernandez and Castillo. In doing this you will show your respect for the fundamental code."[25]

Colonel Carvajal also corresponded with his commanding officer, General José Urrea, on 31 July 1847, to express his exasperation with the appointed public officials of Tamaulipas:

> It is impossible to pass over in silence, any longer, the calumnies pub-lished in the official periodical of the city of Victoria, against the defend-ers of the frontier.
>
> They show the spirit of Governor Fernandez. No man can fight against the Americans, without being called a rascal, robber, worthless scamp, or the companion of savage Indians. The citizens of Tamaulipas know very well (and the Governor knows it also) that we are patriots, and men of honor, with ample authority from your excellencies, to per-secute the enemy . . . but Governor Fernandez has endeavored to make it generally believed that we are without authority, and that the people ought to regard and persecute us as robbers.
>
> Oh! General! Must we, after so many sacrifices for the honor of our country, suffer such outrages from vile and infamous cowards? I there-fore ask you to certify publicly, if I and my squadron act under your orders and instructions.[26]

Urrea wrote a response to Carvajal's public letter, published in the same issue of the *Independente*: "I have seen the article to which you refer in your note of 31st July, and perceive clearly that it is intended to exasperate the public mind against the servants of the nation. I beg you to repose in the testimony of your conscience, of your general, and of the public, who see clearly that the acts of you and your brave riflemen are very different from those attributed to you by those infamous scribblers."[27] But by this date the war in northern Mexico had ground completely to a halt. General John Ellis Wool, now commanding the U.S. Army forces in northern Mexico, had taken special efforts to control the activities of Mexican irregular militia. All supply trains were now furnished with large military escorts, and Wool issued a special order that levied fines on those municipalities supporting guerrilla forces.

The war in central Mexico would also cease by 14 September 1847, with the American occupation of Mexico City. General Winfield Scott, who had landed American forces at Veracruz on 9 March 1847, advanced on the national highway from there toward Mexico City. After a series of battles the principal city of Mexico had been captured. The politicians and diplomats now labored to create a peace. The Treaty of Guadalupe Hidalgo, the result of their efforts, was ratified by the U.S. Congress on 30 May 1848, and the war between Mexico and the United States was over. In return for fifteen million dollars and U.S. assumption of all claims by its citizens against Mexico, the Mexican government ceded lands that would eventually become the states of California, Nevada, Utah, most of New Mexico and Arizona, and part of Colorado and Wyoming.

José María returned to Camargo at the end of the Mexican-American War to resume his civilian life in a depopulated countryside that had been devastated by the war. Civilians had fled from their haciendas and villages into the mountains to avoid the wrath of the combatants. Mexican guerrilla forces demanding provisions from the rural populace could not be refused, lest they kill the owner for treason and burn his dwelling to the ground. U.S. forces, hearing that this same owner had supplied the guerrillas with provisions, would accuse the owner of being a guerrilla and likewise burn his dwelling. One traveler from Monterey to Camargo in 1847 described the road as "dotted with the skeletons of men and animals. Roofless and ruined ranchos, and many a dark and smouldering [*sic*] heap of ashes, told the disasters."[28]

Carvajal continued in his Federalist beliefs, but from the condition of the war-weary populace and the wrecked state of the economy of northern Mexico, he knew that it would be impossible to mount another revolution at this time. Carvajal and the other Federalist leaders sensed that they would need to bide their time and suffer the Centralist government then in power. But he continued to be a party to the development of further plans to form an independent republic in northern Mexico. He was, almost certainly, involved in some manner with the plans of the "Buffalo Hunters" and the "Ousel Owls," which are discussed in Chapter 5.

Immediately after his return to Camargo, Carvajal began the construction of a lavish home in Villanueva, which would come to be known as Carvajal's Castle. Remembering that he had written to Gómez Farías in 1845 that he was working as a surveyor and literature teacher, "to survive," one must wonder at the source of his newfound wealth. Perhaps not all of the "tariffs" he had charged trade caravans during the war had reached the coffers of the state treasury.

Construction on this residence was probably begun in 1848, and the resulting efforts created the largest and most ornate structure then located along the Rio Grande. The palatial home was constructed in Villanueva on the seven lots Carvajal had received for surveying the town site. From the front a large portico was seen, supported by great stone columns that caused the mansion to resemble the type of plantation house seen in the American South. Quite likely Carvajal's design was inspired by the plantations he saw in Kentucky when he visited there as a student. Ernesto Garza Sáenz, the *cronista* (historian) of Camargo, offered a more detailed description:

> Carvajal constructed his building using local materials. The foundation was not deep, because the base was situated over a quarry. He used bricks for the walls and mortar of lime and sand. The columns were more than a meter in thickness, constructed of special bricks in the form of wedges. The roofs were of concrete, supported by big pine beams brought from New York.
>
> The floors were constructed of a concrete made from gravel mixed with lime and sand, a mixture known locally as *tipichil*. The rooms upstairs were reached by indoor staircases and were spacious, being lit by imported candelabras. The tax rolls of 1852 listed this mansion as worth six thousand pesos, by far the most costly domicile in the entire region.[29]

With the completion of his "castle," Carvajal christened it in a grand style. Anna Kelsey, early day resident of Rio Grande City and Camargo, described Carvajal's home as "a two-story tesselated palace," attended the christening and reported that "the occasion was the blessing of the home. . . . Streamers of ribbon were attached to the chandelier and extended to the four corners of the room, where the sponsors stood holding the ends of the ribbons. The priest sprinkled holy water in each corner of the room and said a prayer. After the ceremony of blessing at the home there was dancing until midnight when a delicious banquet was served."[30] One writer remembered that "the palace proper was on top of the hill and overlooked the beautiful San Juan River, beyond which the towers and spires of Camargo's churches sparkled in the morning sunlight."[31]

But the politics of northern Mexico would soon reach down from Monterey to affect the tranquil domestic scene now enjoyed by José María and his family. Don Santiago Vidaurri, the so-called Lion of the North, was busy in 1855 extending his rule over northeastern Mexico. Vidaurri, with the aid of his brilliant military commander, Juan Zuázua, conspired to seize the state government of Nuevo León. The current governor of that state, General Jerónimo Cárdona, seemed powerless to stop the Vidaurri-led revolution. Monterey was captured by 23 May 1855, and from there Vidaurri declared himself governor and military commander shortly thereafter. He proved to be an efficient administrator but was not satisfied with his new domain and set out to form his own version of the Republic of the Rio Grande. Vidaurri soon moved to extend his political and military power over the northern states of Coahuila, Tamaulipas, and San Luis Potosí. Almost immediately after Vidaurri's seizure of Nuevo León, Colonel Zuázua began recruiting a large standing army loyal to Vidaurri. On 25 May 1855, Vidaurri proclaimed the Plan de Monterey a new constitution for Nuevo León. This document was reminiscent of the Mexican Constitution of 1824, with strong states' rights provisions.

After defeat of the Coahuilan state forces by Zuázua's army in July 1855, that state accepted Vidaurri's constitution, and his dominance. The army was then turned against Tamaulipas, defeating troops of that state under the command of General Adrián Woll. Tamaulipas was also forced to accept the Plan de Monterey. But the cost of keeping a large and well-supplied army in the field was draining the resources of Nuevo León. The state's poor people were neither accustomed to nor able to pay taxes; the source of funds for the Nuevo León state army usually came from the customs receipts of the border crossings, money that was supposed to be appropriated for use by the Central government. The port of entry at Piedras Négras furnished a large amount of funds for Vidaurri's army, especially with Vidaurri offering merchants "discounts" for entering goods through that port. But Vidaurri's large standing army needed more funds than Piedras Négras could supply. He turned to Tamaulipas for the needed funds, pressuring the ports of Camargo, Mier, and Matamoros for a larger portion of their customs duty receipts. All of these cities responded by enlarged tribute payments to Vidaurri except Camargo, which stubbornly refused to yield to his threats.[32]

In mid-October 1856 an army under the command of General Martín Zayas was sent to Camargo by Vidaurri to take over the customs house. The city's defenders, led by Colonel Don Guadalupe García, put up a spirited defense for fifteen days, highlighted by the extensive use of artillery by both forces. Zayas was driven from Camargo by 1 November 1856 but not before doing extensive damage to the Villanueva de Camargo. A prominent target for Vidaurri's artillery was the famous "castle" of Carvajal. Carvajal, the outspoken Federalist, must surely have been a critic of the tyrannical tendencies of the self-proclaimed Liberal Santiago Vidaurri. His criticisms of Vidaurri and his refusal to accept the extension of Vidaurri's power into Tamaulipas was probably an important reason for Camargo's failure to allow Vidaurri to loot the Camargo customs house receipts. Thus it was that Carvajal's castle became a target of revenge, and the beautiful edifice was razed by Zayas's artillery attacks during the two-week battle.

The ruins of the castle, prominently located at the crown of a hill by the road entering Villanueva de Camargo, now presented a forlorn sight to travelers, one of whom composed this short poem:

RUINS OF CARVAJAL

Of all the houses that he builded
Yon ruin stands alone.
There a heavy silence: gaunt weeds
Through windows pry.
And down the vale at Carvajal
Old echos, wailing die
—*Unknown poet*[33]

Carvajal would express an intense hatred for Vidaurri during the remainder of his life, both for political and personal reasons. But according to Garza Sáenz, José María would later gain the supreme revenge on his adversary (this is detailed in Chapter 10). The castle was never rebuilt, and after Carvajal's death his heirs sold the ruins for salvage. Only two columns remained until 1929, when they also were taken from the site.[34]

By 1855, Carvajal and his family were living in exile in Piedras Négras, across the Rio Grande from Eagle Pass, Texas, and did not participate in the defense of Camargo from the forces of Vidaurri. The reason for this change in residence is unknown, but it is suspected that his filibustering activities in Tamaulipas during 1851 and 1852 had made him subject to arrest in that state. In October 1855 a gang of adventurers led by Texas Ranger James Hugh Callahan invaded Piedras Négras from across the Rio Grande, claiming to be in hot pursuit of a war party of Indians.[35] The invaders were in fact slave hunters, hoping to recover the many fugitives from Texas who had claimed refuge in Mexico. The invaders were met with an attack from a large party of Seminole Indians south of Piedras Négras that drove the Callahan party back into that city. To cover their retreat across the Rio Grande to sanctuary in the United States, the gang torched Piedras Négras. Carvajal now ironically became a victim of filibuster violence, as his residence was burned to the ground in the resulting fire.

José María filed a claim for damages against the U.S. government in which he stated that he was a citizen of Mexico, his house had been burned, and he and his family had been forced to flee to the woods. They "wandered three days exposed to death under the tomahawk of the barbarous Indians." He claimed damages that totaled $21,792, which were disallowed by a U.S. government reparations commission convened to investigate the claims of Mexican citizens for the damages created by Callahan and his men.[36] Carvajal's fortunes had now reached the lowest point of his life, with no home, no possessions, and in the leadership of a defeated Mexican political movement that lay in ruins. But a better day was soon dawning for this remarkable idealist and his dream for an independent northern Mexican Republic governed by the principles of liberalism.

FIVE

The Texas-Mexico Border
in the Mid-Nineteenth Century

I believe that more men of desperate character, desperate
fortunes, and evil propensities, were congregated here on
this frontier from 1846 to 1848 than ever got together in
any other place.

WILLIAM A. NEALE,
Brownsville, Texas, as quoted in Chatfield 1876
on the occasion of the U.S. centennial

The armed incursions into Mexico from Texas by José María Carvajal and
his followers that came to be known as the Merchants War were the direct
result of several problems that had plagued South Texas for many years.
For a deeper understanding of the causes for the Merchants War and more
generally of life in South Texas and northern Mexico in the mid-nineteenth
century, it is important to examine these issues in some detail.

The Treaty of Guadalupe Hidalgo, adopted by the United States and the
Republic of Mexico on 4 July 1848, formally ended the war between these
two countries. The problem of Indian incursions from the new territories
of the United States into Mexico was addressed in the first paragraph of
Article 11 of this treaty. The United States pledged to control the "savage
tribes" residing in its newly acquired territory of Texas. As such, Indian
raiding parties launched from Texas into Mexico were to be "forcibly
restrained," and if the raids could not be prevented, the raiders would be
punished the same as if such raids had been committed against U.S. citizens.

Such a guarantee by the U.S. government was insisted upon as a condition for peace by the legislatures of those northern Mexican states that

would border the new boundaries of the United States. Nicolas Trist, a clerk in the U.S. Department of State who headed the peace negotiations with the Mexican government, anticipated resistance in the U.S. Congress to this article, but after spirited debate, this portion of the treaty was approved. Secretary of State James Buchanan, in a letter to the Mexican minister of relations, assured him that the United States had "both the ability and the will to restrain the Indians within the extended limits of the United States from making incursions into Mexican territories."[1]

But the government in Washington, D.C., had failed to understand the magnitude of their commitment to Mexico. The Rio Grande wound for more than a thousand miles as a boundary between Mexico and Texas, through a vast wasteland populated north of the river by nomadic tribes of Plains Indians. The Comanche, Lipan, and Kiowa tribes living in this new region of the United States were warlike hunters accustomed to raiding the more populated areas of northern Mexico on forays to steal cattle and horses, to kidnap women and children, and to murder the peaceful farmers and ranchers residing in that area. These raids occurred frequently along a well-defined trail from north of the Rio Grande into Mexico. The Horsehead Crossing on the Pecos River was so named because the many Indian raiding parties returning from Mexico would tarry there to prepare their favorite food, horseflesh. Pacifying the Indian population residing in Texas would not be a trivial task. The number of Indian inhabitants in Texas in 1850 varied from a low estimate of twenty thousand to as high as thirty thousand.[2]

Initial plans by the U.S. government for the protection of Texan and Mexican citizens called for the erection of a chain of forts extending across Texas. These forts, forming a part of the 8th Military District, were visited by Lieutenant Colonel William G. Freeman on an inspection tour in 1853. His findings provide a good picture of the problems the U.S. Army faced in Texas.[3] From a detailed breakdown of the Freeman report, several conclusions are apparent. The 1,997 troops assigned to Texas constituted a third of the total personnel of the U.S. Army. Only 553 (28 percent) were mounted troops, elements of either the Regiment of Mounted Rifles, or the 2nd Dragoons. The 1,444 remaining were companies from the 4th Regiment of Artillery, or the 1st, 3rd, 5th, 7th, or 8th Regiments of Infantry.

The typical military company Freeman found in Texas was staffed at about half strength. But infantry and artillery troops were essentially useless: it was a maxim of the Texas frontier that "a soldier afoot in Texas is no soldier at all." The soldiers stationed on the Texas border from the mouth of the Rio Grande to Eagle Pass, Texas, were mostly afoot. The U.S. Army had stationed 355 unmounted men and 155 mounted men to patrol this three-hundred-mile stretch of an uninhabited shallow river boundary that could be crossed almost anywhere. These few troopers would be ordered to confront a formidable foe. Comanche and Lipan warriors were practically born on horseback, and when riding in a raiding party, they arguably formed the finest light cavalry in the world.

In a letter to the editor of the *New Orleans Picayune*, a citizen of the Rio Grande Valley wrote: "But what, Messrs. Editors, does our Government mean by sending no dragoons to the Rio Grande? What can a few companies of infantry and artillery . . . do in repressing . . . depredations on the other side? . . . Without dragoons . . . men will not be able to travel in safety."[4] The arrival of mounted soldiers to protect the citizens of South Texas was eagerly anticipated in a letter to the *Corpus Christi Star*: "It is rumored that Capt. E. Deas' company of Artillery . . . will be relieved by two companies of the 2d Dragoons. We are highly gratified to hear of this order on account of the necessity for mounted forces."[5] But the editor put matters more bluntly: "Telegraphic dispatches from Washington, of the 3d instant, state that the President has ordered some more troops to the Rio Grande. We sincerely trust that no more infantry will be stationed on this line."[6]

Enterprising garrison commanders set out to acquire mounts and train their infantry soldiers to ride. The 7th Infantry, stationed at Rio Grande City, listed at least one of its companies as "mounted." John S. Ford described the lack of competency of such troops in his memoirs:

> It was rather an unfortunate experiment to mount infantry soldiers, many of whom had never been on a horse in their lives, to operate against the best horsemen in the United States—the Comanche. Yet the United States Army tried it. . . . One day news came to Fort Duncan, near Eagle Pass, that a party of Indians was on the Rio Grande about twenty miles below. Lieutenant Brewerton was sent out very promptly, at the head of a detachment of mounted infantry, to find and chastise the

savages. He moved at a good pace. After having marched eight or ten miles, he passed a deep ravine. The lieutenant halted to verify. He found all the horses in their proper places, but about nine of the men were missing. A squad was sent back to the ravine; they found the bold riders right where they had tumbled from their horses."[7]

Unable either to protect the citizens of South Texas or to honor the provisions of Article 11 to keep Indian raiding parties from Texas out of Mexico, General George M. Brooke, commanding the 8th Military District, wrote to Texas governor George Wood on 11 August 1849 requesting aid.[8] The Ranger Companies—led by Captain John S. Ford, John J. Grumbles, and Henry McCulloch—were mustered into federal service for six months and at the end of this term, General Brooke, in a message to Governor Wood, wrote: "I have determined to offer these companies a renewal of their engagements for six months more, . . . The murders and robberies lately repeated by the Indians and the season now approaching when a renewal of the same atrocities may be expected, the exigencies of the case appear to me to demand the continuance of the force already in service."[9] The actions of Ford's Ranger Company against the Indians in South Texas are well documented in Ford's memoirs and did much good, but northern Mexico continued to suffer from Indian raiding parties.

In 1873 a Mexican commission was established to document the violent history of border relations between the United States and Mexico. A section of their report, titled *Reports of the Committee of Investigation Sent in 1873 by the Mexican Government to the Frontier of Texas,* related to the damages to Mexican citizens caused by Indian incursions from Texas. The report is lengthy and outside the scope of this book, but a few raids are discussed here, to give the reader some flavor of the problem. On 12 April 1849 a "cattle station" owned by a citizen of Reynosa was attacked by savages from the American side of the river, resulting in the death of a man and a woman, with three men and one woman carried off as captives. Similar attacks occurred in that vicinity on 11 June and 27 August. The city of Camargo suffered greater damage than Reynosa, being invaded on 4 April and 5 May of that year by Indian raiding parties. But the committee singled out the city of Mier as being the hardest-hit town on the border: "It was four times invaded in 1848, between June and December, although it had organized a half company of National Guards for the repulse of the Indians, who in that year killed five persons, carried six into captivity, and took all the horses they could find. . . . During the above mentioned period the city of Mier was twenty times invaded. Its citizens were moreover frequently slaughtered at the cattle stations by assaults from the other side of the river, where the Indians organized, obtained arms and ammunition, and passed over to employ them against Mexicans."[10]

Nor was Mier particularly singled out for Indian depredations, as towns throughout Tamaulipas, Nuevo León, and Coahuila were attacked by Indian raiders from Texas. The Mexican commission documented thirty-three encounters with Indian raiders in Nuevo León from 1848 to 1853 and more than forty in Coahuila during that same time period. The bleak conditions in northern Mexico resulting from Indian intrusions were summarized by a Mexican journal: "The first thing that meets our eye is always something about savage Indians. Agriculture, industry and commerce relapse into insignificance, the revenues cease, tranquility is lost in the constant fear of the peril which threatens life, honor, and family interests; all in short present the most doleful picture of misfortune and desolation."[11]

By the fall of 1851 the U.S. government began to understand the magnitude of the responsibilities it had assumed in Article 11 and concluded that it could not honor these obligations. Secretary of State Daniel Webster, in a communication to Robert P. Letcher, the U.S. minister to Mexico, authorized Letcher to begin negotiations with the Mexican government for release from its Article 11 treaty obligations and would pay the Mexican government for such a release.[12]

Letcher met with José F. Ramírez, Mexico's minister of foreign affairs, in February 1852 to bring up the topic of abrogation of Article 11. Ramírez stated that his country expected the United States to pay for all losses sustained by Mexicans from Indian attacks, to remove all Indians from the Mexican border, to furnish troops to protect the border from further incursion, and to be repaid for the money expended in defense of its borders from Indian raiders. Letcher thought that Ramírez "talked like a madman" and that his demands were "nonsense."

By 1 March, Letcher met with Ramírez again, offering two million dollars to Mexico for release of the United States from the responsibilities of

Article 11. Within the month Ramírez informed Letcher that Mexico expected eight million dollars in claims for Indian depredations on the border, and an additional eight million dollars that would be needed to strengthen the country's military forces on the border to withstand further Indian incursions. The United States responded by declaring that the "high expectations" in regard to the monetary claims could never be fulfilled.[13]

By late 1852 the Mexican Congress cloaked the president with special powers to raise money for an impoverished country but stipulated that no treaty was to be made with the United States that would release it from obligations assumed under Article 11. However, the desperate economic conditions of the Mexican government encouraged the United States to continue negotiations, which it did.[14] The United States not only failed to protect its citizens along the border; it also failed to honor its treaty commitments with Mexico. The Gadsden Treaty, signed with Mexico on 30 December 1853, released the United States from the terms of Article 11, but the U.S. government continued to fail in its efforts to protect the Texas frontier between 1850 and the end of the American Civil War. It is therefore not surprising that when Texas ratified the Ordinance of Secession on 5 March 1861, removing the state from the Union, that at the head of that document was this grievance: "Whereas the Federal government has failed to accomplish the purposes of the compact of union between these States, in giving protection either to the persons of our people upon an exposed frontier or to the property of our citizens."

In April 1848, while the U.S. Congress was struggling over the provisions of the Treaty of Guadalupe Hidalgo, mysterious advertisements for volunteers began to appear in U.S. newspapers. A fair example is this notice found in a Philadelphia newspaper: "Wanted: Men of an adventurous nature to join others of a like kind, for an expedition into Mexico for buffalo. Volunteers must supply themselves with blanket, rifle and powder and ball sufficient for a long campaign. Address Box X, New Orleans, La."[15]

A conspiracy was being played out by adventurers in the United States and northern Mexico to separate that region from the Central government. U.S. support for this scheme came from two shadowy groups of men forming the secret societies that came to be known to the public as the "Buffalo Hunters" and the "Ousels Owls." The chief newspaper to support the movement, the *New Orleans Daily Delta*, explained that "it is not important to inquire how or when this scheme originated. It is sufficient for us to note the evident signs of a concerted effort in quarters which give assurance of its success, to dislocate and separate the northern states of Mexico from the rest of the Republic, and establish these as an independent American Republic. . . . Mind our prediction—the Republic of Sierra Madre will be the legitimate offspring of the Trist Treaty."[16]

The roots of the movement to "liberate" the states of northern Mexico can be traced back to the actions of Santa Anna in renouncing the Mexican Constitution of 1824. The Liberals of northern Mexico, such as Antonio Canales Rosillo and José María Carvajal, had campaigned for a return to the ideals of 1824 for many years. When a peaceful change could not be brought about, a revolutionary movement to separate northern Mexico from the Centralist government and form the so-called Republic of the Rio Grande was unsuccessfully attempted from 1838 to 1840. This latest movement for separation had its antecedents during the Mexican-American War in the occupied city of Tampico during the term of General James Shields, military governor of the city. Influential Mexicans, such as Carvajal, approached Shields with the idea of a separatist movement. Accompanying Carvajal were leading citizens of Tampico and the states of Coahuila, Tamaulipas, and Nuevo León who supported the movement for independence.

The movement for an expanded southern border also found support from General Zachary Taylor, then commanding the U.S. forces occupying northern Mexico. In response to the question as to where the boundary line between the United States and Mexico should be established at the end of the war, General Taylor recommended the Sierra Madre Oriental mountain range.[17] While the U.S. Senate wrestled with the question of the ratification of the Treaty of Guadalupe Hidalgo, Senator Sam Houston proposed as an amendment to the treaty that "the dividing line should start one league south of Tampico, in a straight line to the south of San Luis Potosi, thence to the Sierra Madre, and following the 25th parallel to the east coast of lower California, this and the islands in the Pacific to be embraced within the limits of the United States."[18]

While the U.S. Senate was considering the bill establishing a commission to settle the boundary between the United States and Mexico, Senator Daniel Webster proposed that a time limit of three years be set for the life of the commission. In response, Senator H. S. Foote stated that "it would not make much difference what time was fixed, for before the end of three years they would have to run a new boundary line along the Sierra Madre."[19]

But among the Buffalo Hunters there was no singleness of purpose. A group of army officers, supposedly in the secret society, reported that no complete scheme had yet been adopted for "revolutionizing the Northern Provinces," but they will go, and "when they do go to take the country for their own exclusive purpose and to annex it to the United States." The aims and goals of the annexation plot, if it can be called such, had sympathetic supporters not only in the army but in high places within the U.S. government as well.

By August 1848 the movement appears to have been gaining volunteers. A reporter of the *Baltimore Patriot,* writing on 14 August, reports that "the proposed Buffalo Hunt in Mexico . . . is going forward. There are men here now, brave, fighting, roaming, adventurous spirits, Texas Rangers, &c who are bent on the enterprise and forwarding its movements."[20] The editor of the *Daily Delta* reported that he had been informed by a "good authority" that at least six hundred persons were already enrolled for the Sierra Madre expedition and in a jingoist vein recommended the employment of at least seven hundred wheel barrows "to roll off the dead Mexicans."[21]

By 12 September this same editor reported that he had learned from sources in Philadelphia "that fifty gay and gallant young fellows in that city are ready to embark and participate in the coming sports on the banks of the Rio Grande." The column ended by noting that "at the young town of Brownsville, opposite Matamoros, as we are informed, a former mayor of Mobile, who lately raised a company of volunteers in that city, at the head of which he went to Mexico, is now forming a company of Buffalo Hunters, and at last accounts had already some forty in his crowd."[22]

The *Charleston Courier* of Charleston, South Carolina, published a letter on 8 September, written from New Orleans, describing the progress made in that city to mobilize the movement against northern Mexico. In part, it stated that "the resources of this association of Buffalo Hunters (who hold their meetings as a society of owls,) are immense, the treasurer in this city having at his command a sum approaching closely to a half million."[23] The leaders of this movement were shrouded in mystery, but it is suspected that the so-called Grand Scribe of the Ousel Owls was Memucan Hunt of Texas, ably supported by Colonel Lewis DeRussy of New Orleans, Louisiana.[24] The name of Henry L. Kinney, then residing at Corpus Christi, Texas, later became associated with the plot, over his vigorous protests. The conspiracy violated the U.S. Neutrality Act of 1818, so that subscribers and volunteers struggled to keep their names from being linked with the Buffalo Hunters or the Owls.

However, the choice of field commander for the expedition was made known in a note appearing in the *St. Louis Republican* of 9 August: "Not only will Gen. Shields, but other distinguished military officers of the Mexican War, stand pledged, and are expected to participate in this new echelon . . . if he does not accept the post of leadership of the 'Buffalo Hunt' on the Rio Grande, or chairmanship of the 'Order of Ousel Owls,' another brigadier-general of the volunteer service will take the position."[25]

A letter appearing in a Hartford, Connecticut, newspaper related to the public that "there are enrolled now upwards of five thousand men. . . . Shields is to take command, if he do not play false; if so, Gen. [Joseph] Lane. You have no idea of the number of influential men this plan embraces in its ramifications."[26] Some sources even reported that President James K. Polk expressed approval of the plot to invade northern Mexico. Sometime between 12 and 14 June 1848 a special agent of the Buffalo Hunters, a person holding an army commission, met with Polk and his cabinet to brief them on the proposed expedition. Polk was reported to have responded that "the scheme met his approval, and that he would be happy to see the northern provinces of Mexico dismembered from the Central Government, . . . if it could be effected without the direct and formal sanction and co-operation of the United States Government."[27]

The U.S. government, aware of the illegal conspiracy of the Owls and Buffalo Hunters to invade northern Mexico, took actions to alert its agents. On 30 August the secretary of state issued circular instructions to federal district attorneys of the southwestern states, directing them to enforce the provisions of the U.S. Neutrality Act of 1818. Major General Zachary Taylor, now commanding the Southern Military Division of the United States, was issued orders by the president to "cause vigilance to be observed along the Mexican frontier, within the geographical division under your command. Should you discover any attempt by any portion of our citizens to invade Mexico, you will employ the military force to prevent it."[28]

Plans for the invasion of northern Mexico had not been completely formulated, and due to a miscommunication, eager young volunteers took premature actions. On 9 September the schooner *Col. DeRussy* arrived at St. Joseph's Island, a barrier island off the coast of Corpus Christi, Texas. On board were about two hundred Ousel Owls, under the command of one Captain Besançon, determined to set out on a "buffalo hunt."[29] The editor of the *Corpus Christi Star*, J. H. Peoples, wrote that "but as none of the animals were to be found in these diggings, they came to the conclusion of returning to New Orleans, from whence they came. They were not only on the wrong trail, but out of season . . . the only conclusion we can offer is—bide your time."[30]

Besançon was planning to link up at this point with a supposed fellow conspirator, Henry L. Kinney, for further actions, but Besançon's timing was bad. He dashed off a note to Kinney on 11 September before embarking on the return voyage: "Dear Sir—I regret exceedingly having brought down men for the purpose of engaging in what is and has been called the Sierra Madre expedition. Had I been aware of your own opinions, and not relied upon Madam Rumor, I should have been saved the expense of subsistence and transportation of a large body of men." The *Corpus Christi Star* reported that the schooner *Col. DeRussy* returned to New Orleans with only about eighty of the one hundred ninety volunteers that arrived on St. Joseph's Island. The majority that remained were determined not to return, and some few remained in Corpus Christi engaging in business activities. But the majority ominously departed in small parties, destined for Brazos Santiago, Matamoros, Rio Grande City, and other border locales.[31] An embarrassed Kinney, whose plans had now become public knowledge, had the note written by Captain Besançon published, in the *Corpus Christi Star*, and added his own disavowal of any part in the Sierra Madre expedition.[32]

While Kinney was opposed to violating U.S. neutrality laws, he would be willing to violate this same law if and when "the people of northern Mexico are convinced that their system of government is illiberal and oppressive, and that a change would be conducive to their welfare, and they make a formal declaration of independence, then, and not till then, have their neighbors the right to interfere." Kinney's letter had expressed the policy adopted by the Buffalo Hunters: they would "come to the aid" of the states of northern Mexico only if requested.[33]

Evidently popular support for the intervention of U.S. filibuster forces into Mexico had reached a low ebb, and such an invitation was never received. Thus the plans for the Republic of the Sierra Madre failed to reach maturity. But many of the mercenaries and speculators who had been attracted to the border by prospects of an invasion of Mexico remained on to create a nucleus of lawless adventurers, ever ready for any scheme that promised gain.

In early June 1849, in response to the Mexican government's plans to garrison Matamoros with troops, the citizens of that city issued a *pronunciamiento* calling on the people of the city to prevent the entrance of troops and requesting assistance from the United States. In response, more than a hundred well-armed U.S. volunteers were rapidly assembled in Brownsville. A spokesman for the volunteers ventured into Matamoros to request more information and was promptly arrested by Mexican authorities. The Brownsville volunteers were disbanded only after the arrest of one of their leaders, Colonel Manuel Domínguez, a Brownsville resident, on charges of violation of the neutrality act. Domínguez, a Mexican citizen, was the well-known commander of the Mexican Spy Company in the U.S. service during the war with Mexico. He was considered a traitor by Mexicans. Domínguez was later released after the volunteer force disbanded.[34]

Gangs of lawless men, some brought to the border by the failed conspiracy to invade Mexico and others who had lingered behind after the Mexican War, created problems for law enforcement on both sides of the Rio Grande. By 31 October 1848 a correspondent to the *New Orleans Picayune* from Corpus Christi reported that "as a matter of course, the termination of the Mexican war has thrown upon the border many bad men of both nations, but so far their depredations have been confined to the other side of the Rio Grande, where a band, reckoned to be entirely composed of Americans, has plundered many of the haciendas and small pueblos, between Laredo and Sabinas."[35]

A correspondent from Rio Grande City to the *Corpus Christi Star* reported the lawless scene in that city: "There has been much excitement in this community of late growing out of the arrest of a band of robbers who had, after various acts of wholesale plunder and theft set at defiance the civil authorities of Star [*sic*] County. There appears to have been a well organized scheme of robbery, principally directed against our Mexican citizens and from all the facts elicited during the examination, but for their arrest and imprisonment, their operations would not have been confined to this side of the Rio Grande."[36]

William A. Neale, a longtime resident of Brownsville, Texas, wrote of his recollections of the lawless history of that frontier border city from 1848 to 1876: "You may call upon your imagination to picture the quality of the material left here, after the war, for the formation of a new community. I believe that more men of desperate character, desperate fortunes, and evil propensities, were congregated here on this frontier from 1846 to 1848, than ever got together in any other place. When I say any other place, of course I mean on the earth, since the deluge. Many of these men had no respect for human life. They thought nothing of it . . . how desperately they would fight, and for what ridiculous trifles they would sometime fight, to the death."[37]

The Republic of Mexico, almost from its beginnings, developed policies that outlawed traffic in slaves. While the Mexican Constitution of 1824 made no specific reference to slavery, it did declare the civil equality of all its inhabitants, without regard to national or ethnic origin. By 13 July 1824 a federal act came into force prohibiting the commerce and traffic in slaves from any country and declaring that residence in Mexico was tantamount to being free, as all people living in Mexican territory were so declared.[38]

Slaveowners in the United States, fearing the close proximity of a nation offering sanctuary to fugitives, pressed their government to negotiate some sort of arrangement with Mexico to return fugitive slaves. In 1825, under direction from Washington, D.C., Minister Joel Poinsett negotiated a "Treaty of Amity, Commerce, and Navigation" with his Mexican diplomatic counterpart. Article 33 of the proposed treaty provided for the

mutual restoration to legal owners of any slaves escaping from one country for sanctuary in the other. Authorities of either country were to be
required by legal owners to bring about the arrest and detention of fugitive
slaves. Article 33 was rejected by the Mexican Chamber of Deputies in
1827, and the sense of the congress was expressed by Erasmo Seguín, a representative from Texas: "[Congress] resolved to decree the perpetual extinc-
tion in the Republic of commerce and traffic in slaves, and that their introduction into our territory should not be permitted under any pretext."[39]

By 15 September 1829, President Vicente Guerrero signed a decree abol-
ishing slavery in the Republic of Mexico, but after strong political pressure
was brought to bear, he exempted Texas from the provisions of the decree.
Continued attempts by the U.S. government to negotiate a fugitive slave
treaty with Mexico failed, being rejected in each case by the Mexican
Congress. Thus Mexico left open the door to blacks fleeing slavery and
became a place of sanctuary that offered citizenship and equality.[40]

The slave population swelled in Texas, and by 1840, 11,323 Negroes
resided in Texas as slaves, with a white population of 54,088. Negro slaves
soon became aware of the legal status of slavery in Mexico, and the number of runaways began to increase. Newspaper advertisements began to
offer sizable rewards for the return of runaways: one planter offered twelve
hundred dollars for the return of six Negroes who escaped from his plantation and were assumed to be heading for Mexico.[41]

As early as 1843, Thomas Jefferson Green, then a Mier Expedition prisoner, reported that in Matamoros, Mexico, "were a large number of negros
who absconded from Texas." In the crowd Green had spotted two prominent ones, Tom and Esau, formerly the property of General Sam Houston.[42]
By 1850, in response to the need to cultivate large tracts of fertile Texas
lands, 58,161 slaves were residents of Texas, as opposed to 154,034 white residents. Slaves became big business in Texas, a healthy male field hand bringing as much as $1,500 and a female $1,250. The number of runaways to
Mexico began to dramatically increase, as did the size of the rewards offered
for their capture. Thus came to be that most feared, hated, and despised class
of citizen in Texas, known commonly as the "nigger hunter."

Blacks not captured by the time they reached the border could live in
freedom in Mexico without fear of legal recapture. Legal recapture, accord-

ing to one observer, was sheer folly: "You often meet your own property in Matamoros." By 1860 the U.S. consul in Matamoros described its citizens as follows: "These people are, and always have been, deadly hostile to every American (unless they are Negro or mulatto) from the commencement of this town."[43] Escaped blacks traveled south to the freedom of Mexico. John S. Ford, writing in his memoirs, estimated that by the mid-nineteenth century, at least three thousand Negroes who were owned by Texans were living in freedom in Mexico north of the Sierra Madre.[44]

The recapture of these former slaves for their reward and resale were the powerful economic motivations that explained Ford's alliance with José María Carvajal in the latter's attempts to separate northern Mexico from the Central government. Ford asserted that if Carvajal's plans for the separation of northern Mexico had been successful, Carvajal would have surrendered these refugees to their Texas masters, and would have supported a law in this new republic making it a felony "for a person in involuntary servitude to escape therefrom and take refuge upon Mexican territory." Apparently Ford aligned himself with Carvajal's forces in order to play the role of a "nigger hunter" on a grand scale in northern Mexico and reap rewards by trafficking in human misery.[45]

But others living in Texas at this time took pity on the fleeing fugitives and illegally aided in their covert flight to Mexico. The immigrant population that had been driven from Europe to Texas by the uprisings of 1848 and 1849 were highly educated, liberal-minded people who did not support slavery. Mostly of German and French extraction, these industrious and fiercely independent people, known as "Freethinkers," settled west of San Antonio in such settlements as Castroville, Comfort, Quihi, and Sisterdale. The trail from San Antonio west to Eagle Pass was the shortest route to the Rio Grande border, and although parts of this route passed through desolate and harsh country, it contained much less of this type of geography than other trails that wound through South Texas to the Mexican border. This trail became a literal underground highway to freedom for blacks escaping a life of slavery in Texas.[46]

At Eagle Pass author and adventurer Jane Storms Cazneau in 1852 reported seeing "hundreds of runaway slaves, who are tempted to escape from Texas into Mexico. . . . [In Mexico they] have all the social rights and honors of the most esteemed citizen." This vast number of blacks could not have made their exodus to the border without the aid of some charitable souls.[47] Frederick Law Olmsted, a visitor to Eagle Pass during this time, reported talking to a black fugitive in that town who stated that he could not "guess how many came in a year, but he could count forty that he had known of, in the last three months." Olmsted hastened to point out the perils of the journey: "There is a permanent reward offered by the state for their recovery, and a considerable number of men make a business of hunting them. Most of the frontier rangers are ready at any time to make a couple of hundred dollars, by taking them up. If so taken, they are severely punished, though if they return voluntarily they are commonly pardoned. If they escape immediate capture by dogs and men, there is then the great dry desert country to be crossed, with the danger of falling in with savages, or of being attacked by panthers or wolves, or of being bitten or stung by numerous reptiles that abound in it; of drowning miserably at the last of the fords; in winter of freezing in a norther, and, at all seasons, of famishing in the wilderness from the want of means to procure food."[48]

The dangers inherent in a flight to freedom by an escaped slave were many, but there were also many dangers to be risked by those good souls who offered aid to the fleeing pilgrim. Olmsted reported that these good Samaritans, whom he termed as "Germans," were not eager to discuss their illegal activities with strangers. But Olmsted learned, indirectly, that aid and comfort were being supplied to escaping slaves. Slaveholders repeatedly charged the immigrant Germans with aiding slave flights, and as punishment the liberal-minded new arrivals were often brutally treated by gangs of "ruffians" on suspicions of aid to blacks.[49]

But despite the perils for both blacks and whites, an underground railroad was operated from San Antonio westward to Eagle Pass that funneled many fugitive slaves to freedom. Reward for the return of these Negroes to slavery in Texas created an important incentive for incursions and filibustering expeditions into Mexico. Little documentation on the efforts by Freethinkers to pilot fugitive slaves to Mexico has been found, but as most letters between Freethinkers were written in an archaic form of German, their importance may still be unrecognized by some researchers. This subject would be worthy of more extensive investigation.

Only a glance at the history of South Texas is necessary to understand that a vast cloud of uncertainty hung over the titles of many land tracts in this region. Land ownership could have been claimed by a patchwork of overlapping grants that included royal grants from the king of Spain, grants and sales from the Republic of Mexico, or grants and sales from the Republic of Texas. In each of these governmental systems that held sway over South Texas for a period of time, a separate complex set of laws existed to govern the title to land. Many of these grants had not ever been surveyed accurately, and metes and bounds were often located by such temporary designations as a pile of stones or the location of a certain tree.

Many land sales in Texas made by the state government of Coahuila y Tejas, such as the so-called Eleven League grants that resulted from the struggle for power between the central and state governments, were controversial in both Mexico and Texas. Their legality would later be challenged in U.S. courts. The cash-starved treasury of the Republic of Texas issued land scrips to investors in the United States to raise money and granted portions of its public lands to soldiers in lieu of pay. As if this were not enough, hordes of land speculators descended on South Texas, buying up existing land claims, often inferior in nature and in some cases fraudulent.[50]

As early as June 1847, land speculators were making plans to profit from the confusion that resulted from the patchwork of laws governing land ownership in South Texas. From an issue of the *American Flag,* this advertisement for land services by attorney Rice Garland reads as follows:

LAW OFFICE AND LAND AGENCY

The Legislature of the State of Texas at its last session, by express enactment, extended the jurisdiction and laws of the State over the country east of the Rio Grande. Mexican authority and laws are forever at an end, on that side of the river, if not further west. . . . By the laws of Texas, no alien enemy can hold real estate within its limits, nor can any non-resident foreigner except under certain conditions and under restrictions. Persons claiming under Mexican grants will do well to give prompt attention to them, as preparations are now being made, to locate other claims on the lands covered by such titles.[51]

The advertisement was quite misleading, however. At this time the war between the United States and Mexico was still being fought, and it was known neither if the territory south of the Nueces River would become part of the United States nor if terms for peace would be a result of the termination of this war. Article 8 of the Treaty of Guadalupe Hidalgo, which superseded all state and local laws, guaranteed the property rights of all persons residing in the newly annexed territories. This article in part read: "In the said territories, properties of every kind, now belonging to Mexicans not established there, shall be inviolably respected. The present owners, the heirs of these, and all Mexicans who may hereafter acquire said property by contract, shall enjoy with respect to it guarantees equally ample as if the same belonged to citizens of the United States."

But much confusion to land titles existed. The Texas Legislature acted in 1850 to resolve the issue. A law was passed to appoint two commissioners, one of whom was conversant in Spanish, to investigate land claims in the South Texas counties of Cameron, Kinney, Starr, and Webb. The two commissioners, William H. Bourland and James B. Miller, were appointed by Governor Peter H. Bell. By the terms of the law, they were given the power of subpoena and expected to travel to the county seat of each county to personally conduct a hearing and examine all witnesses. An abstract of each claim and the commissioner's recommendations were to be submitted by the commission to the legislature, with the final disposition of each claim to be handled by the legislature. Sales of lands whose ownership was in question was halted until the legislature's final decision.[52]

A hearing was held in Brownsville in early November 1850, and the resulting reports, in Miller's possession, were sent to Austin. But disaster overtook the commissioner and his reports. In a letter of 28 November, Miller described the events to Governor Bell: "I left Brazos Santiago on Sunday last at 4 o'clock, we found the sea very rough on Monday night about 10 o'clock the Steam ship *Anson* filled and sunk in the Breakers about two hundred yards from the beach, and fifteen miles from Matagorda. I lost my trunk containing all of the original titles presented at Brownsville." The letter went on to report that the citizens of Brownsville were pleased with the "government of the state" and recommended that the legislature amend the present law so as to make the decision of the commissioners final with the right of appeal. "If that is done, I will immediately return, and the loss of these papers can be repaired . . . the Mexicans are anxious to sell a portion of their land and the Americans are equally anxious to purchase."[53]

But not everyone in Brownsville shared in the confidence for the state government as Miller reported. Bell, in a letter to the legislature on 21 November 1851 on the subject of the land title commission, confided that "I am gratified in announcing to the Legislature that the most beneficial results have been derived. . . . Much dissatisfaction prevailed for a short period of time after its enactment, arising mainly from a misapprehension of its provisions and true meaning."[54] This dissatisfaction came to a head in Brownsville, on the evening of 2 February 1850, in a meeting held in the schoolhouse of one R. N. Stansbury. A crowd of citizens including Stephen Powers, Elisha Basse, R. H. Hord, Samuel A. Belden, F. J. Parker, and Joseph Palmer—men either deeply involved in land speculation or the agents of land speculators—met to propose actions to counteract the intervention of the state legislature into the business of determining land titles. The members of the meeting voiced the fear of many speculators that the state government was seeking to annul land titles between the Nueces and the Rio Grande.[55]

A petition was directed by the membership to the U.S. Senate that requested that the lands between the Nueces River and the Rio Grande be separated from the state of Texas to form an independent territory of the United States, to be governed by an appointed territorial government. The Anglo speculators felt that their political influence in Washington, D.C., would enable them to have a voice in the appointment of territorial courts, which they could control. The Brownsville Separatists, as they were denoted by historian Frank H. Dugan, wrote that "the country lying East of the Rio Grande and South of the line of New Mexico, distinct from the former province of Texas, of right belongs to the Government of the United States, and that the state of Texas has extended her jurisdiction over it without our consent."[56]

The separatists argued that this portion of the state was an isolated area, without protection from the Indians and without any roads to the interior of the state. Officials of the state government, they protested, had ignored these problems. A first petition by the separatists was presented to the U.S. Senate on 27 February 1850 by Senator William H. Seward. The petition to create the proposed "Territory of the Rio Grande" had appended to it 106 names, of which only 3 appeared to be Anglo-Saxon. Eight names were "x," with the person's name added, and about half of the names having the appearance of being misspelled, giving the petition the suspicious air of a fraudulent document. None of the original separatists had signed the petition. In defense of Texas, Senator Thomas J. Rusk rose to speak in reference to the Brownsville Separatists: "What their object is I do not know . . . they have taken charge of the Mexican population, and are engaged in directing their action to their own purposes."[57]

The *Texas State Gazette,* representing the opinion of many Texans, attacked the messenger as well as the message: "The organ selected by our Rio Grande patriots is a tollerably [*sic*] clear indication of their sentiments in relation to slavery, Mr. Seward being a rank free soiler."[58] A second petition, identical to the first, was introduced on the Senate floor by Henry Clay on 11 March 1850. Senator Clay washed his hands of the matter by stating that "I know very little on the subject. . . . I had no information whatsoever that there was any dissatisfaction prevailing in that portion of the Country."[59] This petition had seventy-four signers, including many of the movers in the separatist cause, such leaders of the Rio Grande Valley as Charles Stillman, Richard King, and Mifflin Kenedy. Those signers later directly involved in Carvajal's invasion of Mexico included Joseph Moses, James O'Donnell, Francis N. Gracesqui, F. J. Parker, F. R. Taylor, E. Basse, R. H. Hord, and Samuel Belden. Senator Rusk again rose to defend the state of Texas, claiming that the Mexican people of that area were duped by "individuals who never were, or were never until recently inhabitants of that section of the country," men who were exploiting the prejudices of "Mexicans who were originally and always adverse to Texas."[60]

A 5 February 1850 meeting of Brownsville citizens opposed to separation from Texas graphically indicated that a majority of the population favored remaining a part of Texas.[61] The separatist movement, never popular with the majority of Brownsville citizens, died a quick death, thanks to the honest dealings of the Bourland-Miller Commission as well as the efforts of such Cameron County leaders as Israel B. Bigelow. Many of its leaders later recanted their decision to support the Territory of the Rio Grande: "We are gratified to notice that Jack R. Everett, Esq., who participated in a meeting held in Roma, on the Rio Grande, in favor of the establishment of a Territorial Government in that portion of Texas, has frankly acknowledged himself to have been in error, and explicitly disclaims any further connection with the movement."[62] Jack R. Everett would later be involved in Carvajal's conspiracy to invade northern Mexico.

But title to newly acquired U.S. lands was a thorny issue. The controversy concerning the ownership of the lands upon which Brownsville is located offers a fair case in point. This land, a portion of the "Espiritu Santo grant," had been received by the ancestor of Rafaél Garcia Cavázos, José Salvádor de la Garza, as a royal grant from the king of Spain in 1781. In 1826 the city of Matamoros negotiated to purchase this portion of land, lying on the north side of the Rio Grande, from the owner at that time, Francisca Cavázos, widow and heiress to the land. The land was needed to form a town commons, required by Mexican law of all cities. The negotiations were never completed, however, and the Cavazos family was never paid for the property.[63]

By the end of the Mexican-American War, speculators swarmed into South Texas, thirsting after profits from the possession of Mexican property. Señor Cavazos posted this warning in the *American Flag* of 14 June 1848:

> All persons are hereby notified, that I, Rafael Garcia Cavazos, am the owner possessing a valid and indisputable title to a certain tract of land . . . which . . . embraces the entire front from opposite the City of Matamoros on the said Rio Grande.
>
> Notice is hereby given that all documents emanating from the Honorable Ayuntamiento of the City of Matamoros, purporting to be titles to labors as exidos [*sic*] are of no value, as said Ayuntamiento are not, nor ever have been possessed of any legal right to grant said labors or any part of said tract of land.
>
> All persons purchasing or attempting to hold said land, or any part thereof, except by titles emanating from myself are hereby notified that they will do so at their own cost, and will subject themselves to damages as trespassers, as I am determined to appeal to the law for the protection of my just rights.[64]

Regardless of this warning and the evident public knowledge of rightful ownership, wealthy merchant and entrepreneur Charles Stillman bought inferior titles to this portion from tenants farming this parcel of land, Texas headright certificates, and land scrip: some 4,676 acres that were located on the Cavazos grant.[65] Stillman, with partners Samuel Belden, Simon Mussina, and William W. Chapman, formed the Brownsville Land Company and began to develop the town site and sell town lots. In opposition, Cavazos retained attorney W. G. Hale and filed suit *(City of Brownsville v. Pedro J. Cavazos)* in federal district court. The lengthy case was settled on 15 January 1852 in a decision rendered by Judge John C. Watrous, who issued a judgment against the Brownsville Land Company and enjoined it from further operation.[66]

Dugan states that attorneys Elisha Basse and Robert H. Hord, acting as agents for Stillman, subsequently offered Cavazos a sum of thirty-three thousand dollars for the land, which Cavazos accepted. However, there is no evidence that Cavazos ever received any money from Stillman and his cohorts for this land. The titles to Brownsville town site lands remained clouded. By 1876, William Neale, in a speech to Brownsville citizens that traced the city's history, noted that "some unscrupulous men got a footing among us; they made vast claims to landed property and instituted suits at law; they in fact claimed all land donated to the city by the state Legislature, that lay within the corporate limits. These rival claims discouraged many persons who had intended to settle here, and prevented them from doing so; it also deterred those who did stay here, from putting up good and substantial buildings, and this accounts for the very inferior class of buildings that grace, or to speak more truly, disgrace some of our public thoroughfares."[67] The claims and counterclaims for the ownership of the Brownsville town site continued until 1921, when Stillman's heirs concluded a $325,000 settlement with the City of Brownsville. Some land claims continue in the courts to this day. Most notably are those by the heirs of Padre Nicolas Balli to the title of South Padre Island, which at the time of this writing are still in the process of litigation.[68]

The early American victories at Palo Alto and Resaca de la Palma and the subsequent occupation of Camargo, Matamoros, and Reynosa by May 1846 offered opportunities for the duty-free importation of American goods into Mexico. By 30 June 1846, Secretary of Treasury R. J. Walker had advised American customs officers that U.S. vessels arriving at the Port of

Matamoros carrying either the articles of "growth, produce or manufacture of the United States," or vessels carrying imports from foreign countries upon which import duties to the United States had already been paid, would not be required to pay any import duties for Mexico. Anticipating the capture of more Mexican territory, Walker further stipulated that any other Mexican ports or places that shall be in the possession of the United States shall also be governed by the same rules that affected the imports to Matamoros.[69]

Such economic incentives brought many merchants to the Rio Grande and a flood of American goods into Mexico to be eagerly received by the native populace. Before the war, oppressive Mexican import duty schedules had choked off trade between the two countries. The lower-cost U.S. goods, such as calico and gingham cloth, were very popular and sold well. Some Americans prophesied that the Mexican public would never permit the resumption of the old high-tariff rates after the war. With the capture of Monterey in late September 1846 by U.S. forces, Matamoros assumed a larger role of importance in the importation of goods to Mexico. Vast amounts of duty-free American goods landed at Matamoros that would be carted by wagon and mule trains overland for sale in Monterey. The editor of the *American Flag* noted that "the area of trade has been enlarged, and the whole country between here and Monterey will be supplied with goods from this place [Matamoros]. There will be some handsome fortunes made."[70]

By early 1847 it became apparent that the cost of the war with Mexico was draining the U.S. treasury. Steps were taken to increase the revenues, one of which was the so-called Walker tariff. President James K. Polk, assured by his advisers of the legality of collecting duties as military contributions under the laws of war, approved the Walker plan. This plan also lowered Mexican duties into Mexican cities controlled by the U.S. military by more than one half and substituted for all port dues and charges a uniform rate of one dollar per ton. Mexico responded by declaring that goods imported into Mexico under the Walker tariff would be confiscated, but this declaration was ignored by many of the more aggressive merchants.[71]

Walker's original edict to the customs officers regarding goods imported into Mexico through Matamoros was altered by his orders of 30 March

1847. The *American Flag* reported that as a result of this new restrictive change, border merchants were "winding up their business and preparing to leave the country." The editor felt that this new tariff had been conceived in "ignorance of the effect it would have upon the enterprise and prospects of citizens of the United States."[72] The Polk administration partly relented on the strict terms of the new regulations and on 10 June 1847 reduced the "military contribution" on manufactured cotton goods to 30 percent ad valorem.[73]

With the introduction of the practice of collecting "military contributions" by customs officers, despite the reduction put into effect on 30 June 1847, the smuggling of goods by American merchants into Mexico became a prevalent practice. In an effort to stem the flow of illegal goods into Mexico, Colonel William Davenport, the U.S. military governor of Matamoros, issued an order on 5 July 1847 creating an office for the collection of tariff duties at Matamoros.[74] By 19 August 1847 smuggling had increased to such a level that Davenport issued the following public letter to his newly appointed tariff collector: "Sir: It was reported to me yesterday that the steamers Aid and Lama are engaged in the business of transporting goods from the mouth of the river to points above this place, on the Texas side of the river. . . . There being so few consumers of goods above this, on the Texas side of the river, the object, it is almost certain, is to smuggle them into Mexico, and it is the duty of all custom house agents to prevent this by all lawful means."[75]

A punishment for smuggling, although of a vague nature, was set by Davenport, who ordered that all contraband goods be seized and sold with one half of the proceeds going to the person or persons who might inform on the smuggler. The preceding order was legal, as Matamoros and occupied northern Mexico had been placed under military rule, and this order was accordingly enforced.[76] The collection of Mexican tariffs by the U.S. military had come to an end by 1 July 1848. Order No. 26, by General John Ellis Wool, pronounced a resumption of peace between the two countries: "1. Peace being happily restored, and orders being expected withdrawing the troops from Mexico, it becomes necessary to turn over the custom house to the Mexican authority without further instructions."[77]

The economic and political control of northern Mexico was returned to the Central government of the Republic of Mexico at this time. Mexico found itself in a strapped economic condition. With the exception of hides, wool, and specie, Mexico produced no export goods. There were almost no producers of manufactured goods in Mexico at this time. However, a notable exception was an infant industry producing unbleached cotton goods, known as *manta*. To raise a protective tariff barrier on this product as well as others, Mexican import duties were set to an almost prohibitive level, especially on textiles. But American merchants on the border, having once gotten the taste of profits from Mexican trade that accrued during the Mexican-American War, did not accept these prohibitive tariffs without opposition. On the other side of the border, consumers in northern Mexico had become accustomed to the variety and low cost of American goods, and likewise they were opposed to any exclusion of such goods.

With no other alternatives available, smuggling became the major practice by which goods were introduced into Mexico. Many Americans on the Texas side of the river abandoned their trades to take up the economically rewarding and "meritorious" profession of smuggling, which came to be "identified with the best part of the population." Mexican merchants also became involved in smuggling foreign goods into the interior of Mexico. With an almost empty treasury, the Mexican government could not afford to hire enough customs officers to enforce its laws along the wild Texas-Mexico border, and the U.S. government turned a blind eye to the smuggling parties often organized on the left bank of the Rio Grande. The three official sites for imports into Mexico along the lower border were Camargo, Matamoros, and Mier, but there was an extreme amount of rivalry among these sites for imports; corrupt officials were always eager to offer a modified form of smuggling by concluding an informal agreement for lower rates than those specified either by Mexican law or their rival ports of entry.[78]

P. W. Humphries, a purchasing agent for the army, described a border smuggling incident:

> Some merchants desiring to cross goods, applied to those in authority in Camargo, who required 25 per cent;—deeming that price too high application was made to those at Mier who agreed for a much less sum. According to arrangement the Guard being removed, the goods were

crossed and were about to be conveyed to the interior, when a Custom-house-officer from Camargo accompanied by a Guard of 37 soldiers captured them and were proceeding with them to the latter place for confiscation, when a party of Texans under promise of pay $2000, re-captured and took them to the other side of the river without actual bloodshed.[79]

Lieutenant A. P. Hill, stationed at Fort Brown during 1851, wrote this impression of the brutal state of life along the Rio Grande:

One who has not been here and daily mixed with the people living in this frontier can have no conception of the state of society, the quintessence of ruffianism and scoundrelism that has been squeezed out from the states and sprinkled along this Rio Grande—Human life is but held as a feather in the list of possessions and he who can must recklessly expose his own, or must murderously take that of a fellow being is pointed out as one deserving of all praise—Tis the distinctive mark of each individ-ual when you ask the question "Who is he?—Oh, he is the man who killed so and so," and the larger the number the greater the admiration expressed in the manner of telling and the tone of voice—I was in Brownsville but some ten days and four men were severally shot down in the streets.[80]

The grim picture of the societal conditions along the Texas-Mexico bor-der in the mid-nineteenth century presented in this chapter can be sum-marized succinctly in the words of the English social philosopher Thomas Hobbes, who in his book *Leviathan* described a society without law as "poor, nasty, brutish, and short."

SIX

The Merchants War

I am now before the city with an armed and organized force and
without delay I intend to attack the troops of the Government.

GENERAL JOSÉ MARÍA CARVAJAL
near Matamoros, 19 October 1851,
as quoted in the *New Orleans Picayune*, 18 November 1851

By 1851 the violent nature of life along the Texas-Mexico border was about
to become even more violent. Newspapers from the United States were
filled with rumors of covert plots to invade Caribbean and Central American
can countries with private filibuster armies. An unsuccessful attempt,
under the leadership of Narciso López, to liberate Cuba from Spanish rule
had already been attempted, and a second army of liberators had set sail
in the early months of 1851 from New Orleans for another try. Along the
Rio Grande grumblings could be heard from the Brownsville merchants
about the prohibitive Mexican import duties that had strangled a lucrative
trade built up during the palmy days of the Mexican-American War. From
the south side of the river Mexican consumers, accustomed to the quality
and low cost of imported foreign goods, likewise registered their complaints to their government, but to no avail. It appeared to many that the
Central government in Mexico City had ignored the welfare of their citizens in the north (known as *norteños*). The norteños were left to defend
themselves as best they could against Indian raids that had become the
scourge of northern Mexico. Repeated petitions from the north for military forces to combat the Indian menace continued to be ignored.

Thus it was that a plot developed to separate northern Mexico from the
Central government, forming an independent state that would come to be

known as the Republic of the Sierra Madre. The plan drew support from border merchants as a remedy for the costly import duties that were ruining their business with Mexico. More important, however, an independent northern Mexico was sanctioned by Mexican Liberals, weary of the unfulfilled promises of their government, to loosen the millstone of an unresponsive government from the backs of the people of northern Mexico.

The first hint to the general public that an armed incursion into Mexico was in the offing is found in the *New Orleans Picayune* of 17 August 1851 in a column noting that the editors of the *Brownsville Sentinel,* Joseph Palmer and Edwin Scarborough, had sold that newspaper to Ovid F. Johnson and Francis J. Parker. The new paper, *The Rio Bravo,* was to become the official organ for José María Carvajal's anticipated revolutionary movements in Mexico. The column further reported that "we have of late seen some indications and heard many surmises of another approaching revolution in Mexico." It predicted that the struggle to found the Republic of the Sierra Madre would be successful and that Mexico would lose territory equal to that which it had already lost to the United States. Under way was a plan by a group of conspirators headed by Carvajal to separate Mexico's northern states from the republic. As with most illegal conspiracies, the details and planning were covert—both to assure the element of surprise and to leave no record behind as evidence to be used in a legal proceeding. But what information on the conspiracy that exists today can be found as the result of an investigation carried out by the U.S. district attorney for the Eastern District of Texas, William Pitt Ballinger, seeking indictments of the conspirators.

By June 1851, Carvajal had entered Texas as an agent of several Mexican citizens who claimed title to "large grants of land between the Rio Grande and the Nueces River." This vast expanse of land, identified by Ballinger as the "Carasillas grant," was most probably either the Conceptión de Carricitos grant, in which the present-day town of San Benito is located, or the San Juan de Carricitos grant, which now includes the towns of Raymondville and Lyford. Carvajal approached Brownsville merchants, suffering from the prohibitive Mexican tariff, with an offer, according to Ballinger, to "exchange the grant for merchandise to introduce into Mexico, free of duty at the Custom House." In addition, he proposed that if his separation of the

northern states of Mexico was successful, he would allow Brownsville merchants to "send goods into Mexico, paying Carvajal 35 to 40 percent of the
amount, a considerably lower amount than the Mexican tariff."

Ballinger estimated that Carvajal had made five hundred thousand dollars in the land sales and the same amount by the introduction of goods
into Mexico, once he had captured the little Mexican border town of
Camargo. The exchange of land for merchandise that Carvajal proposed
was not illegal, according to Article 8 of the Treaty of Guadalupe Hidalgo.
This article guaranteed that Mexicans living in territories acquired by the
United States as a result of the war could retain their prewar properties or
could dispose of them, "and removing the proceeds wherever they please,
without their being subjected, . . . to any contribution, tax, or charge whatever." Carvajal had proposed a very clever method of finance, using an
interpretation of Article 8 that its authors had probably never envisioned.
This money was to be used to finance and supply an army of mercenaries
that would soon invade northern Mexico.[1]

By 18 August more than two hundred men were concentrated at Rio
Grande City. Some were reported to have come from recently disbanded
Texas Rangers companies active in South Texas against Indian raiding parties. This force lay camped at Rio Grande City, quietly awaiting "the proper
time to cross the river and participate in the revolutionary movement."[2]
Sinister movements of men were reported throughout the state. The
Galveston Journal reported that a dozen of the disbanded Cuban volunteers who had missed a rendezvous with a ship transporting mercenaries
for Narciso López's second invasion of that island had passed through the
city on their way to the Rio Grande to join up with a group forming a
"buffalo hunt" in that part of the country.[3]

The Nueces Valley, a newspaper of Corpus Christi, Texas, reported on 7
September that numerous delays had prevented a party of men camped on
Mustang Island from going to Cuba to participate in the López Expedition.
The editor opined that "a lack of funds in New Orleans prevented the
transportation of these men. Some of these Filibusteros have become very
restless waiting and have abandoned Mustang Island for more prosperous
settings." On 29 September this same paper reported that seventy or eighty
of the men had been mounted and left for some destination on the Rio

Grande to join the revolution in Tamaulipas. This party of men—led by Major McMacken [J. Smith McMicken], Major [Alfred Howell] Norton, and Captain [Joseph Davis] Howell—were reported to have few firearms. Another party of sixteen or seventeen well-mounted and well-armed men, under the leadership of Colonel Robert [Chatham Roberdeau] Wheat, joined up with the expedition as they headed south. The men, according to the editor, were thought to be "mostly Kentuckians."[4]

The U.S. Department of State had become informed of a plot to invade Mexico and on 24 September 1851 directed a note of warning to Luis de la Rosa, Mexican minister to the United States: "The President [Millard Fillmore] has been induced by recent information to apprehend that efforts are making or will be made, to fit out for the invasion of that Republic, armed expeditions from Mustang Island or other places within the United States, in violation of the laws of the United States and of obligations to a friendly power."[5]

On 3 September 1851, at the Hacienda de La Loba, near the town of Guerrero [Viejo], José María de Jesús Carvajal and José María Gonzales initiated the uprising against the Republic of Mexico by issuing a *pronunciamiento* (pronouncement): the Plan de La Loba. The twelve points of the plan, endorsed by many prominent citizens of Guerrero, were reminiscent of the states' rights provisions of the liberal constitution of 1824:

> The subscribers, all citizens of the city of Guerrero, in the State of Tamaulipas, convinced that the national representation has paid no attention to the repeated petitions which they have sent to that sovereignty, through the corresponding sources, for the abolishment of prohibitions and the reduction of the tariff; the protection due to stop the depredations of the Indians, already unsupportable, as well as the oppression they suffer, owing to the restriction together with the hostility of the barbarians, are the complete destruction not only of those who speak, but of the whole frontier, have decided and resolved to sustain with their arms the contents of the following articles.

The pronunciamiento listed demands, which included the removal of all permanent troops from the border; soldiers were described in the plan as "pernicious, oppressive, and useless." The plan also contained provisions to protect the civil and property rights of all citizens and to embrace proportional representation. The plan recognized the need for changes in the national constitution, which included a clause much like the tenth amendment of the U.S. Constitution: "reserving to the States all the powers and enjoyments not granted to the General Government." The prohibition of foreign goods into Mexico was abolished, and a limit of 40 percent ad valorem on customs duties was to be set. The proceeds of the customs duties were to be dedicated to funding forces that would be "created for the exclusive and sacred purpose of making war upon the savages." Smuggling was to be vigorously prosecuted as a criminal act, and a customs house for foreign goods was proposed for the city of Reynosa.

In addition to these twelve articles, in his memoirs John S. Ford maintained that Carvajal favored the sale of the mortmain property of the Catholic Church and the use of the proceeds to support the government and to apply to the national debt. These reforms would later be enacted into law by the Liberal president of Mexico, Benito Juárez. Ford, whose interests lay with stopping the flight of fugitive slaves to Mexico, claimed that Carvajal would, if successful, advocate a law making it a felony for a person living in involuntary servitude to seek sanctuary in the territory of Mexico.

The Mexican border towns of Camargo, Guerrero, Mier, and Reynosa strongly supported the sentiments expressed in the pronunciamiento and became adherents of the Plan de La Loba.[6] The first orders Carvajal issued to his army, titled "to the Defenders of Mexican Liberty, who under my orders, swear to combat against Tyrants," addressed the many weaknesses of the current government. According to Carvajal, the recent war with the United States had left northern Mexicans destitute and without property, which was taken from them. He estimated that forty million dollars would not pay for the losses in land and other property. His general orders further stated that "the savage murders our parents and brothers, violates our wives, and carries off our children [as] captives. . . . The government has not done enough to help the northern states, and . . . remains deaf to our lamentations. . . . Its troops, far from occupying themselves in defending or consoling us, rob and murder our countrymen, under the frivolous pretext that they are smuggling, although these troops, when before the enemy, fly coward-like." Carvajal's general order concluded by expressing the determination that "my subordinates swear to sustain, generally with all their might and boldness, fighting gallantly and with fidelity . . . until we expel the enemy from our territory . . . and make the despots who inhabit the palace of the Montezumas understand the claims and rights of freemen shall be respected. . . . Viva la Libertad! Death to the tyrants!"[7]

Recruits swarmed to the banner of the so-called Liberators, as they were offered twenty-five piastres a month for their services; however, men of questionable backgrounds were not accepted for service. Colonel Manuél Domínguez, then living in Brownsville, Texas, was rejected by Carvajal on two occasions. Domínguez had commanded the famous Mexican Spy Company, composed of Mexican citizens who had sided with the U.S. forces of General Winfield Scott in central Mexico during the Mexican-American War. Domínguez offered to raise and equip two hundred men for service in Carvajal's army under the condition that he be given a separate command. Carvajal surprisingly refused Domínguez's offer, stating that he would not employ the services of a traitor to his country.[8]

Those men approved to serve in Carvajal's army had to swear to obey orders, to respect the ownership of private property, and to not molest any peaceable persons. Private property taken in battle was to be distributed among the soldiers in the army, while captured public property was to be used to support the cause. Soldiers that completed their term of service, for either three months or six months, were to receive a bonus of two months' extra pay. The pay was the same as received by Texas Rangers who had served in South Texas against the Indians.[9]

An observer in Carvajal's camp noted that during his stay, several Mexican citizens had approached the general with complaints of being robbed by soldiers from his army. In each case the general had ordered an investigation into the circumstances of the case, declaring that he would not permit such behavior by any man in his command. A court-martial was then in session for a soldier found with stolen property among his possessions. The stolen articles were returned to their owners, and the general expressed an intention to remunerate the owners for property that could not be found.[10]

But with such a large group of undisciplined and high-spirited men, disputes were inevitable. In the little town of Edinburgh (present-day Hidalgo) a fatal argument arose. A Captain Ross, leading a company of men from New Orleans on their way to join General Carvajal, was insulted by a Dr. Emswiller, one of the men in the company. The doctor urged the men of the company to depose Ross as their leader and instead elect him as captain. Several offensive words were traded between Ross and Emswiller, causing Ross to advance on the doctor with a pistol in hand. The doctor shot Ross twice, who died twenty-four hours later from the wounds.[11]

An anxious Mexican minister to the United States, Luis de la Rosa, penned a note to the U.S. secretary of state. The note thanked the United States for the message of 24 September informing his government that an armed expedition against Mexico was then in the offing. Minister de la Rosa made it clear that he expected the United States to act swiftly against the filibustering party: "The Undersigned is persuaded that the Government of the United States has all the power, all the authority, and all the forces necessary to restrain the adventurers who intend to organize and arm themselves within the territory of this Republic [the United States] for the purpose of invading Mexico."[12] But the Liberator Army, so named by Carvajal, had no intention of arming and organizing their forces while in the United States, for such an act would have been a clear violation of the Neutrality Act of 1818. Rather, the mercenaries would cross the border into Mexico in small parties, and when safely on the south side of the Rio Grande, would complete the organization and arming of the troops.

On 19 September, at 2 p.m., General Carvajal crossed the Rio Grande near Rio Grande City and led his army in an attack on Camargo, a village about three miles south of the river. The attackers consisted of three companies: the company from Guerrero, under the command of José María Canales, was placed in front; the second company, made up of sixty Americans from the border towns of Roma and Rancho Davis (present-day Rio Grande City), led by Captain Robert C. Trimble, was placed in the center; while on the right flank was the company from Camargo, led by Tomás Cavazos.

The Liberator Army quickly drove the Mexican army garrison troops, under the command of Vicente Camacho, to the town center, where they took refuge in the customs house and the church. The Mexican troops had a four-pounder cannon, while the Liberator Army was without artillery. Carvajal's forces encircled the defender's strongholds and "every Mexican soldier who dared to make an appearance above the house tops was immediately shot by the Texan rifles." By midnight the Mexican army detachment surrendered and the customs house, filled with "mantas and imperials," fell into the hands of Carvajal. Reported casualties included sixty Mexican soldiers killed, including four officers, and four Americans and six Mexicans of the Liberator Army wounded, but none mortally.[13]

The victorious Carvajal dictated a surrender agreement:

CAPITULATION

In the town of Camargo, on the 20th day of the month of September, 1851, the officers under the commandant of squadron, Don Vicente Camacho, agreed to enter into the following capitulation with Col. Don Jose Maria J. Carvajal, in accordance with the army regulations and actual circumstances. It is as follows:

Art. 1.—That the forces under Commandant Comacho shall surrender their arms, horses, and equipments, as well as the 4-pounder, with all its ammunition, arms, and other warlike stores, allowing them to carry off only ten muskets and two rounds of cartridge.

2. That the equipage and arms belonging to Senor Camacho and his officers be allowed to them in consideration of the determined valor with which they sustained themselves against very superior forces.

3. That the forces of the said Senor Camacho shall be marched through Monterey to San Luis Potosi, all the officers giving their word of honor for themselves and troops not to take up arms against the cause at present headed by Col. Carvajal . . .

The surrender document, signed by Mexican army officers and members of the municipal government, included the names of Vicente Camacho, Policarpo Marulando, Francisco Ledesma, Francisco Carillo, Rafael Cervantes, Apolinar Morales, Isidro Garcia, Francisco Losada, and Augustin M. Saavedra. A town meeting was held in Camargo, under the direction of the first *alcalde* (mayor), Secúndio Récio, and the twelve articles of the Plan de La Loba were approved by acclamation. A copy of the pronounciamiento was signed by about a hundred citizens.[14]

Now in command of Camargo, one of General Carvajal's first acts was to drastically cut the import tariff rates for goods passing into Mexico through this city. This new schedule provided, for example, for white and brown cotton goods at 30 percent ad valorem, colored cotton and linen goods at 25 percent, silks at 45 percent, groceries at 15 percent, and medicines and lumber admitted free of charge. Merchants in the vicinity of Rio Grande City took immediate advantage, and it is estimated that from two hundred thousand to three hundred thousand dollars in goods crossed the river into Mexico at this point. The Camargo customs house receipts became a needed addition to the funds required to supply the Liberator Army.[15]

Carvajal's chief opponent, General Francisco Ávalos, the military commander of the border, knew he must move quickly to slow the revolutionaries' momentum. Many of Carvajal's financial supporters were merchants living in Brownsville and Matamoros, and Ávalos had to gain their support. By 8 October 1851, Ávalos announced that he considered Matamoros to be under siege and that he would match Carvajal's tariff schedule for all goods entering Mexico through the port of Matamoros. Merchants in Brownsville were overjoyed by this action, and American goods rapidly flowed into Matamoros. Goods entering Mexico through this port not only appeased Carvajal's Brownsville supporters, it also denied revenue to the revolutionary movement at Camargo.[16]

By early October 1851, Carvajal's forces at Camargo had been reinforced by several companies of new American recruits. A company of eighty filibusters from Corpus Christi, under the command of Captain Joseph Davis Howell, the son-in-law of Jefferson Davis, arrived in Camargo, and a company of men under the command of the famous mercenary Colonel Chatham Roberdeau "Rob" Wheat reported for duty. Last but not least, a company of about thirty Texas Rangers, led by Colonel John Salmon "Rip" Ford, freshly mustered out of six months of federal service on 23 September 1851, joined the Carvajal army. A few U.S. Army deserters from posts at Ringgold Barracks, Fort Brown, and Paso del Aguila (Eagle Pass) who were living near Lampazos, Mexico, and under the supposed command of a Captain John C. Tod completed the complement of new recruits.[17]

Carvajal's forces began to appear more and more "Americanized" to critical Mexican observers as a result of this influx of new soldiers, causing them to describe the revolutionary army as "muy agringado" [sic], a charge incidentally that had also been leveled against Carvajal by his critics for his Anglo manners and speech.[18] A note of protest from the Mexican minister of foreign relations was directed to the U.S. Department of State on 5 October 1851. This hurried note read in part: "I send you [Daniel Webster] by British express . . . a copy of a note . . . touching the disasters suffered by troops of the Mexican Government on the river Bravo from the insurgency of Carbajal and the support alleged to have been given him by armed persons coming directly from the American territory."[19]

A more complete message of protest was sent on 23 October 1851 that appealed for American action against the filibusters: "It will be impossible to prevent the commission of hostile acts against Mexico, on the part of a large portion of the inhabitants of the American frontier, while those who are guilty of such excesses, are not tried and punished, according to the laws of the country. . . . The love of gain, on the part of a great number of smugglers, residing in villages, situated on the frontier of this Republic, is the principal cause of all the depredations and aggressions which are so frequently committed against Mexico."[20] Carvajal's revolutionary army, despite the pleas from the Mexican government for American action, was now poised for a descent on Matamoros.

By 6 October 1851 the revolutionary army had captured Reynosa, in a bloodless victory. The alcalde of Reynosa, Manuel de la Viña, was an adherent of the Plan de La Loba and surrendered the town and its military garrison, which yielded up one cannon and a considerable supply of ammunition, provisions, and supplies to Carvajal's forces, then desperately in need of these important sinews of war. The single captured cannon, a six-pounder, placed under the command of Colonel Rob Wheat, was the only artillery piece in the revolutionary army.[21]

Alarming reports now filtered back to Washington, D.C., that armed parties of American and Mexican filibusters were crossing and recrossing the U.S. border on the Rio Grande. These attacks against Mexico, a coun-

try with which the United States was now at peace, were expressly pro-
hibited by the U.S. Neutrality Act of 1818. The U.S. government seemed to
ignore the volatile situation then being played out on the border. One
source claimed that no advance warning had been given to the president
by his many agents in South Texas, which was a very unlikely proposition.
A more likely scenario is that this news had not filtered up through the lev-
els of government below the president, or more ominously that some parties had suppressed the information.

Be that as it may, a resolute President Millard Fillmore was finally awakened to direct this tardy proclamation to the Liberators on 23 October
1851, "warning all persons who shall connect themselves with any such
enterprise, in violation of the laws and national obligations of the United
States, that they will thereby subject themselves to the heavy penalties
denounced against such offenders; that if they shall be captured within the
jurisdiction of the Mexican authorities, they must expect to be punished
according to the laws of Mexico, and will have no right to claim the inter-
position of this Government."[22] Notes of warning had already previously
been dispatched to the commanding officers of the U.S. Army garrisons
near the Rio Grande. One such note, issued to the commander of Fort
Brown, ordered that "you will do all in your power to maintain and carry
out the treaties between the United States and Mexico, & prevent directly
or indirectly the support of the insurgents by men & arms."[23]

But while the politicians and diplomats continued to alert forces, warn
of consequences, and threaten doom, José María Carvajal and his Liberator
Army advanced on Matamoros from along the Mexican side of the Rio
Grande. On the evening of 16 October 1851 the Liberator Army, estimated
to be as large as eleven hundred men, was encamped six miles west of
Matamoros at Rancho Guadalupe making preparations to attack the city.
The beleaguered defenders of Matamoros were feverishly preparing that
city for an imminent attack. Streets were barricaded and holes drilled
through the masonry and adobe walls of the houses for gunports. Yet
despite these dangers, a flood of goods continued to pour into the city
from merchants across the river in Brownsville. One observer estimated
that since General Ávalos had reduced tariffs, more than three hundred
thousand dollars of goods had been imported into Matamoros.[24]

The forces of General Ávalos, the National Guards, were commanded in the field by General Macedonio Capistrán de la Garza. Capistrán was a leader of forces that resisted the many Indian raids in that area and had fought against the Americans during the Mexican-American War. Matías Longória and José María Cavázos, both promising politicians who would later hold important positions in the city government of Matamoros, served as Capistrán's lieutenants. Rafaél Quintero served as a colonel, and Colonel Nicolás de la Portilla led the National Guard cavalry.[25]

A delegation of politicians and church officials from the city traveled to the rancho of Las Rucias to hold a parley with Carvajal and discuss possible terms for keeping the peace. Civic leaders considered a bloodless surrender of the city, but only under the condition that Carvajal discharge his American mercenaries; one source stated that he was offered upwards of fifty thousand dollars to rid his forces of the hated *norteamericanos*. But the offer was refused. Carvajal countered by entreating city officials to pronounce in favor of the Plan de La Loba, but the counteroffer was rejected. Local politicians in the delegation doubted Carvajal's good faith, while the church members could hardly think of throwing their support to any Mexican professing to be a Protestant.

On 19 October, Carvajal addressed a letter to each of the foreign consuls in Matamoros: "I am now before the city with an armed and organized force, and without delay I intend to attack the troops of the Government. . . . I desire to protect the persons and property of any peaceful citizens and particularly those of the nations who are at peace with the Mexican people, I desire that you will immediately take the necessary steps to place the persons and property of your countrymen in safety." The consuls—J. F. Waddell, U.S. consul; M. Bousigues, vice consul of France; A. Uhade, Her Brittanic Majesty's vice consul; and Dímas de Tórres, vice consul of Spain—promptly returned a note the same day declaring that "we have hoisted the flags of the respective nations we represent." Their consular offices, sitting beneath the flags of their countries for identification, were not to be the target of any attacks from the Liberators.[26]

The Liberators attacked the defenses of Matamoros on 20 October. From across the river, Helen Chapman, wife of Brevet Major W. W. Chapman, stationed at Fort Brown, noted: "[Oct. 21] . . . Yesterday, Carvajal took possession of Fort Paredes. . . . Brownsville is crowded to overflowing and I suppose great numbers are without shelter. . . . For a week or fortnight past, Brownsville has been filled with wild, strange looking beings, many of whom, probably in spite of all the vigilance of troops from the garrison, have effected a passage to the other side."[27] Observers estimated that between a thousand and fifteen hundred women and children fled Matamoros, seeking refuge in the streets of Brownsville, many destitute.[28]

The commanding officer of Fort Brown, Captain J. W. Phelps, with his small complement of men, struggled desperately to prevent parties of armed men from crossing the Rio Grande into Mexico to reinforce Carvajal's army. He mounted a piece of artillery on the deck of the *Corvette,* a government-owned river steamer, and with twelve men and an officer aboard, steamed up and down the river to interdict illegal crossings. A guard and a piece of artillery were placed at each of the ferry crossings, but Carvajal's Brownsville contingent was able to effect crossings at ranchos above and below the city by the use of canoes, forcing their horses to swim.[29]

Members of the Brownsville Company of the Liberator Army, led by Captain Edward C. Hord, an attorney residing in Brownsville, would cross the river in the evening to fight with Carvajal's forces and return to their homes in Brownsville early the next day to rest and conduct business during the daylight hours. At this time of the year the Rio Grande was so low that despite the efforts of the U.S. Army to guard the crossings, the river could be forded almost everywhere.[30] Helen Chapman wrote that "the position of the Regular Army here [Brownsville] is by no means pleasant." Citizens of Brownsville, sympathetic to Carvajal's cause, had become hostile to the officers and men of the U.S. Army, whose duty it was to patrol the river and enforce U.S. neutrality laws.[31]

Hostilities commenced on Monday, 20 October, in the afternoon, when a patrol of Liberators, probing the city's western defenses, discovered that Fort Paredes was lightly manned. An attack dislodged the defenders from that earthen fortress, and an enthusiastic Carvajal ordered the band that accompanied the Liberator Army to celebrate this victorious occasion with music. There was a pause in the chattering of musketry for a few moments as the sounds of stirring marches and sweet waltzes filled the air. The one piece of Liberator artillery, a six-pounder, was placed inside the walls of the earthen fort and commenced firing on selected targets within the city. By Tuesday the entire Liberator Army, estimated at this time to be a thousand men, was headquartered at Fort Paredes, from where they skirmished with the National Guard defenders throughout the balance of the day. Liberator casualties were one killed and three wounded, all Americans. General Ávalos's losses were seven dead and a large number wounded.[32]

The sounds of the fighting could be clearly heard in Brownsville, across the river. Helen Chapman reported that "all day yesterday [21 October] we heard the rattle of musketry and the roar of cannon. Last evening, riding through Brownsville, we saw, as usual, crowds of Mexicans and the whole American population in a state of most intense excitement. All business was suspended, and the highest houses were covered with people witnessing the battle."[33]

This day also witnessed a unique test of U.S. neutrality laws. In the morning the charter steamer *Neptune* appeared off Brazos Santiago. On board were about 150 Mexican troops and two cannons, sent from Tampico by General Garay to reinforce General Ávalos's defenders in Matamoros. The Mexican troops requested permission to land there and proceed across U.S. soil to Matamoros. Captain J. W. Phelps, commanding at Fort Brown, denied this request, citing possible violations of the neutrality laws. The Mexican troops then chartered the river steamer *Mentoria,* a private boat, to transport them, via the Gulf of Mexico to the mouth of the Rio Grande and hence up the Rio Grande to Matamoros. Phelps agreed to such a movement of Mexican troops, feeling that such an action did not violate neutrality laws. The *Mentoria* was proceeding to Matamoros, loaded with the Mexican troops, when intercepted by an express boat with a message from Phelps. He had suddenly withdrawn his permission and ordered the *Mentoria* to return immediately to Brazos Santiago. The Mexican troops, unable to reach Matamoros either by land or sea, were then reboarded on the *Neptune* to return to Tampico. It is quite likely that pressure from Carvajal had caused Phelps to relent on his earlier decision.

As the *Mentoria* steamed in the Gulf of Mexico with its cargo of Mexican reinforcements, Carvajal had fired off a bombastic letter of protest to Phelps. Phelps, upset by the letter's angry tone, penned an unfriendly response to Carvajal on 25 October from Fort Brown that questioned a right of protest, as Carvajal occupied no official position with the recognized government of Mexico. Phelps further charged the Liberator Army with violations of the rights of American neutrals residing in Matamoros.

Carvajal responded to Phelps's note with a second diatribe in which he described himself as the appointed agent of Camargo, Guerrero, Reynosa, and "other independent towns of the north" to lead their struggle for independence. He specifically denied responsibility for several fires that had destroyed buildings in Matamoros, claiming that the fires had been started by the defenders of Matamoros to burn his headquarters, which housed a large supply of ammunition.[34] Carvajal further protested the use of river steamers plying the international waters of the Rio Grande to secure the many river crossings. "I have seen troops wearing the uniform of the United States" halting civilians crossing the river on the ferries and subjecting them to rigorous search and examination. He reminded Phelps that any violators of the civil and criminal laws of the United States should be prosecuted by the civilian courts. He protested that "I am not aware that the military department of that Government [United States] has any particular right to interfere in the punishment of a crime, whatever power it may assume to prevent its commission."[35]

A heavy attack on the city occurred on Wednesday, with Carvajal's forces capturing the customs house despite heavy cannon fire on the attackers from the six twelve-pounders and two six-pounder cannons in General Ávalos's arsenal. The Liberator Army, led by Colonel Ford, penetrated to the buildings fronting the northwest corner of the main plaza while Ávalos's forces occupied the church and other buildings on the opposite side. By evening the defenders had placed cannons across the plaza opposite Ford and his Texas Rangers and had begun to rake them with heavy fire. Cannonballs began to shatter the masonry walls that sheltered Ford and his men. A wall struck by one shot fell on Captain Andrew "Andy" Jackson Walker, with bricks and masonry raining on his head. Walker dug himself out of the debris cursing, "Damn them, they have mashed my new hat." Ford wryly remarked that the hat had cost Walker $1.25.[36]

Leading a reconnaissance of Mexican positions, John E. Wilson, one of Ford's men, had climbed onto the roof of a cabin for a better view. A cannonball came tearing through the building, and Wilson jumped down, exclaiming to his fellow Rangers that he had been struck in the side by the six-pound ball. He left for the rear ranks after reporting to his amazed comrades that he advised retreat if the firing got any hotter, but being as he was disabled, he would need to leave immediately.[37] During this attack Major Alfred Norton was severely wounded by a cannonball that tore off his arm. Exact casualties were unknown, but it was thought that the defenders had suffered heavily.[38]

After dark, Ford moved his men back to the customs house, where he received an order from General Carvajal to retire from the city center and return to Fort Paredes. Ford ignored the order, and soon a second order to retreat was delivered to him personally by Colonel John L. Haynes, in a low voice so as not to be heard by the men of Ford's command. Again Ford refused to obey the command, and the third command to retreat was soon delivered to Ford, this time in a loud voice. Both Ford and his men protested the order to give up the part of the city they had taken during the day, knowing that on the morrow they would have to battle again to retake the same ground. But Ford yielded to Carvajal's command, saying to his men: "Gentlemen, if we were in the service of a regularly organized government, I would disobey and be court-martialed. Insomuch as we are acting in a revolution, and as yet without a government, I shall obey because obedience is the only tie which can hold this army together."[39] Carvajal justified his action in withdrawing the troops by citing the actions of General Zachary Taylor during the attack on Monterey during the Mexican-American War. Ford disagreed with Carvajal's order, as had Colonel Jefferson Davis done with General Taylor's order to evacuate Monterey some five years earlier.[40]

That evening Carvajal summoned a Catholic priest residing in Brownsville, the French Abbé Domenech, to his headquarters at Fort Paredes. The general begged the Catholic priest to return the next day and tend to the spiritual needs of his wounded soldiers. On Thursday morning a Mexican guide brought the good father across the river into the strife of Matamoros. Father Domenech was led up the "Rue du Commerce" in the direction of a barricade manned with cannon. As this party progressed to their destination, a large ball struck a brick building behind them, which crumbled in a cloud of dust. Shortly thereafter, Father Domenech's Mexican guide fell from the effects of a mortal wound, a cannonball had carried away his thigh and abdomen. As the padre was giving the last rites to his dying guide, an officer of the Liberator Army appeared and led Father Domenech to the Liberator hospital. The hospital was described as a "wretched hovel" in which six mortally wounded men were being treated by an Irish surgeon. Father Domenech dispatched the surgeon to treat his fallen guide and then proceeded to administer the last rites to the stricken men. Five of the wounded men died shortly thereafter.[41]

On Thursday an attacking party of 250 Liberator troops, led by Colonel John S. Ford, returned to the northwest corner of the main plaza. True to Ford's suspicions, Ávalos's defenders had, in the mean time, heavily reinforced the plaza. Sandbag revetments had been placed on the rooftops of buildings on the south side of the plaza, and cannons were mounted to place the north side of the plaza in a deadly crossfire. From their forward position Ford's men faced a tremendous barrage from the massed cannons and small arms of Ávalos's forces. With such a strongly fortified position across his path of advance, Ford cancelled plans for any further forward movements onto the plaza during the remainder of the day. As Ford peered from a door that fronted on the main square, a ball struck him on the head, "cutting his hat band and passing out at the top of the hat." Claiming that the three-inch scalp wound had "affected his mind," Ford turned command of the Rangers over to Major James Taylor, his subordinate, and crossed the Rio Grande for treatment in the Brownsville home of Dr. D. Dunlap. General Ávalos was struck in the same action by a spent bullet and his aide, Colonel Zapata, was slightly wounded.[42]

During Friday daytime, 24 October, the city was quiet, but by 9 P.M. the Liberator Army launched a massive attack on the city's defenses. A destructive fire began after twilight and some of the city's finest buildings were reduced to ashes. The fire commenced in the Devine Building, which was quickly consumed, as was the adjoining Resaca House. Both buildings contained merchants' goods estimated at a value of forty thousand dollars. There is little doubt that much of this merchandise had been brought into Matamoros in response to General Ávalos's order reducing excessive import duties. American Consul J. F. Waddell struggled to save an estimated twenty thousand dollars in goods in the burning Resaca House, the property of an American citizen. A number of the National Guard had set aside their arms to aid the worthy consul, and one Mexican citizen displayed the American banner for protection. Despite the banner, however, Carvajal's forces fired on Waddell's party, disregarding the promise to honor the flag of neutrals. A buckshot, fired by Texas Ranger A. J. Mason, wounded Waddell in the cheek. Waddell retreated from the scene, but as neither side would allow the other to tend to the fires, they continued to burn out of control and consume other buildings.

In answer to the charge that his forces had wounded Waddell, Carvajal stated that "his [Waddell's] flag and official residence were scrupulously respected," but that Waddell had only himself to blame. He had abandoned his sanctuary and mixed with the throng of spectators, assisting porters in securing bales of merchants' goods within the range of the attackers' guns and was thus wounded. Carvajal claimed that Waddell's wounding was his own fault, and that he had no right to complain.[43]

There was a lull in the fighting on Saturday, but Sunday found Carvajal's forces mounting an unsuccessful attack designed to gain a position near the Grand Plaza, where Ávalos's headquarters were located. But the intense cannon fire again drove the Liberator Army away. Hard fighting continued throughout Monday, but the defenders stubbornly held their ground. No large-scale attacks occurred on either Tuesday or Wednesday.

As of Tuesday, 28 October 1851, among those casualties reported as killed were Peter Culver, a Brownsville merchant, and Alexander Langstroth, a Matamoros merchant shot by a sniper as he struggled on the roof of his store in Matamoros to control a fire. However, it is quite possible that Langstroth was assassinated by one of the Mexican defenders for his defiance of Ávalos's orders. As the former collector of customs in Matamoros, Langstroth had directed opposition to the reduced Ávalos customs schedule and had been arrested and imprisoned on 7 October 1851 for his opposition. Among the wounded were one F. R. Gracesqui, who lost his right arm to a cannonball, and one R. Finley, who later died from his wounds.[44]

In a letter of 29 October a correspondent from Brownsville reported that the city was desperately in need of the services of a federal marshal and a U.S. attorney. The correspondent reported that the patriotic zeal surrounding Carvajal's attack had all but vanished in Brownsville, and it was considered now to be no more than an armed invasion from the United States. The Liberator Army's sole mission had now become looting, robbery, and other excesses. The plunder taken from the peaceful residents of Matamoros was being ferried across the river for storage in the United States.[45]

But to another observer it was not clear that the soldiers of the Liberator Army were the looters. He reported, as had Helen Chapman, that "a considerable band of marauding scoundrels hang about . . . Matamoros, ready to rob and murder all who fall in their way." To enforce discipline among his troops, Carvajal ordered two of his soldiers who had been caught looting to be severely whipped, and he issued the most stringent orders for the punishment of any others caught in the act of looting.[46] After more than a week of piecemeal battles between the National Guard and the Liberator Army, General Ávalos's hospital contained more than 108 wounded men. The number of dead was unknown but estimated to be at least half that number.

One writer, so close to the action that he did not have to raise his eyes from the sheet to see the "flash of every discharge," reported that Carvajal's army has lost the enthusiasm that it had when it initiated the attack on Matamoros almost ten days earlier. There is a great reluctance on the part of the Liberator Army to carry the city by storm, "they evidently have a great horror for Avalos' big guns."[47] One of the decisive factors in the battle was the big superiority in number of cannon by Ávalos's forces, which reportedly included six twelve-pounders and two six-pounders, as opposed to the single six-pounder in Carvajal's stock of artillery. The lone six-pounder simply did not have enough power to crumble the solid masonry walls on the Grand Plaza.

Carvajal's sole artillery piece was commanded by Colonel Chatham Roberdeau "Rob" Wheat, the six foot four inch, two-hundred-sixty-pound veteran mercenary who admiringly referred to Carvajal as "our youthful general." Despite the small number and caliber of his artillery, Wheat had done fearful execution on the Matamoros defenders. When all artillery ammunition for his piece had been expended, Wheat ordered a blacksmith to cut bars of iron into a proper length and fired these in his cannon. But the massive masonry walls were simply too strong for the smaller cannon. Wheat wishfully exclaimed to Carvajal that he had converted his six-pounder to a twelve-pounder by taking half the distance.[48] During these ten days of siege, Ávalos's artillery expended between four hundred and five hundred cannon rounds, canister, grape, and shot. In reply, Wheat had fired only about one hundred rounds.[49]

Ávalos's forces had captured four soldiers of the Liberator Army—Robert McDonald, a Texian and member of Colonel Ford's Company; George Williams; and two Mexicans, Estanislao Villegas and Jesús Gómez. A suggestion was made to Ávalos that the prisoners should be shot but, according to Ford, Ávalos replied: "It will not do. Shoot these two Texians and a thousand will come to their funeral."[50]

On the morning of 30 October, after ten days of siege, Carvajal surprisingly ordered his forces to abandon the attack on Matamoros and started their retreat to the west. The Texas Rangers, now under the command of Andy Walker, were placed as a rear guard of the army and soon came under a strong attack.[51] About eight miles west of Matamoros, a force of two hundred Mexican cavalry under the command of General José Nicolás de la Portilla formed into a line and charged the Texan rear guard. The Texas horsemen counterattacked, striking the line of attackers in the center, rolling up both ends. The Mexican cavalry lost about thirty men in the attack, while the much smaller Ranger force lost two men. General Portilla and his cavalry returned to Matamoros without any further action, reporting to General Ávalos that "your enemies have gone like dogs with their tails between their legs."[52]

The cavalry attack had created a panic in the ranks of the Liberator Army, and many men abandoned the more or less orderly retreat to swim the river and claim sanctuary in the United States. Colonel Rob Wheat was left with only two men in his artillery company to service the cannon. The cannon's harness had broken, and the piece was being pulled along from horseback with lariats. A decision was then made to abandon the cannon, which was spiked and rolled over the bank into the Rio Grande. A disorganized group of stragglers was now all that remained of the proud Liberator Army that had advanced on Matamoros just ten days earlier.[53]

Carvajal had ordered the retreat in response to reports that two powerful military columns were bearing down on Matamoros to relieve the siege. The first column, with three hundred militia organized from the towns of Victoria and Tula, arrived in Matamoros on 31 October. This army was led by General Antonio Canales, who commanded the National Guard of Tamaulipas.[54] A second army of eight hundred men from Monterey, under the command of General José López Uraga, arrived in Matamoros by mid-November. Uraga's army was supported by several pieces of artillery and a mortar.[55]

The relationship between Antonio Canales and José María Carvajal was indeed puzzling. Both were strong Federalists and had fought together almost hand in hand during the Federalist War of 1838–40 in northern Mexico. They had both resisted the American invasion of northern Mexico during the Mexican-American War, where each had led a division of troops. Two of Canales's sons, José María Canales and Servando Canales, were soldiers in the Liberator Army. The youthful Servando Canales had been raised by Carvajal, who loved him as his own son. Servando would grow up to lead a force that aided in the defeat of the French at the battle of Santa Gertrúdis, fought near Camargo, and would later become governor of Tamaulipas. José María Carvajal's son, José María Jr., would later marry Mamela Canales, daughter of the Mexican general. Perhaps this was why General Canales's relief column tarried so long in marching to the relief of Matamoros. Some observers believe that if the Liberator Army had captured Matamoros, Canales would have transferred his allegiance to the Liberators. But in an address to the city governments of Camargo, Guerrero, and Laredo, Carvajal would later refer to him as that "faithless traitor Canales" for his actions in defeating Carvajal's army at Camargo during the upcoming year.

William Pitt Ballinger, the federal district attorney who would prepare the indictments against Carvajal and his followers for violation of the Neutrality Act of 1818, believed that the Carvajal movement had the clandestine support of "Cardenas [Jesus Cardenas, governor of Tamaulipas], Canales [Antonio Canales Rosillo, commanding the National Guard of Tamaulipas], and Macedonio Capistran [de la Garza], the commander of the National Guard at Matamoros, and other persons of influence." However, with the arrival of John S. Ford and his ex-Rangers to the Carvajal command in September 1851, trouble began. Ford and the Texans refused to be commanded by Canales, whom they classified as a traitor and a coward for his surrender of Federalist forces ending the Federalist wars of northern Mexico in 1840 and his betrayal of the Texan Auxiliaries in Saltillo during that same year. Thus Carvajal decided not to turn over command of the Liberation Army to Canales, and Canales Rosillo "turned his arms in favor of the government."[56]

A note of 13 November 1851 from the Mexican minister Luís de la Rosa to Daniel Webster, secretary of state, registered official Mexican protest to the attack on Matamoros and generally cast a suspicious eye at the United States for a lack of activity in apprehending Carvajal and his men: "The Government of the Undersigned does not believe it possible, that expeditions of adventurers, against Mexico, could be organized on the frontier of the United States, and those adventurers be provided with arms, ammunitions, and provisions, without the most culpable dissimulation and sufferance, on the part of those authorities and functionaries, whose duty, it ought to be, to prevent those excesses. It, therefore, considers the government of the United States, responsible for those excesses."[57]

The defeat of the Liberator Army at Matamoros marked the downturn of Carvajal's reputation in the press. Articles now appeared critical of Carvajal's generalship, and the U.S. public began to realize that "American" fighting men were not invincible against Mexicans. Ovid Johnson, editor of the pro-Liberator newspaper *Rio Bravo,* even headlined an article on Carvajal's retreat as "General Caravajal's pale faced flight."[58] The blame for the unsuccessful attack on Matamoros lay squarely on Carvajal's shoulders. He had demonstrated a complete lack of military skills, withdrawing his forces in the evening of his greatest success from the hard-won forward positions on the Grand Plaza, and thereafter fought his battles in the streets of Matamoros as a series of small armed skirmishes, refusing to commit his entire force to a single assault. His attacks were uncoordinated and ill-timed. But above all, Carvajal had lost the most important struggle of the campaign by failing to gain the hearts and support of his countrymen living in Matamoros.

Mexicans were turned against him by his use of a large force of American mercenaries. Mexicans who hated the Central government hated only one other thing with greater passion: Americans. Carvajal had antic-ipated that he would receive great support from the citizens of Matamoros, who would join him in rebellion as soon as he entered the city. But his army, "muy agringada," was led by the "muy agringado" Protestant Mexican, José María, who was eyed with distrust by his countrymen. Many Mexicans felt that the Central government might not be any worse than surrendering to another army of Americans who might again annex their lands. And last but not least, Carvajal, a Protestant, could gain no support from the Catholic Church, who would not willingly place their city into the hands of an *hereje* (heretic).

In a story Carvajal related to John S. Ford a proposition was presented to José María by Mifflin Kenedy. Kenedy, of the powerful firm of Kenedy and King, representing several American border merchants, offered to advance credit for the supplies and ordnance needed by the Liberator Army if Carvajal would relinquish command of the army and accept the position as president of a provisional government. It was probably certain that this cartel of "investors" wanted Ford to command the army instead of Carvajal, but José María refused the offer. Carvajal's refusal was worded in the simple sentence that tells a great deal about the idealistic nature of the quixotic José María: "I told him [Kenedy] my ambition was to be the Washington of my country."[59]

The Republic of Mexico was proud of the successful struggle put up by the defenders of Matamoros. On 7 November 1850 the Tamaulipas state legislature passed a proclamation stating that hereafter the title of the city would become "Leal Invicta y Heroica Ciudad de Matamoros," or the Loyal, Unconquered, and Heroic City of Matamoros. The National Congress passed the same proclamation on 28 May 1852, and the grand city of Matamoros retains that same title even to this day.[60]

Carvajal's forces were reported to be in Reynosa on 12 November 1851, where he continued to recruit soldiers for his Liberator Army. With him in Reynosa were the Texas Ranger force, led by Captain Andy Walker, and other officers that included Captain E. R. Hord, Majors McMicken and Everett, and Lieutenants Brown and Garza.[61] Carvajal's many friends in Texas had promised to raise a regiment of infantry and another of cavalry and had attempted to negotiate through Memphis, Tennessee, for a badly needed supply of cannon.[62] In a letter to his mother, written from Camargo on 21 November, Roberdeau Wheat observed that "the general is for the time being recruiting his forces. We may remain here two weeks; but shall then move towards the enemy who are very much afraid of us. . . . I am anxiously awaiting the arrival of some heavy pieces from the United States. . . . My pay is $200 a month and I can save something out of that."[63]

Carvajal returned to Camargo at a later date, residing at Villanueva, while many of his American mercenaries crossed the Rio Grande to camp near Rio Grande City at the ranchos in that area. On 22 November the peace and quiet of the countryside was broken by Major Jack Everett, who rode into Camargo from his ranch, near the conjunction of the Rio Alamo with the Rio Grande, to report disquieting news. The Centralist General Antonio María Jáuregui had arrived in Mier from Monterey at the head of an army of five hundred soldiers supported by two pieces of artillery. The soldiers consisted of Mexican regulars interspersed with Seminole and Kickapoo Indians. Major Everett, who had completed a reconnaissance of Mier on the preceding night, reported that Centralist forces were fortifying the village and Jáuregui had set up his headquarters on the village's principal square. Later reports placed the force at 350 Mexican troops, mostly regulars, fifty Seminole Indians, and two cannons.[64]

A correspondent to the *New Orleans Picayune,* writing from Corpus Christi, Texas, expressed concern about the use of Indians to fight in the ranks of the Centralists: "It is absurd to think the United States can restrain and govern these tribes, when Mexico hires them to do her own internal fighting. . . . There can be no doubt of their being in the regular employ of Mexico, and there is as little doubt that one day Mexico will complain of the United States, and ask indemnification for the spoliations these very fellows may commit."[65]

But the Mexican government had granted lands to the Seminole Indians provided that they would defend the republic in time of peril. A rumor was being circulated at this time in San Antonio, Texas, to the effect that Seminole Chief Wildcat was in Eagle Pass, Texas, offering a two-dollar bounty for Americans to join his command. The chief was there to recruit a unit of irregulars for service in the Centralist Army of the North against the Carvajal revolutionaries.[66] Carvajal immediately issued orders for those of his soldiers who were camped north of the Rio Bravo to cross over and join him in Camargo. By the next morning Carvajal's Liberator Army, with a force of two hundred cavalry and one hundred infantry, advanced in a forced march on Mier, some thirty miles west of Camargo. Two hundred additional volunteer soldiers from Rio Grande City, Alamo, and Roma joined Carvajal's forces on the march.[67]

On the night of 24 November 1851, Carvajal arrived at Punta Aguda, about five leagues from Mier, to find that Jáuregui and his forces had fled Mier. The Centralists were retreating to Monterey to avoid being cut off from that city by the advance of Carvajal's forces. Carvajal's forces were exhausted by the rapid pace of the march, but smelled blood and were rallied by the oratory of an impassioned Carvajal. By the next morning the Liberator Army had abandoned its baggage to move more swiftly and had left the main road, taking to the chaparral to overtake the forces of Jáuregui. Carvajal's army returned to the main road to Monterey about five leagues from Cerralvo, near the little village of Papagallo. The forced march had placed Carvajal's army between Monterey and the retreating forces of Jáuregui. A clash of arms was now inevitable.[68]

On the outskirts of Cerralvo, Carvajal received a message from the alarmed alcalde begging him not to fight in the village. Carvajal replied that he wished also that the battle would not be fought in Cerralvo; his greatest desire was to meet the Centralists in an open field. But Jáuregui took refuge in the city, fortifying the town by cutting loopholes in the adobe walls of the buildings that lined the street to the principal square. Carvajal's forces, in a bitter two-day house-by-house struggle, forced the Centralists to the principal square. In desperation, Jáuregui's Centralist forces sought refuge in the cathedral located there, an excellent defensive position surrounded by a stone wall. Carvajal's forces rushed the cathedral grounds, leaping over the stone wall with muskets in hand, often landing head first among their enemies. The Centralists retreated in panic, rushing in all directions from the church, but were soon reformed in a large stone building nearby, known locally as La Cureña, that served as a nunnery. The building had an interesting history, serving as an American quartermaster's depot during the Mexican-American War and sheltering American soldiers during a siege by the forces of General Urrea in early 1847.[69]

Carvajal controlled the remainder of the city and had captured Jáuregui's baggage train, provisions, and most of their ammunition. But the Centralists still maintained possession of their two pieces of artillery, which fired on the Liberator Army from the protection of the stone nunnery with rocks and scrap metal when their supply of cannonballs had been exhausted. As the Centralist position was too strong to take by direct assault, it was decided to lay siege to the nunnery and starve Jáuregui's forces into submission.

During this attack Carvajal's casualties were ten men killed and twenty-four wounded, including Captain Christopher C. Chinn, Lieutenant Graham, and Colonel Roberdeau Wheat, who was shot in the arm while leading the charge on the cathedral. The total extent of casualties for Jáuregui's forces was unknown, but it appeared that most of the Seminole Indians had been killed as well as their chief. The Texas Ranger Company, bearing a special hatred for Indians, concentrated their fire on the Seminole warriors. Two Negroes, a part of the Seminole force, were killed in one house. Private Clark of the Rangers, with unerring aim, shot a Seminole chief and stripped him of his headdress of buffalo horns. Lugging the Indian headdress into Carvajal's headquarters, Clark announced to the surprised staff that he had "taken in the sign of the big bull of the rancho."[70]

In his memoirs John S. Ford reported the loss of an "Old Ranger," Plas McCurly, in the battle with the Seminoles. McCurly had a dream the night before, seeing himself killed by a musket ball through the neck. The popular McCurly reported the vision to his fellow Rangers, who had struggled unsuccessfully to keep him out of the fight that day. Taking turns firing from a loophole in a stone wall at Seminole positions, McCurly advanced to the loophole, discharged his musket, and immediately received in turn a ball fired through the loophole. The ball struck McCurly in the neck, as prophesied in his dream, and he fell dead.[71]

During the battle that raged in Cerralvo, Carvajal's forces captured Major Camacho and his men, the Centralist defenders of Camargo that Carvajal had captured in September. Camacho and his officers had signed a parole at that time in which they swore that they would not take up arms again against Carvajal and his Liberator Army. Under the conventions of war Carvajal now had the right as a belligerent to execute these men, but instead released them after refusing to accept their offer of a second parole. Total Mexican casualties were not known, but nine of the Centralist artillerymen had been killed, and their captain wounded and captured.[72]

A hasty note from Major Jack Everett on 29 November 1851 expressed the high morale of the Liberator Army:

> I promised to write you when anything of importance occurred. I do so now to say that we have routed the enemy in every sense of the word. We have driven them through every house in the town to a large stone building formerly occupied by the American army's quartermaster store. Today we expect to capture their whole force and then prepare to meet the troops of Uraga from Matamoros. If, however, we are unsuccessful, we will harass the approaching army at every turn in the road. Our men have proven themselves to be the right stamp. 'God and Liberty' is our cry, and will be until the banner of Carvajal, the liberating chief, shall wave o'er the ruins of prostrate despotism.[73]

A final assault on La Cureña was planned for 27 November 1851, when news reached Cerralvo that Centralist General José López Uraga with a force of one thousand men and six pieces of artillery was bearing down on Cerralvo from Matamoros on the Aldamas road to relieve the siege. Not strong enough to battle both forces and low on ammunition, Carvajal ordered a retreat northward to the border town of Guerrero. The battle fought in Cerralvo had been costly to the Liberators. Captain Chinn, Lieutenant Graham, and Lieutenant Plas McCurly had been killed, as well as a private in Walker's Ranger Company, and six Mexicans of McLean's and Garcia's companies. Among those wounded were Colonel Roberdeau Wheat and Captain Joseph Davis Howell, not seriously, and seven privates. The Liberator Army dallied in Guerrero for several days, but as General Uraga's army neared, Carvajal's army fled to the Rio Grande. The Liberator Army, with an estimated 210 men crossed the Rio Grande, returning to the United States on 3 December 1851. Carvajal was shortly thereafter reported to have made his headquarters in the United States at the Hacienda of Agua Nueva, about fifteen miles north of Davis's Rancho (Rio Grande City).[74]

SEVEN

Defeat at Camargo

The revolution is no more, "for the present." The brave little
General [Carvajal] has been deserted by his Mexican friends.

MAJOR JACK R. EVERETT,
Liberator Army, in a letter to the *National Intelligencer,*
17 March 1852

The U.S. federal government, in early 1852, struggled to rebound from the crisis instigated by José María Carvajal's incursions into northern Mexico. Since the secession of the lands between the Nueces River and Rio Grande from Mexico by the Treaty of Guadalupe Hidalgo, no federal marshals or other federal civil officials had been appointed to enforce laws in this vast region. Moreover, this area had received insufficient protection from the understaffed forces of the U.S. Army, and consequently a state of virtual anarchy existed among the citizens living along the Rio Grande. Carvajal's invasion of Mexico had literally caught the U.S. government in Washington, D.C., unprepared to govern this region and dispense federal laws. But the administration of President Millard Fillmore was finally jarred into action by the strident Mexican diplomatic protests of this unwarranted invasion of Mexican soil by a country that claimed to be at peace with it.

By February 1852, at the urging of Washington, the federal district judge for the State of Texas, John C. Watrous, convened a federal grand jury in Brownsville, Texas, the first to ever meet south of the Nueces River. Even before sufficient evidence against Carvajal and the men of his army could be gathered, Federal District Attorney William Pitt Ballinger presented a hurriedly prepared case against Carvajal and his lieutenants that convinced a majority of the grand jurors to vote a true bill. Ballinger then dispatched newly appointed deputy federal marshals into the countryside to gather the evidence against Carvajal that would be needed for a conviction. Broadly speaking, the officers of Carvajal's Liberation Army had been bound over by the grand jury for trial on charges of violating U.S. neutrality.

To understand the indictments brought against Carvajal and the men of his army by the U.S. government, it is important to examine portions of the U.S. Neutrality Act of 1818. Sections 1, 2, 5, and 8 of the act are of primary importance in the Carvajal matter. Section 1 prohibits citizens living within U.S. territory from accepting commissions to serve against any nation with whom the United States is at peace. Section 2 prohibits all persons living in the United States from enlisting or hiring other persons to serve against any nation at peace with the United States. Section 5 prohibits any person from setting on foot any military expedition from the United States against any nation at peace with the United States. Finally, Section 8 empowers the U.S. president to employ the forces of the army and the navy to enforce the provisions of the neutrality act as shall be judged necessary. The U.S. government based their hasty indictments against Carvajal and his cohorts almost exclusively on Section 5 of the Neutrality Act, ironically the only section of the act that Carvajal had bothered to comply with.[1] In a more general sense the United States, as a signatory to the Treaty of Guadalupe Hidalgo, was bound by provisions respecting the boundary lines of the Republic of Mexico. Article 5 of this treaty laid out the boundary lines between the two republics, and the last paragraph of this article stated: "The boundary line established by this article shall be religiously respected by each of the two republics."

In early September 1851 the U.S. government had done essentially nothing to extend federal laws into South Texas. The only civil federal agents on the border were revenue officers Frank Latham, stationed at Brownsville, and W. B. Brashear, an attorney directing revenue collection at Rio Grande City. The newspaper *Rio Bravo* asserted the pressing necessity for an immediate session of federal courts at Brownsville: "The revenue officers have made many seizures, some of which have brought them and the State officers into immediate collision, and nothing but a high degree of forbearance and prudence has prevented bloodshed. These questions, in a great degree, belong to the federal court."[2] The government in Washington, D.C., had still not become alarmed by the rumors of a filibuster army, led by Carvajal, massing in the United States to invade northern Mexico.

The army posts on the border had been neglected and the garrisons undermanned. The post at Fort Brown consisted of Companies B and K of the 4th Regiment of Artillery, with an aggregate strength of eighty-nine privates and noncommissioned officers. The officers at this post were Captain John W. Phelps, commanding; Nathan Jarvis, surgeon; Lieutenants Julius P. Garesche, Henry M. Whiting, John Gibbon, James Holmes, Rufus Saxton Jr., Hugh E. Dungan; and Paymaster Henry Hill. Ringgold Barracks, ninety miles above Brownsville at Rio Grande City, was garrisoned by Companies C and E of the 1st Regiment of Infantry, with an aggregate strength of 102 privates and noncommissioned officers. The officers at Ringgold Barracks were Captain and Brevet Major Joseph H. LaMotte, commanding; Nicholas L. Campbell, assistant surgeon; Captain William E. Prince; and Lieutenants George D. Brewerton, Egbert Viele, Daniel Huston, and Samuel Holabird. With this aggregate of soldiers the federal government made a futile attempt to guard all border crossings on the Rio Grande for a distance of more than two hundred miles. To complicate matters, the river was very low at times of the year, and a crossing could be made on the Rio Grande at almost any point.[3]

When rumor became fact in late September 1851, and the Liberator Army moved across the Rio Bravo at Rio Grande City to capture Camargo, there was hand-wringing in Washington, D.C. Information on the delicate situation then playing out on the Texas border had evidently been kept from President Millard Fillmore. By 22 October 1851, however, Fillmore was moved to action and published a warning to the belligerents now engaged in fighting in northern Mexico—but he could do little else. The U.S. Army could only stand by as interested spectators while events unfolded.[4]

One such spectator of the events, Captain LaMotte, recorded his impressions of the Carvajal incursions into Mexico. In a letter of 27 September 1851 from LaMotte to his wife, Ellen, Carvajal's capture of Camargo was noted: "The Mexicans opposite have set on foot another revolution and with the aid of some of our loafing population have dislodged the troops from Camargo and are at this time in possession of that town. It is understood they will soon march upon Reynosa and Matamoros. If successful along the Rio Grande it is confidently believed that the territory this side of the mountains will proclaim itself independent and so reenact under the shadows of the Sierra Madre the grand texan drama."[5] LaMotte expressed no sympathy for any filibustering actions and reserved special criticism for the ill-fated López Expedition to drive the Spaniards from Cuba.[6]

By 25 October 1851, LaMotte noted that "the revolutionists on the frontier of Mexico having taken Camargo are now concentrating about the ancient city of Matamoros—the insurgents are 1,000 strong—a day or two will settle the question."[7] The thin blue line of the U.S. Army, who was patrolling the frontier against Indian raids, had been stretched even thinner by the Carvajal incursion. In a letter of 25 November 1851, LaMotte reported the circulation of "a rumor to the effect that Gen. [Persifor F.] Smith who commands this Department designs pushing the Infantry farther out, into the indian country, the invasion of a neighboring Mexican State and the delicate duties required of our troops along the Rio Grande, will perhaps cause some delay in this contemplated change of position."[8]

With the failure of Carvajal to capture Matamoros, LaMotte wrote of the success of Mexican forces: "There is very great excitement on the Rio Grande yet growing out of the efforts making by the fillibusteros, to revolutionize the adjoining States of Mexico. It is far from being settled yet the Mex. troops are at present in the ascendent [sic] and I think will be able to rule the storms tho' much is said of the indomitable energy and perserverence [sic] of the Saxon race—I hope the affair will soon terminate one way or the other—this state of hostilities is ruinous to the business portion of the community and, I am sure, anything but agreeable to us."[9]

But steps were slowly being taken to enforce federal laws in South Texas. John Charles Watrous, U.S. federal district judge for Texas, responded to a direct plea from the president to take action against the filibusters. He arrived in Brownsville in early 1852, accompanied by Ben McCulloch, federal marshal for the Eastern District of Texas, to impanel a grand jury. Judge Watrous set about organizing his court in Brownsville, holding the first sessions at the Botica del Lion, at Twelfth and Elizabeth Streets, on 22 January 1852, with F. W. Fount Le Roy as clerk of the court. Watrous immediately issued writs to convene grand and petit juries, and on the next day grand jury members were impaneled. The newly appointed deputy marshal, Brownsville resident John K. Leman, was dispatched into the countryside to collect evidence concerning any possible violation of federal laws associated with Carvajal's two invasions of Mexico.[10]

Lieutenant A. P. Hill met U.S. Deputy Marshal Leman while the latter was busily attempting to collect evidence of neutrality violations along the Rio Grande. Hill was then stationed at the Rio Grande crossing near Edinburgh (now Hidalgo), a small village on the Rio Grande opposite Reynosa. He had been ordered there with a squad of troops to prevent armed American filibusters from crossing into Mexico. After meeting with Leman, Hill expressed skepticism on the success of the marshal's mission: "The Deputy Marshal, who remains with us to night, on his route to Brownsville—He is hunting up evidence against Carvajal and the Filibusters to present to the grand jury now sitting in Brownsville, but from the evident sympathy manifested by almost every one on behalf of these scoundrels the grand judiciary formality will no doubt end in a farce." Lieutenant Hill's company of the 1st Artillery was staffed by Second Lieutenant James E. Slaughter, described by Hill as "a terrible Filibusterer," who was to later return to the Rio Grande region of South Texas.[11] The Virginian, after having been dismissed from the U.S. Army on 14 May 1861, tendered his services to the Confederacy and rose to the rank of brigadier general in that service. He became Confederate commander of the Rio Grande District, much to the displeasure of Confederate Colonel John S. Ford, a rival. Ford disliked General Slaughter personally, picturing him as an indecisive leader.[12]

During the latter days of December 1851, the Liberator Army lay inactive, dispersed in camps at the ranchos of Agua Nueva Wells, El Sauz, and Escobares. Carvajal was rumored to have his headquarters at the latter location. But armed incursions into Mexico continued. On Christmas eve eight or ten men crossed over from Rio Grande City into Mexico and attacked a party of fifteen or twenty Mexican soldiers guarding the river crossing. Three Mexican soldiers were slain in the affray, brought on, it was claimed, by the guards' display of insulting manners to Americans. One source claimed that on this very day, ladies crossing over into Mexico had been "grossly insulted" by the guards, who wanted to search them and their possessions. The attacking party returned to the U.S. side of the Rio Grande with the horses, saddles, and personal effects of the Mexican soldiers. The names of the Americans composing the attacking party were "not known," although two men were arrested as suspects in the attack and after extensive questioning were released. One American in the attacking party was severely wounded and later died.[13]

At the other end of the lower Rio Grande Valley, the citizens of Brownsville attended a grand ball on Christmas evening, held in the second story of the new Market House. Officers from Fort Brown were in attendance, but the invited party of Mexican officers, which was to be led by General Ávalos, failed to attend. This mysterious no-show was attributed to rumors that Carvajal's forces were again advancing on Matamoros.

On 25 October 1851, President Millard Fillmore, alarmed by continued reports of a buildup of filibuster forces in South Texas, was finally moved to action. Under the authority of the Neutrality Act, Fillmore authorized General Persifor Frazer Smith, commanding the 8th Military District, to take action against the filibuster army of Carvajal: "You are hereby authorized and empowered . . . to take all proper measures . . . as may be necessary for the purpose of preventing the carrying on of any such expedition or enterprise from any port or place within the limits of your command. . . . You will, in cases of doubt, act under the legal advice of the District Attorney of the United States for your district."[14]

General Smith immediately forwarded the order to General William S. Harney, then camped on the Llano River and in the process of negotiating a treaty of peace with the Indians of that region: "I beg you will, as soon as you can conveniently . . . hasten to the Rio Grande, and . . . use all the means in your power to prevent any breach of the act referred to [the Neutrality Act of 1818]."[15] Harney arrived at Ringgold Barracks on 22 November 1851 with an escort of twenty-two soldiers from the 2nd Dragoons and immediately set to work on plans to guard the river crossings. From Brownsville a company of the 4th Artillery, under the command of Major Haskins, was dispatched to guard the crossing at Edinburgh, across from Reynosa.[16]

Captain Prince, with a company of mounted infantry, was sent from Ringgold Barracks to Roma with strict orders to preserve U.S. neutrality and prevent all armed and organized bodies from passing the river at any point. Prince left a detachment at Roma to guard the ferry there, subject to the orders of a Mr. Durgan, the U.S. revenue officer stationed there. Prince's squad continued up the river as far as the ancient crossing on the Rio Grande opposite the Alamo River, near Everett's rancho, placing detachments of men to guard all likely crossing points. Another detachment of men were placed at Belleville, a small village opposite Guerrero, a site that was destined to become a permanent garrison for the U.S. Army. The guard was too late to intercept Carvajal's forces, however, which had crossed at this point from Guerrero on 3 December 1851, after being closely pursued by the Mexican forces of General Uraga.[17]

Army forces, now spread paper-thin along the river, were gradually receiving some reinforcements. A company of the 2nd Dragoons, under the command of Lieutenant Tyler, arrived at Belleville on 9 December, and two mounted companies of the 7th Infantry, under the command of Brevet Majors Paul and Garnett, arrived at Ringgold Barracks.[18] General Harney, aboard the river steamer *Corvette*, proceeded from Ringgold Barracks to Roma, the nominal head of navigation on the river, on 9 December to inspect the river crossings. He had guardedly stated in an earlier interview with the *American Flag* that he was determined to enforce the neutrality laws so far as it lay within his power.[19] Harney was uncertain as to how he should carry out his orders when confronting Carvajal's armed filibuster army. On several occasions the boisterous Harney, a man not known to suffer in silence, questioned the scope of the power given him by the Neutrality Act, expressing doubts of his authority to use violence against civilian violators of the act without the express order of a proper civil officer of the U.S. government. He aired these views publicly on many occasions, and it is quite likely that Carvajal's forces knew of the U.S. Army's reticence to enforce neutrality on the Rio Grande. Harney's public doubts became a hot topic for debate among the junior officers along the Rio Grande with most sharing Harney's doubts.[20]

Even with the new reinforcements, Harney had been given an inadequate force of men to guard the river crossings and patrol this harsh brush country. The river historically was at its lowest level of flow during the winter months, and this year was no exception. There were simply too many fording places on the river to guard. Carvajal and his men knew the river well and would have no difficulty in finding an unguarded crossing place should they wish to cross into Mexico again.

On 29 November, Mexican forces under the command of General José López Uraga occupied the village of Camargo. The Mexican force sounded a parley, and Harney received three of their officers on board the *Corvette*. Their spokesman, Guadalupe García, commandante of the National Guard of Matamoros, functioned as the group spokesman. The purpose of the meeting was to determine if the American forces on the river would carry out the terms of the proclamation of 22 October 1851 by President Millard Fillmore. With assurances from Harney the Mexican delegation appeared satisfied on this point. The Mexicans informed Harney that the border had now officially been closed to all Americans.[21]

On this same day two proclamations were posted in Camargo under the authority of the military officers commanding the Mexican frontier along the river. On 25 November 1851, General Francisco Ávalos, then commanding the frontier, issued a proclamation closing the border to all trade between the United States and Mexican cities then in rebellion. The only crossings on the river that remained open to trade and passenger traffic were La Garita de la Cruz and those located at Freeport, near Brownsville. Any foreigner found armed in Mexico was to be executed, and any unarmed smugglers were subject to four months' imprisonment and a loss of their goods.[22] The second proclamation, from Ávalos to the Mexican soldiers on the border, ordered that no quarter be given for any "foreigner" invading the Republic of Mexico and that persons "shall be put to death immediately if caught with arms in his hands."[23] Uraga further issued an order of confiscation, and was selling off the homes and other property of the Carvajal insurgents who were Mexican nationals.[24]

Meanwhile, at Brownsville the federal grand jury had been sworn in and were busy listening to testimony concerning violations of the Neutrality Act. A large number of witnesses were examined, according to one observer, nearly half of all Brownsville residents, and a large number of subpoenas had been issued for the "denizens" of Rio Grande City, Roma, and other sites on the river. On 7 February 1852 the river steamer *Camanche* arrived in Brownsville from Rio Grande City with a number of witnesses summoned to testify before the grand jury. The U.S. federal district attorney, William Pitt Ballinger, feverishly presented the hastily gathered evidence on Carvajal's activities to the grand jury, and later confided to his wife: "After only one day of deliberation, and after I had presented the court with the most thorough account on their [Carvajal's army] looting & plundering, the grand jury ruled in our favor."[25] The grand jury adjourned on 11 February 1852 after bringing sealed indictments against certain parties for "alleged" violations of the neutrality laws. The court promptly adjourned; Watrous and Ballinger departed by ship to return to Galveston, Texas.[26]

Around January 1852, Teresa Viele, wife of Second Lieutenant Egbert Viele, stationed at Ringgold Barracks, met José María Carvajal while riding near the post. The young impressionable lady left us this description of the then forty-two-year-old Mexican revolutionary: "When we met Carvajal, I knew him in an instant, by the stylish way in which he wore his black felt sombrero, by the silver-mounted pistols, and by the pure English accent of his salutation. . . . He was a small man, with a dark complexion and an eagle eye, the beauty of his excessively ugly face—like a Scotch terrier— consisting of this very ugliness combined with an expression of great intelligence."[27]

Carvajal was now actively moving about the country recruiting soldiers for his army in preparation for another invasion of Mexico. He did not have to travel far to find volunteers. A correspondent traveling the Rio Grande at this time found the ranchos on the U.S. side of the river filled with refugees. General Canales, commanding the Mexican National Guard, had issued an order to organize and arm all Mexican civilians, and his forces were busy impressing the peaceful farmers and ranchers into the military. The refugees had fled to the United States to avoid being forcefully placed in the Mexican National Guard. Many of the people interviewed publicly stated that they wished to serve under Carvajal, and that if they must fight, they reserved the right to choose the side for which they would bear arms.[28]

Rumors surfaced in the press that Colonel Ford was soon to return to the border, leading an army of eight hundred filibusters with two cannon to replenish the ranks of Carvajal's army, and that Carvajal's friends had sent off to Memphis, Tennessee, for artillery to bolster his army. This newly recruited and supplied Liberator Army was to swing into action by about the middle part of February.

The border was indeed ripe for revolution at this time. The streets of Brownsville were again crowded with refugees from Matamoros, who anticipated a second attack on that city from Carvajal's forces. From across the river in Matamoros crowds of protesters cursed the Central government, and shouts of "Viva Carvajal!" could be heard in public places. The Central government had refused to ratify the tariff reductions instituted by General Ávalos in September 1851 to compete with the reduced rates Carvajal offered in Camargo. The Central government had restored the old prohibitive tariffs levied on the border. Furthermore, all goods that had entered Mexico during the period of tariff reduction were ordered to be revalued on the old system. Brownsville merchants who had taken advantage of the lowered tariff rates had poured more than two million dollars' worth of goods into Mexico during this time.

Many of these hastily imported American goods were now sealed in Monterey warehouses by the Mexican government, awaiting payment of the higher tariff rates by their owners. Failing the additional tariff payment, the government threatened confiscation and sale to the highest bidder. An angry Central government also imposed a new tax on merchants doing business in Mexico. A tax of 4 percent was levied on invested capital in addition to a 4 percent sales tax. Prominent citizens of Matamoros who had opposed Carvajal in October 1851 vigorously protested this new act of financial oppression by the Central government, and now openly supported the revolutionary movement. Carvajal's partisans on both sides of the river expressed confidence in his renewed prospects for success.[29]

The defenses of Matamoros were being strengthened. General Ávalos, expecting a second attack on Matamoros to occur shortly, had fortified a position outside of the city, concentrating many of his troops there. The Mexican War steamer *State of Mexico* arrived off Brazos Santiago on 13 February 1852 with a large supply of arms and ammunition for the Matamoros garrison. The river steamer *Grampus,* a vessel owned by the company of Kenedy and King, however, refused to off-load the cargo. The owners claimed that the Mexican government needed to post bonds to ensure the security of the *Grampus* and its crew. The Mexican government refused to post such bonds, and the *State of Mexico* left port on the same day without having made the arms delivery to Ávalos's forces.[30]

The U.S. Army garrison at Brownsville was still in no condition to oppose the passage of any army wanting to cross the river. Helen Chapman wrote, on 17 February 1852, that "the Regular [U.S.] Army here is too small to offer the slightest check to the sympathizing movements on this side of the river." The U.S. Army had been charged by some of the U.S. press with sympathy for Carvajal and his aims and that many of the rank-and-file soldiers had deserted their posts to join Carvajal's army the previous fall. The army responded by issuing an official disclaimer: "The War Department has received no official confirmation of the desertion of soldiers from our army stationed on the Mexican frontier, to the revolutionary bands now seeking to overthrow the authority of the Mexican government."[31] But Teresa Viele reported that the September 1851 attack on Camargo "by a mixed army of Americans and Mexicans, led on by Carvajal, roused to so high a pitch of enthusiasm, that men from the ranks were daily deserting the garrison of Ringgold Barracks to join them."[32]

The garrison at Fort Brown was surprised on 16 February 1852 by the mysterious burglary of a "large number" of twelve-pound cannon balls. According to one source, the garrison at the fort was so small at that time that the guard at the gate was removed at night in order to guard the magazine. Anyone wanting to enter the fort either through the gate or from the river could do so without being challenged. The balls were apparently taken across the river to Matamoros, as the tracks of several men and mules were clearly visible from Fort Brown on the Matamoros side of the riverbank.

This theft became the source of some amusement from Brownsville citizens, one of whom posted a sign requesting volunteers to help guard the U.S. property in Fort Brown. But the theft took on more sinister overtones, when in a few days Carvajal's army took the field again sporting a single twelve-pounder artillery piece. Who supplied Carvajal with this armament and how was he able to take possession of such a large weapon? The overland and river passages leading to his camps were supposedly heavily guarded by the U.S. Army. Carvajal did not have this cannon as late as December 1851, or he would have used it in his attack on Cerralvo. Sometime between that date and the early part of February 1852, Carvajal took delivery of this artillery piece from party or parties unknown. Although we can only speculate on who furnished this armament, we can easily surmise the source for its ammunition.[33]

Rumors of Carvajal's plans for the imminent invasion of Mexico stirred General Harney to action. Hoping to move against the filibusters before they could completely organize, he issued an order on 31 January 1852, to Brevet Major Gabriel Paul: "He [Harney] furthermore directs that you [Major LaMotte] instruct Major Paul to re-examine the country lately passed over by him, and, if possible, find the camp or camps of these men, (avowed adherents of Carbajal,) to seize their arms and ammunition, and to order them to disperse in the name and by the authority of the U. States . . . before Major Paul resorts to force, if such extremity should become necessary, that he will secure the names of as many of these men as possible that they may be subsequently be brought to trial before the civil tribunals of the country."[34] Major Paul refused to obey these orders and was placed under arrest, pending a court-martial.

By 1 February 1852 these same orders were issued to Major Robert Garnett.[35] Garnett responded the next day to Harney. He agreed with Paul's decision that the order was an illegal one, and by the articles of war "I deem it to be my duty, for the reasons set forth, . . . also, respectfully . . . [to] decline obeying the General's instructions."[36] Garnett was also placed under arrest to await future court-martial proceedings. These same orders were issued to more compliant officers, and patrols set out from Ringgold Barracks to the north, combing the countryside for Carvajal and his men. But the veteran Carvajal had been over this country many times during the Federalist and the Mexican-American Wars and knew it and the people living there too well to ever be caught.

On 6 January 1852, Captain William E. Prince led a patrol to Agua Nueva and found the supposed Carvajal headquarters deserted. Twenty miles to the west, the patrol came upon a large abandoned camp who, "doubtless, informed of my approach, had seasonably broken up."[37] Two weeks later, Captain LaMotte, on patrol twelve miles northeast of Agua Nueva, reported finding two Mexican peons tending cattle: "They said they were very much afraid of 'Los Comanches' but they were paid for their labor etc.—one of them told me that Carvajal had killed 26 of their beeves and taken some horses for which he had left an order on his Quartermaster Peter Dowd."[38]

The only direct contact with Carvajal's men by a U.S. Army patrol occurred on 5 February 1852 by a party of forty troopers led by Lieutenant Egbert Viele. He reported:

> I went onto San Antonita . . . where I found a body of men about thirty five in number encamped and living in "jacals." I rode up to the camp and asked who was the leader of the party. I was informed that they were under Captain Adams. I then called Captain Adams and asked him for what purpose he had such a large body of men encamped at that place. He replied that he was there with a commission for the Governor of Texas, and empowered to arrest certain negroes who had escaped from the Seminole Indians. At the same time he showed me his commission. . . . I then told him that I had been informed that he was commanding an organized body of men who belong to the party of Carvajal and that if such was the case, that he must deliver up to me all his arms and ammunition. He told me that I could take all that I could find, at the same time offering me his pistol. I then had the whole camp searched thoroughly, and could not find either arms or ammunition of any kind. . . . On the morning of the 6th instant they had all gone. I then had the camp and its vicinity searched and found one keg of powder, two muskets, one rifle, a sabre, and some cooking utensils.[39]

Carvajal, at the head of the Liberator Army, crossed the Rio Grande into Mexico on 20 February 1852, a little below Rio Grande City, landing at the rancho of Estradeña, about two leagues from Camargo. His forces were held up one day until proper transportation could be found to move the heavy twelve-pounder cannon and its ammunition across the river. The river steamer *Tom Kirkman,* a private vessel thought to have been owned by Peter Dowd of Rio Grande City, brought the cannon and supplies across the Rio Grande.[40]

Lieutenant J. B. Holabird and a patrol arrived at the scene too late to halt the river crossing, but from his position near the crossing site he reported: "I plainly heard a bugle said to be in the camp of Carvajal, and a little after daylight I should think some two or three hundred discharges of firearms and one cannon. I inferred it was for the purpose of cleaning them."[41] With the crossing completed, Carvajal marched to the right bank of the Rio San Juan and commenced to move on Camargo. The size of this Liberator army, depending on the source considered, was between two hundred and five hundred men. General Antonio Canales, commanding the defenders of Camargo, claimed that Carvajal's forces consisted of 438 men, but a more accurate estimate of Carvajal's strength was about 244.[42]

Canales, headquartered at Camargo, commanded a defending force of about five hundred National Guard troops from Ciudad Victoria, Tamaulipas; the battalion of the First Light of Ciudad Victoria, commanded by Colonel Valentín Cruz; and the Second Corps of Cavalry, commanded by Captain Don Pedro Díaz. Supporting these troops were two twelve-pounder howitzers and two six-pounder cannons.[43] Canales, not known for being an aggressive fighter, surprised all by ordering an immediate attack on Carvajal's advancing forces. He reasoned that the past defense of the city, conducted from behind the city walls, had failed and that more active steps were required to prevent the capture of Camargo.

The clash of arms occurred about a half mile from Camargo at 3 P.M. on 21 February 1852. Carvajal's men were advancing through an open field, with forces strung out in a long line, in a movement of the type that might be expected from undisciplined troops. Suddenly, from a chaparral brush fringe that rimmed the field, a volley was fired into the ranks of Carvajal's army. The Liberator Army had not advanced skirmishers on the march and was no more than four hundred yards from Canales's troops before they discovered the trap. Before Carvajal's forces could recover from the effects of the volley, thundering hooves announced the approach of 250 lancers bearing down on the disorganized Liberator Army in an earth-shaking charge. Well-trained troops equipped with bayonets might have deployed into hollow squares to defeat the cavalry charge, but the untrained Mexican and Indian volunteers that constituted a large portion of Carvajal's army panicked at the sight of the oncoming horsemen. A detachment of sixteen

Carrizo Indians were the first to flee in terror, followed by from seventy to a hundred men from the battalion of Major McLean, led by the company of Captain Núñez. Those who fled the field in panic never returned during the remainder of the battle, and several were drowned in the Rio San Juan attempting to escape their pursuers.

The balance of Carvajal's forces, now estimated to be no more than eighty men, retreated with their twelve-pounder cannon into a chaparral thicket with the Rio San Juan to their back and prepared to receive further attacks from the National Guard troops. Canales's men charged this thicket on three attacks during the next three hours with cavalry and a company of the Second Light Infantry, led by Lieutenant Antonio Izaguirre. With bayonets and lances glittering in the afternoon sun, National Guard forces advanced on Carvajal's men, only to be repulsed by the deadly fire of double-shotted canister from the twelve-pounder cannon, commanded by Colonel Roberdeau Wheat. The remainder of Carvajal's forces, now surrounded, stood in imminent peril of being captured and summarily executed.[44]

What happened next depends on the source reporting the action, but the eyewitness account by Teresa Viele appears most credible. She had mounted a high hill near Ringgold Barracks, and from there she could see the clouds of white smoke rising from the battlefield in Mexico. The sounds of guns, the wild yell of the combatants, and the neighing of horses were clearly audible to her from this vantage point. From fugitives that had fled the fight, the electrifying word came across the river to Rio Grande City that Carvajal and his men were now surrounded and fighting for their lives. Viele reported that "the greatest excitement prevailed. Every American not in the army, armed himself for the rescue. The regular soldiers would have gone had they dared. Even the women wanted to go."

Henry Clay Davis, prominent merchant of Rio Grande City, set about to organize a relief party. Riding north of town to a Carrizo Indian encampment, Davis, with his face daubed with red warpaint, returned leading a war party of Indians to effect a rescue of Carvajal and his men. Some of the Indians were carrying tomahawks and spears, but many were armed with rifles supplied by the citizens of Rio Grande City. The Indians were "dressed in the skins of wild animals, bound around their loins, their hair parted in the center of their head, and braided down their backs." The war party soon gathered into boats and were drawn across the river, disappearing on the other side into the chaparral. The eerie silence which now replaced the earlier sounds of rapid firing caused the worried citizens across the Rio Grande to fear that Carvajal and his men had surrendered. But with the arrival of Davis and his Carrizo soldiers, loud cheers were heard and the sounds of firing commenced again with great rapidity.[45]

Late in the day, Canales's forces retreated back into Camargo, leaving the remnants of Carvajal's Liberator Army to occupy the ground formerly held by his attackers. Colonel Wheat pronounced this act as evidence of a filibuster victory over the National Guard. But Canales viewed the action differently. In his official report of the battle to Ávalos, entitled "Defeat of the Filibusters under command of the traitor Carvajal," Canales regarded his retreat as an attempt to draw Carvajal's forces from their secure spot into the open, where they could be destroyed by his forces. But the tattered remains of the Liberator Army would not advance from their secure position, according to Canales, because they had been "panic stricken by the brilliant charges of the battalion of the National Guard of C. Victoria and the second corps of regular cavalry, sustained by the dextrous fire of our artillery."

After dark the Liberator Army could count fewer than a hundred effective troops remaining in its ranks. A deep depression fell over the remainder of Carvajal's army, and by about 10 P.M. the officers began deserting the field in small groups, returning to the U.S. side of the river. The twelve-pounder cannon and its ammunition, abandoned on the field by the Liberator Army, was recovered the next day by a gleeful Canales, who reported that "the gun is in good order, and I shall very soon have the satisfaction of sending it to you [Ávalos]." In addition to the cannon, Canales captured 143 muskets and sapper's tools.[46]

The casualty report issued by Canales to Ávalos claimed that the defenders had lost only four soldiers killed with seven officers, subalterns, and soldiers wounded. In turn, he claimed that Carvajal's forces suffered forty-eight killed, not counting those who drowned attempting to swim the Rio San Juan, and twenty-four wounded. Colonel Roberdeau Wheat issued what was probably a more accurate count of the losses, reporting

Carvajal's casualties as ten killed and twenty-three wounded, including himself. The next morning, when reports indicated that both sides had abandoned the battlefield, the Liberator and Centralist armies both hastened to return to the scene and claim victory. But Canales's army reached the scene first, and the bedraggled remnants of the Liberator Army fled, crossing the Rio Grande again to return to the United States by the evening of 22 February 1852.

A later published account of Carvajal's men slain in the battle included W. D. L. Pannell of Alabama; James Reese, James Lovatt, and William Bonner of Texas; James H. McGroin of New York; Henry Crossman and George Liston, addresses unknown; and Frederick Backus, formerly of the 8th United States Infantry. In addition to these casualties, W. T. Cake, the clerk of Starr County, who had accompanied Carvajal's forces into Mexico, was missing. It was rumored that he had been captured by Canales's forces and hung.[47]

The situation that now existed on the border was succinctly summed up in a letter from Major Jack R. Everett, an officer in the Liberator Army:

> The revolution is no more, "for the present." The brave little General [Carvajal] has been deserted by his Mexican friends. On the 21st we attacked a large force of Government troops. . . . At the first onset all our Mexican friends deserted, and left about sixty of us to do the fighting. We fought bravely—not for the cause, but for our lives—and gained a complete victory, having driven the enemy from their pieces and dispersed their cavalry. It was then that we discovered that we were fighting the people of Mexico, for what we did not know, and left the field after dark, entirely disgusted with our wrong-called patriots—General Carvajal being the only one left to back us. . . .
>
> As far as regards my humble self, I have to say that our miserable neighbors are not capable of self-government, and ought to be furnished with such overseers as Texas has—a good Constitution—but a good thrashing first, to jog their memories. I am on hand and in for it; and last but not least, damme [sic] if ever I vote for another Whig President unless he swears right out, publicly, that he is a good and true Filibuster.[48]

This rout of the Liberation Army outside of Camargo by the forces of the Mexican National Guard marked the last dying gasp of hope for the

Republic of the Sierra Madre. José María Carvajal was now a fugitive attempting to evade arrest in both the United States and Mexico. With no further funds to pay the filibuster army, it evaporated into the chaparral heading for other fields of glory and profit. But many of Carvajal's filibuster army had not lost their taste for that occupation. Roberdeau Wheat became a general in the army of General Juan Alvarez in southwestern Mexico and fought to drive Antonio López de Santa Anna from power in 1854.

Still seeking glory on the field of strife, Wheat next joined the forces of William Walker in Nicaragua and was engaged in Walker's losing bid to seize that country. Giuseppi Garibaldi's campaign to unite Italy next excited Wheat's romantic spirit, and he became one of the red-shirted "immortals" fighting on the Italian peninsula. In his last bid for fame as a soldier, Wheat was killed by a sniper at the head of his famous Zouave-clad Confederate States battalion known as the Louisiana Tigers at the battle of Gaines Mill in Virginia in 1862. The infamous one-armed "Major" Alfred Norton is listed as a passenger aboard the S.S. *Promethius* on 21 June 1852, bound for Graytown, Nicaragua, en route to the gold fields of California. His profession was listed as "miner," the same as every other male on the passenger list. J. Smith McMicken, another officer in Carvajal's army, led a life shrouded in mystery but is known to have engaged in filibustering plots as late as 1856. John Ford was known to have been a party to other Carvajal plots to invade northern Mexico that never passed the planning stage and similarly became a conspirator in a plan developed by ex-Mississippi governor John Quitman to invade Cuba. With the untimely death of Quitman in 1858, however, no further plans materialized.

José María Carvajal now went into hiding in the area around Rio Grande City but was soon to be arrested by the U.S. government.

EIGHT

The Indictment and Trial
of José María de Jesús Carvajal
and His Men

My ambition was to be the Washington of my country.
JOSÉ MARÍA DE JESÚS CARVAJAL,
1852, quote appearing in Oates, p. 203

By early 1852, Texas federal district judge John Watrous and federal district attorney William Ballinger were under great pressure from the Fillmore administration in Washington, D.C., to take some action against Carvajal and his filibuster army. Rumors abounded that Carvajal had reconstituted his army and was poised on the Texas-Mexico border near Rio Grande City for yet another incursion into Mexico. Diplomatic pressure from Mexico was squarely focused on the U.S. Department of State, with angry notes that accused the U.S. government of aiding Carvajal and planning to recognize the infant Republic of the Sierra Madre immediately after it won independence from Mexico. Once diplomatic recognition was extended, Mexican diplomats predicted that it was only a short step to the annexation by the United States of the former northern states. Thus Watrous and Ballinger took bold steps, even though Ballinger did not have the time to either perfect the indictments or develop evidence against the leaders of the Liberation Army sufficient to win a conviction in the courtroom.

The indictments that had been issued by the Brownsville federal grand jury in January 1852, supposedly sealed until June, mysteriously became public knowledge on 17 February 1852. Those indicted for violation of the Neutrality Act of 1818 were Peter Dowd,[1] A. J. Mason,[2] R. N. Stansbury,[3]

Alfred Norton,[4] J. M. J. Carvajal, Captain McLane, R. H. Hord,[5] E. R. Hord,[6] J. D. Howell,[7] R. C. Trimble,[8] Captain Wheate [*sic*], and J. R. Everitt [*sic*].[9] The federal government then took immediate steps for the arrest and arraignment of these men. But the grand jury was not finished and would subsequently hand down other indictments in the Carvajal matter. The reader might wish to speculate why other important figures, such as John Ford and Henry Clay Davis, were not also indicted for their actions in the Mexican incursions, as well as the merchants who most likely furnished the finances and supplies needed for a filibuster army. Suspicious by virtue of their sympathies for the Carvajal movement were such merchants as Charles Stillman, Mifflin Kenedy, and Richard King, to name only a few.

Since its organization in mid-1851, the *Rio Bravo,* a newspaper edited by Ovid Johnson and published by Francis J. Parker, had advocated filibuster activities into northern Mexico and had been especially sympathetic to Carvajal's cause. Both of these men were subsequently indicted by a federal grand jury. J. S. Waddell, U.S. consul in Matamoros, in a report to Washington, D.C., implicated Johnson in the Carvajal plot: "A paper published in the town of Brownsville called the 'Rio Bravo' and edited by Ovid F. Johnson Esq. is regarded as having done more than any other single cause to incite our peaceable citizens to this undertaking. Openly advocating the cause of Carvajal it has throughout the whole affair assumed the tone and played the part of his official organ." But by December 1851, with the general failure of Carvajal to gain ascendancy in northern Mexico, the paper was sold. The new owner, Edwin Scarbrough, renamed the paper the *American Flag,* and through its new editor, a Dr. Adams, launched a series of editorials highly critical of Carvajal and his cause. The Scarborough editorial of 6 March, which unfortunately cannot be found, raised the ire of Roberdeau Wheat, who had just posted bond for his federal indictment. The giant filibusterer attacked editor Adams on the streets of Brownsville, but the rencontre evidently caused no lasting injury to either party.[10]

During early May 1852 the first State Fair of Texas was held in Corpus Christi. The fair was organized and financially underwritten by Henry L. Kinney, with an organizing committee for the fair that included such famous Texans as Ashbel Smith, Governor Peter Hansborough Bell, William H. Bourland, James Davis, former Texas governors James Pinckney Henderson

and George T. Wood, Henry Clay Davis, Gideon K. "Legs" Lewis, and
Forbes Britton. On 13 May 1852, José María Carvajal gave an invited speech
to the assembled crowds attending the fair after a rousing introduction by
Colonel Hugh McLeod, an active proponent of revolutionary movements
past, present, and future. Carvajal was well received by the crowd, speaking
on the Plan de La Loba, and the need for democratic institutions in Mexico.
It was reported that he "stirred up the crowds at the fair with his speech,"
but his personal appeals for funds to continue the war for the liberation of
northern Mexico were not enough. The money Carvajal raised fell far short
of expectations. One journalist placed the blame for the poor rate of contributions on the crowd of Carvajal's soldiers that had followed him from
the border to Corpus Christi. The Liberator Army soldiers, described as
"about two hundred filibusters," were accused of frightening respectable citizens away from the speech as well as the fair.[11]

A disillusioned Roberdeau Wheat, writing his mother from Corpus
Christi, mentioned: "I saw Gen. Carbajal yesterday, he is downcast but yet
hopes. I shall not move again in the matter unless I am certain of success."
Wheat went from Corpus Christi to Austin in a belated attempt to raise
volunteers and funds for Carvajal's army, where he was "surrounded by
friends and admirers," who unfortunately had neither the time nor the
money with which to aid Wheat's "youthful general"—José María
Carvajal. Wheat then returned to New Orleans and civilian life, still yearning for adventure.[12]

John S. Ford expressed the opinion that one of the purposes of the state
fair at Corpus Christi had been to promote the cause of the Carvajal revolution. Ford must have attended the fair, for he thought that the general
was "a pleasant speaker and handled the English language well." Among
the distinguished Texans attending the fair, there was agreement that
Mexico was a "dangerous neighbor" for Texas, and a great many expressed
the desire to aid General Carvajal in his struggle, as they felt that he had
taken the U.S. government as his model for reform. But alas, no more
money was forthcoming from the Carvajal patrons, and Ford stated philo-
sophically that "as a general rule, war without a well-filled military chest,
degenerates into robbery. Many of us who had spent considerable money
in the revolutionary service and had drawn almost no pay now felt unable

to do anything more. Fate seemed against General Carbajal. The revolutionary movement was virtually at an end."[13] Carvajal's recent attacks on Mexico had set the stage for a period of border unrest that would extend well into the next century. Without a treaty of extradition, brief border raids would continue to be launched from both countries with the raiders returning to seek sanctuary in their country of origin.

On 17 May 1852 an unprovoked attack occurred on the river steamer *Camanche,* captained by Richard King. As the boat passed a point on the Rio Grande near Rancho Santa Anna, shots were fired from the Mexican side. Some twelve shots struck the *Camanche,* seriously wounding Mr. W. B. Brashear, the U.S. revenue officer from Rio Grande City, and his four-year-old son.[14]

The court-martial of Brevet Major Robert S. Garnett, held at Ringgold Barracks, began on 18 May 1852. The court was composed of thirteen of the outstanding officers then serving on the Texas frontier. Garnett was specifically charged with disobedience of the orders of his lawful military superior, Brigadier General William S. Harney. Harney had ordered Garnett on 31 January 1852 to take a troop of mounted soldiers and proceed to the camps of Carvajal's soldiers, located at El Sauz, Escobares, and Agua Nueva Wells. At these camps Garnett was ordered to "seize their arms and ammunition, and order them to disperse in the name and by the authority of the government of the U. States." Refusing to carry out this order, Garnett wrote to Harney that "in order to make this service a proper military duty, it is necessary that it should be made so by Congress, or under existing laws, by the sanction, in due form, of the civil authorities. I am not advised that the General's orders have been issued in pursuance of any requisition from such authorities; and in the absence of this important fact, I am constrained to regard them as illegal—the articles of war and my commission only making it obligatory upon me to obey the 'lawful orders' of the President and my superiors, and making me the sole judge, at my risk, in each case."[15]

Garnett stated in his defense during the court-martial proceedings that he knew of the desperate character of the men that constituted Carvajal's army. The orders that he had been issued could only be carried at the point of a bayonet. At the time that this order had been given, there was only one U.S. deputy marshal in the lower Rio Grande Valley, and he was then at Brownsville, not near enough to accompany Garnett on his mission. Had Garnett gone to one of the camps of the "filibusters," who were civilians, and killed any of them in the execution of his orders, Garnett felt that he would have in turn been tried by a Texas civilian court as a murderer and hung. The order to arrest a civilian would have been legal only when given by an officer of the federal government. However, the proper authority did exist for Garnett to carry out his orders. That authority had come in the form of the order of 22 September 1851 from President Fillmore to General Persifor F. Smith, commanding the 8th Military District, who invoked Section 8 of the Neutrality Act.[16] Smith had transmitted this order to Harney and ordered Harney and his forces to the Rio Grande to bar the river passages.[17]

Court-martial testimony, however, brought out the fact that Harney had failed to inform his officers of the order issued by President Fillmore requesting military aid, a necessary legal requirement of the Neutrality Act. The blustery Harney "considered his rank and position as sufficient for any officer under his command to obey any and all orders that he might give, without exhibiting any extraordinary powers for his authority." Concerning the actions of Major Garnett in this matter, Harney had brusquely stated: "By God, when I give an order, I expect it to be obeyed." On the witness stand, an officer testified that he had questioned Harney on the responsibility of a soldier to follow orders: "I asked him if a superior officer to him, gave him an order to kill a number of citizens, whether he would obey it,—he said, 'Yes, by God, if I was to be hung for it.'"[18]

Major Paul testified under oath that he had heard Harney say that "he [Harney] did not consider it was necessary, or his duty, to communicate to the subordinate officers on this line, that special powers had been delegated to him by the President of the United States."[19] Such an attitude by Harney had created confusion among the junior officers along the Rio Grande, the ones who would have to enforce the Neutrality Act against Carvajal's followers. Under oath, Lieutenant James Holmes, 4th Artillery, testified that it was general knowledge among his fellow officers "that the presence of a representative of the civil authority was necessary before anything could be done against the violators of the neutrality laws."[20] Carvajal's followers were aware of this prevailing opinion among the military at Ringgold Barracks and felt no apprehension until a civilian marshal should appear in the area, only then they supposed would Harney move against them.

With testimony completed, the court-martial was closed on 21 May 1852 and adjourned to deliberate on the testimony. The court returned on 22 May with its findings. On the charge that Garnett had disobeyed the orders of a superior officer, the court found him not guilty. The court found that Garnett had not been duly informed of "the instructions emanating from the President of the United States."[21]

On 14 June 1852 a final disposition was made of the prisoners captured during Carvajal's unsuccessful assault on Matamoros in late October 1851. The four prisoners were Robert McDonald, a naturalized U.S. citizen from Scotland and an army deserter from Ringgold Barracks; George W. Williams, twenty-two years of age, born in Poughkeepsie, New York; and the Mexican citizens Estanislao Villegas and Jesús Gómez.[22] The prisoners were regarded officially by the Mexican government as rebels and assassins, not prisoners of war. Consequently they were condemned to death by order of General Francisco Ávalos under the authority of Santa Anna's order of 17 June 1843. The prisoners felt that they had been kept in cruel suspense for more than eight months as to their sentence and had written to the U.S. consul at Matamoros for support, but by virtue of an earlier warning to filibusters published by President Fillmore, they had received no official reply. At length, an order from Mexico City came to shoot the prisoners at 7 A.M. on 14 June 1852.

Abbé Domenech, a French priest in Matamoros, was charged by General Ávalos with the spiritual interest of the prisoners and their preparation for death. After a visit to the prisoners, Domenech became sympathetic to their plight and decided to actively intervene to save their lives. He visited the English and French consuls in Matamoros to enlist their aid. The consuls visited Ávalos to beg for the prisoners' lives, but Ávalos was furious at the filibusters and vowed to carry out the death sentence. Father Domenech, after a personal interview with Ávalos, described the military commandant of Matamoros in these rather unflattering terms as "a small fat, rather olive-complexioned person. His black beard, and quick, sinister eyes gave him a ferocious look. His father was a Mexican, his mother an

Indian. The savage blood could be seen in the man. With polished, affable, and accomplished manners, he was stern, false, and vindictive."[23] Regardless of his looks, Ávalos was a distinguished military man who was credited with the successful defense of Matamoros against the Liberator Army. For his meritorious conduct he was promoted to the rank of brigadier general, received the thanks of the Mexican Congress, and was awarded a cross of honor from the Sovereign State of Tamaulipas.

Domenech, failing to appeal to the humanity of Ávalos, decided next to try a little blackmail. He visited the general again to seek more time for the condemned. He reminded Ávalos of his "heroic" personal efforts during the battle for Matamoros. Ávalos had been slightly wounded by a spent musket ball that had struck his leg during the first days of the siege. Rather than be taken to his own home for recovery, he had ordered that he be secretly moved to a distant hut, far away from possible capture by the Liberator Army. Ávalos had remained there until the siege was lifted, leaving his troops "to their own guidance." Domenech hinted that if the general did not postpone the execution, he would "publish this story in the journals, adding the names." The general's dark eyes flashed with anger, but he finally answered: "Very good, the execution shall be deferred until I receive orders from Mexico."

Meanwhile, the priest drew up a petition addressed to Mariano Arista, president of Mexico, signed by the ladies of Matamoros, that pled for the prisoners' lives. The petition stated that the executions would be looked upon as an act of vengeance and a political assassination, and that Ávalos's enemies might in retaliation take the general's life. But the petition was met only with silence from Mexico City. In a final effort of mercy, Father Domenech attempted to organize an escape for the prisoners. The prisoners were being held at the Lancers' Barracks in the center of the city under a moderate guard. The plot failed when an important filibuster prisoner, Colonel Núñez, was moved to the barracks and placed under heavy guard. The padre then appealed to certain citizens of Brownsville for action but was met only with "inertness, imbecility, and stupid threats against Avalos."[24]

On the day before execution Mexican priest Don Raphaél brought the Holy Sacrament from the Cathedral to say mass for the condemned men.

The path along which the Holy Sacrament passed was strewn with flowers and branches, and silk handkerchiefs fluttered from the houses along the route. The procession was preceded by a military band playing a dead march; a multitude of townspeople, praying aloud, followed.

At about 4 A.M. of the next day Father Domenech left the prisoners to return to the cathedral and say a mass for the condemned men. During the mass he received a message to come quickly, that the prisoners were being marched to their execution. As he raced down the streets of Matamoros, he heard a sound that chilled his blood: the roar of musketry, followed by a second volley delivered as a coup de grâce. The four men had been tied to a bench and executed in an untilled field, about six hundred yards from the prison. The bodies were then flung onto a dung cart and marched slowly to the cemetery. A driving rain fell upon the funeral party, and Father Domench noted, as he marched behind the cart, that blood trickled from the cart onto the ground. The final burial was in a rude grave without coffins, overlooked by Lancers who were sent to ensure that the bodies would not be taken across the river for burial in Brownsville.[25] The *Texas State Gazette,* with hot anger, headed their account of the execution as "Great Excitement!—Two Americans Shot in Matamoras!!"[26]

General Ávalos, never very popular with residents along the border, now became the widespread target of protest. Citizens of Brownsville and New Orleans organized protests, with the most impressive demonstrations occurring in Brownsville. A scaffold was raised on the bank of the Rio Grande directly opposite Ávalos's home in Matamoros. Two dummies, representing Ávalos and Agustín Menchaca, Ávalos's aide, were mounted on asses and paraded through the streets of Brownsville for three days. On the third day a boisterous crowd gathered to hoist the dummies onto the riverbank scaffold and after a noisy demonstration left to swing in the wind.[27]

The Mexican minister at Washington, D.C., protested the actions of the Brownsville demonstration, writing that "the Mexican authorities being denounced, the public functionaries who performed their duties on the frontier, being laughed at and ridiculed, as it was proved by the farce which was enacted in Brownsville in the month of last June, during which the effigies or statues, representing Messrs Avalos and Menchaca, were paraded through the streets, the crowd breaking out in all sorts of disagreeable demonstrations and insults, followed by volleys of fire; all of which was announced by previous notices and done with the knowledge and permission of the authorities."[28]

Several residents of Matamoros were incarcerated after being accused of serving in the Liberator Army. One such person, John McAllen, who was later to become a prominent South Texas rancher and merchant, described his prison ordeal: "[I worked in Matamoros] . . . untill the first Carbajal war when I was taken prisoner by mistake and 17 sware against me that I was seen fighting against the City party but I had my pasport as a British subject deposited with the Brith. Consul. I sent for him and told him that I did not know Carbajal. He told me to be quite [sic] that he would do all he could to have me released, but he could not. . . . I was a year and aleven monts prisnr. Most of the time could not talk to aney one. At last, I made my escape to this side."

Early 1853 found José María living quietly in Rio Grande City but attempting all the while to raise another force to attack Mexico. Meanwhile, Carvajal's backers had become anxious for him to repay the money borrowed for previous forays into Mexico. James H. Durst, the erstwhile Coahuila y Tejas legislator and land speculator, and H. Clay Davis of Rio Grande City had entered suit against Carvajal for payment for the supplies furnished by Durst and Davis to the Liberator Army. But as Carvajal's filibustering activities were illegal, it was suspected that the plaintiffs would not collect this debt. Carvajal had even borrowed "thousands of dollars" from his mother-in-law, Patricia de la Garza de León, to finance his filibuster army. He never repaid her for the loan, and with the reading of her will after her death, she specified that she left "to Jose Maria Carbajal the $6,000 that he owes me."[29]

Many of the mercenaries of the Liberator Army, sensing that the struggle for northern Mexico had come to an end, and with it their dreams for conquest, began to leave the border in search of other pursuits. But some lingered on to cause even more trouble in Mexico. On 25 March 1853 a party of some fifty American and Mexican freebooters, formerly in Carvajal's command, raided Reynosa, a Mexican town across the Rio Grande from Edinburgh. The American portion of the party was a group of Texas Rangers that had been recently disbanded from service to the state on 6 March 1852. Led by Major Alfred Norton, who had lost an arm in the October 1851 attack on Matamoros, and ably assisted by A. J. Mason and Voltaire Roundtree, they crossed the Rio Grande at Edinburgh and rode into Reynosa.

Their first mission was to capture the town hall and secure all arms and ammunition stored within. This body of robbers then entered the homes of Don Francisco García y Treviño and Trinidad Flores, *alcaldes* (mayors) of Reynosa, and took them to the principal plaza. Both men were flogged and threatened with death by Norton, who demanded a large sum of money "in the name of Carvajal." But finding that the town did not have such resources, Norton limited his demands to four thousand dollars. Finally Norton generously agreed to settle for all the money these two men then had, a collective sum of about fourteen or fifteen hundred dollars, as well as a note from Mr. Elias D. Smith of Edinburgh for a sum sufficient to increase the booty to two thousand dollars. During this negotiation each of the alcaldes had been placed on horseback with nooses around their necks.

Major Norton then led his brave volunteers back across the river, gathering with him as he went "horses, mules, saddles, bridles, blankets, guns— in fact nothing appears to have been too hot or too heavy for him to take."[30] After reception of the news of Norton's raid on Reynosa from the first constitutional mayor of "Reinosa," the Mexican minister of foreign affairs sent a formal note of protest to the U.S. government. He condemned the outrages that had been committed by "Mr. A. N. Norton, Justice of Peace of 'Davis' [Starr] county."[31]

Soon thereafter Norton turned up again in Brownsville and "walked the streets with the air of one whose gallant conduct was the theme of universal approbation." But the Mexican consul there filed a complaint against Norton for his raid on Reynosa, and the latter was quickly arrested on the streets of Brownsville by a federal marshal. Mason and Roundtree were also subsequently arrested by John K. Leman, U.S. deputy marshal, for their part in the Reynosa raid. At their arraignment before U.S. commissioner Franklin Cummings, Norton and his cohorts could not furnish the required bail and were remanded to the guard house at Fort Brown, where they were held until May 1853.[32]

Elias D. Smith, anxious to receive some military protection, wrote: "We are being threatened with an attack on this place [Edinburgh] by a band of men from the vicinity of Reynosa, in retaliation for an outrageous act committed by a party of Americans and Mexicans under the command of Major Norton."[33] A correspondent writing from Brownsville echoed the concerns for adequate military protection expressed by Smith: "We want protection on the Rio Grande. There is an entire regiment of mounted rifles somewhere on the prairies, which should be along our river. From Ringgold down, a distance of some two hundred miles, there is not a single mounted man."[34]

General Harney, motivated by the Norton raid on Reynosa, now moved to serve the arrest warrants pending against Carvajal and his followers. He ordered Company F from the Regiment of Mounted Rifles, then stationed on the Nueces River, to join him on the border. The company reached Roma, Texas, by the evening of 31 March 1853. After 11 P.M., when it was thought that the citizens of Rio Grande City might be asleep, the company rode on to Rio Grande City. Reinforced by Company B of the Mounted Rifles and four companies of infantry, the troopers proceeded to serve the arrest warrants in a house-to-house search, using axes to break open the doors of those that would not yield to inspection. The male occupants were then marched to the main square, and placed under heavy guard. José María Carvajal and Peter Dowd were both taken in bed without a struggle. Those not listed in the arrest order were disarmed and released. One of the soldiers present reported that "they were desperate looking men . . . and had they not been taken by surprise would doubtless have made a bloody resistance."[35]

Carvajal and eleven of his followers proceeded to Brownsville aboard the steamer *Camanche* in the custody of Lieutenant John Gibbon of the 4th Artillery. After their arrival in that city, a hearing was held. After a thorough review of the evidence, U.S. District Attorney Ballinger had to admit that the case against Carvajal and his associates would be difficult to win in a trial. Evidence indicated that the Liberator Army had been organized only after the mercenaries had crossed into Mexico, not in violation of the Neutrality Act. The popularity of Carvajal and his cause on both sides of the border created an environment in which no testimony favoring conviction could be found. Consequently, Ballinger persuaded Judge Watrous, presiding at the hearing, to grant a continuance until the next court session to allow for more time to prepare his case against Carvajal. Ballinger confided in a letter to Secretary of State Daniel Webster that his office could not "pursue them legally any further than what I have accomplished." A bail was set to guarantee their appearance at the June 1853 session of the U.S. District Court, and the indicted men were released. Carvajal's bail was set at five thousand dollars and the other eleven each paid three thousand dollars.[36]

The raids against Mexico continued. Shortly thereafter, on 20 May 1853, a band of men lately of the Liberator Army made a another raid into Mexico. The raiders crossed the Rio Grande near El Guardado, some five miles from Mier, and began to gather up a herd of horses and mules from the ranchos of that area. But the citizens of Mier dispatched an armed force to attack the rustlers. In the subsequent battle, three of the raiders and one citizen of Mier were killed.[37]

Thought to have planned the Norton raid on Reynosa, Carvajal's bond was now revoked. The citizens who previously had guaranteed the appearance bonds for Carvajal and his men now withdrew their pledges, and Carvajal and the others who had been indicted were placed under guard at Fort Brown, until the June 1853 session of the federal district court.[38] The correspondent "Brownsville" reported that sentiment along the lower Rio Grande region had turned against Carvajal and his men: "You may consider the Reynosa affair as a death blow for filibusterism on the Rio Grande, at least for the present." The June session of the U.S. Federal District Court for the Eastern District of Texas opened in Brownsville, without Judge Watrous in attendance. Carvajal and others of the Liberator Army made an appearance before the court. Again, the government discovered that the indictments filed by Ballinger were filled with legal errors, and with no other recourse, another continuance was granted. A remorseful Ballinger described the situation as a "most dreadful debacle . . . the most humiliating experience I have had as a lawyer & servant of the U.S. government." A disgraced Ballinger resigned from his post as U.S. district attorney, effective 1 July 1853. In regard to their indictment for violation of the Neutrality Act, Carvajal, R. H. Hord, E. R. Hord, A. J. Mason, A. Norton, and R. C. Trimble each requested a change in venue to Galveston, Texas, which was granted.

The Mexican minister to Washington, D.C., puzzled by the American system of justice and generally frustrated by a lack of action against Carvajal and his followers, wrote: "The arrest was effected; but the accused remained at liberty by means of a bail which they gave . . . the jury which was to have met again in the month of last June, did not assemble; because Judge Watrous, . . . was then in this city [Washington]; and more than a year has elapsed since Carvajal and his accomplices were ordered to be arrested, and subject to be tried, . . . and this has not been done, up to this moment."[39]

A U.S. grand jury was then in session, investigating the Norton raid on Reynosa and other matters associated with the raids into Mexico. By July thirteen additional indictments were returned for violation of the Neutrality Act. Among those persons was Ovid F. Johnson, a person with a tinctured past. The *Galveston Journal* exposed his career in this article:

> Johnson had served as Attorney General for the State of Pennsylvania during the term of the Democratic Governor David R. Porter, from 1839 to 1845. Johnson was accused of such improprieties as "pardoning offenders of the criminal law before they had even been indicted." The late attorney general then journeyed to Texas on a legal mission to plunder the public domain of that state by establishing a "large number of fraudulent land certificates by suit." He and his backers did not prevail, but he managed to escape the punishment prescribed by Texas law for making, selling, or locating fraudulent certificates or for being either "directly or indirectly concerned in so doing." This punishment in part was to receive thirty-nine lashes well laid on the bare back.
>
> During the election of Gen. Zachary Taylor, Johnson converted from the Democrat Party to become a Whig, delivered a Whig speech or two and was rewarded with a minor post involving revenue matters on the Rio Grande. He moved to Brownsville, but relocated to Washington, D.C. shortly thereafter where he surprisingly wrote several editorial columns for the official organ of the Democrat Party, The Washington Union.
>
> Johnson returned to Brownsville, where he was installed as editor of the *Rio Bravo,* a Democrat newspaper which supported Carvajal's revolutionary efforts in northern Mexico. Carvajal awarded him with the rank of colonel in the Liberator Army, probably an honorary title. It is not known whether he actively participated in the attack on Matamoros

in October, 1851, but he was one of the men who crossed the Rio Grande in February, 1852 for the second attack on Camargo. Carvajal is said to have awarded him the rank of brevet brigadier general for the active role he played in that struggle. He was identified as the author of the letter of 23 February 1852 published in the New Orleans Picayune that described the battle between the forces of Gens. Canales and Carvajal.

With the failure of the *Rio Bravo,* Johnson became a delegate to the Democratic National Convention, meeting in Baltimore, Maryland. At the convention, he offered a filibuster resolution which was promptly voted down, even the delegates from Texas voted against this resolution. Shortly thereafter, Johnson unsuccessfully argued the land certificate case of Phalen and Herman, originating in Texas, before the United States Supreme Court. With the election of Franklin Pierce, he attempted to obtain the position of Collector of Revenue at Point Isabel but failed in that bid because of lack of support from either the Senators or the Representatives of Texas.

In 1853, Johnson moved his residence to Washington D.C., where he was hired as editor of the *Democratic Monthly Review.* He must have been serving in that post when he was indicted by the Grand Jury at Brownsville.[40]

Others indicted included Elisha Basse,[41] Francis J. Parker,[42] Robert Wheat, Edward J. McLane, Andrew J. Mason, Robert C. Trimble, José María J. Carvajal, Alfred Norton,[43] Warren Adams,[44] Joseph Moses,[45] Peter Dowd,[46] Voltaire Roundtree,[47] Papa Gonzales, John H. Allen, Joseph Howell,[48] and Juan Treviño. Fourteen others were also true billed by the grand jury, but the U.S. district attorney entered a *nolle prosequi* on the grounds that they took no leading part but were lured by the more prominent parties. The government wished to concentrate their limited resources on the prosecution of the more prominent filibuster leaders. Additional indictments were also issued against Norton, Roundtree, and Mason for the Reynosa raid.[49]

The list of indictments were in line with the thoughts of Patrick C. Shannon, who in a 9 November 1851 letter to Thomas Corwin, secretary of the treasury, gave a list of Americans whom he felt were backing

Carvajal. These persons were Samuel A. Belden (unindicted), merchant; Charles Stillman (unindicted), merchant; Edward H. Hord (indicted), attorney; Ovid Johnson (indicted), attorney and editor of the *Rio Bravo;* F. J. Parker (indicted), printer and assistant editor of the *Rio Bravo;* Elijah Basse (indicted), attorney; H. Howlett, (unindicted) notary public and "secretary to Carvajal"; Joseph Moses (indicted), merchant; and A. J. [Jo] Mason (indicted) grocer, the "person who is said to have shot the consul."[50]

Still, too little was being done by the federal government to ensure the peace and tranquility of the Texas-Mexico border. The plight of the lone deputy federal marshal was reported by "Brownsville": "The Deputy Marshal for this section of the country, has never yet received a farthing for his services or for the expense of retaining prisoners. . . . Carvajal, Norton, and Roundtree would have to set at large for the want of funds to feed them, were it not that a civil officer of the Government, who has public money in his hands, takes the responsibility of advancing the necessary means, and trusting to fate and the worthies at Washington for the settlement of his account."[51]

More protection for the border was being sent by the U.S. Army, but a correspondent complained that the soldiers were of the dismounted variety: "These troops [U.S. troops] are good of the kind and just such as are wanted here in the forts, but to send them in pursuit of disbanded Rangers and plundering Mexicans is the height of folly. . . . If the Government does not give us protection soon, it is proposed to request Gov. Bell to call the Rangers into service again, thereby giving us peace, by absorbing the idle and lazy."[52]

In the renamed Brownsville newspaper *American Flag,* Carvajal published a most emphatic denial of the charges specified in the indictments brought against him in which he predicted that "the time will soon come when I shall claim a hearing before the American public, when I shall present such facts and documents as will compel all candid minds to do me the justice which my sufferings for the most honorable cause demands."[53] On the one hand, the grand jury had found true bills against many of the conspirators and principal actors engaged in the unlawful invasion of Mexico, but on the other hand, they had failed to act against many of the most powerful men engaged in the plot. Many of these men had furnished the finances that made the invasion possible and were likewise guilty of violating the Neutrality Act.

Rumors of the involvement of the famous financier and border merchant Charles Stillman in the Carvajal revolution echoed from the border eastward to New England. In a letter to his friend James Jewett, Stillman reassured Jewett of his innocence: "I am sorry to see Jim that you thought me so green to be engaged in the Revolution, any further than talking goes; that I would like to see Carabajal succeed is true . . . a great many of my friends are engaged in it, it has not cost me a fraction, neither have I a dollars worth of goods in Mexico."[54]

The firm of Kenedy and King, headed by Richard King and Mifflin Kenedy, were likewise rumored to have furnished financial backing for Carvajal.[55] Other unindicted major players included Henry Clay Davis and John S. Ford. Davis not only furnished supplies for Carvajal's army but actually invaded Mexico on 22 February 1852, leading an armed party of Carise Indians to free Carvajal's surrounded army. Anyone living on the border or even within the state of Texas at the time would have to have been deaf and blind not to know the active part that John S. Ford played in Carvajal's invasion of Mexico. Ford openly touted his part in the October 1851 battle for Matamoros to his friends and to newspaper reporters, but the grand jury apparently turned a blind eye in his direction.

Ford, a staunch supporter of slavery, was appalled that as a matter of policy the Republic of Mexico refused to extradite runaway slaves. He had joined the Carvajal plot to aid in the creation of the Republic of the Sierra Madre because of the personal guarantees Carvajal gave him. Ford would later write that "it is one of the primary articles of agreement between Carvajal and his auxiliaries, in the event of success, to allow owners of runaway slaves to redress their property, within the limits of the territory controlled by the revolutionaries." Ford estimated that about four thousand escaped slaves were then living in northern Mexico, and he characterized them as "healthy and intelligent" for the initiative and fortitude they had displayed in their escape from their owners. Their return would bring a top dollar in rewards, estimated by Ford to be $3,200,000. Thus Ford had a plausible financial motive for his involvement in the Carvajal plot.

Finally, the role played in the Carvajal incursions by the Rio Grande

Lodge No. 81 of the Freemasons requires some scrutiny. Teresa Viele noted that "these plans were confided to many of the Texan lodge of Free-Masons, to which fraternity Caravajal belonged," and as many of the Masons were merchants, "they joined heartily with the revolution."[56] The extensive involvement of the Freemasons in the filibuster invasions of Cuba has been documented by historian Antonio R. de la Cova. The Masons justified such actions as a part of their creed. In the ninth and tenth degrees of Scottish Rite, a Mason takes an oath to "assist those who struggle against oppression." In the twenty-ninth and thirtieth degrees he swears to "wage war against tyranny and despotism," And in the thirty-second degree, he vows to assume the obligation of being "a soldier of freedom."[57] But just how much support Carvajal received from the Masonic Order, a secret organization, will never be known. However, the membership of Rio Grande Lodge No. 81 included José María Carvajal, John S. Ford, and many others who played an active role in the Liberator Army.[58]

Samuel D. Hay, Ballinger's successor as U.S. district attorney, now worked feverishly to meet the January 1854 date for the Carvajal et al. trial in Galveston. But he could muster little support, either from border residents, the administration of President Franklin Pierce, or his predecessor, Ballinger, who flatly admitted that the "jury here [Galveston] is too unfamiliar with their past acts—Hay hasn't enough evidence to put before them to win conviction." Two Brownsville attorneys, A. W. Arrington and Franklin Cummings, had been retained by the government to aid the prosecution, but when additional travel expenses requested by Hay from the Office of Attorney General were rejected by Attorney General Caleb Cushing, the two men resigned, leaving the new district attorney without associate counsel. Hay was able to persuade a Galveston attorney to assist him but without guarantee of reimbursement from Washington, D.C.

The tone of the Pierce administration was decidedly cool on the prosecution of filibusters. Hay wrote Secretary of War Jefferson Davis to clarify the government's position on the trial: "Will the Government give me no intimation as to its policy touching these important trials[?]" Davis responded tersely that he had referred Hay's letter to the offices of the secretary of state and the attorney general, without any commitment as to the policy, and Hay received no further response.

The trials for the Carvajal filibusters began in Galveston on 2 January 1854, with the proceedings against José María Carvajal, defended by attorneys Hale and Allen. A plea of abatement was filed by the defense, alleging that of the original seventeen members of the grand jury that indicted Carvajal, five of those did not meet the legal requirements to be a grand juror. The law required that a minimum of thirteen grand jurors be required to bring an indictment and thus the true bill rendered against Carvajal was invalid. The defendant was summarily discharged by Judge Watrous. The second case against Andrew Jackson Mason, then also under state indictment for murder in Colorado County, Texas, was tried, with a "not guilty" verdict rendered by a jury. After two more of the defendants in the Carvajal matter were acquitted, District Attorney Hay realized that he was fighting a losing cause and moved for dismissal of the remaining cases against the filibusters.[59]

Carvajal returned to Brownsville, where he continued his efforts to organize revolutionary efforts designed at deposing Antonio López de Santa Anna from the presidency. In this location he met Melinda Rankin, a young Presbyterian missionary, who lived near him, in a rather unsavory neighborhood on the outskirts of town frequented by prowling Indians and lawless Mexicans. Miss Rankin found a friend and neighbor in the chivalrous José María, who "took her under his protective and fatherly wing." Carvajal's small jacal was guarded at night by a bodyguard, which he informed Rankin would also be assigned to guard her premises. But Rankin was not reassured by Carvajal's offer: such a controversial figure as Carvajal was bound to be the target of violence and "in case of an attack, my domicil [*sic*], with its slender walls, would as likely be penetrated by bullets as his."[60]

Newspapers reported in late 1854 that a bloody revolution was then in progress in northern Mexico, and the insurgents had called on José María to accept a position of leadership in that struggle. This revolution was in fact occurring throughout Mexico to overthrow Santa Anna's government. Sixty thousand dollars had reportedly been raised from the citizens of Mexico and the merchants of Brownsville to fund another incursion into Mexico. Mexican citizens from as far away as Monterey were reported to have guaranteed a contribution of four hundred thousand dollars to aid an army led by Carvajal and would not object to the employment of foreigners in this army. But the Central government of Mexico had prepared themselves to cope with any future border incursions. A force of one thousand Centralist soldiers with a good supply of artillery, ammunition, and provisions were in garrison at Matamoros, a hundred men stationed at Reynosa, four hundred at Camargo, four hundred at Mier with three pieces of artillery, and a hundred in garrison at Guerrero. General Adrián Woll, commanding government forces in northern Mexico, had cut off all communication between the U.S. and Mexican sides of the Rio Grande. The Mexican army had cleared an eighty-yard strip of land on the right bank of that river from Guerrero to Matamoros. Fences were removed, the posts burned, and corn fields that lay within this limit were cut down.[61]

Roberdeau Wheat returned to Brownsville in the fall of 1854, quite likely to appear before a U.S. commission that had been convened to investigate Carvajal's neutrality violations. Just before leaving New Orleans for Brownsville on 13 October 1854, he wrote John A. Quitman to discuss his future plans: "I received a long letter yesterday from Gen. [Juan] Alvarez inviting me to emigrate to Guerrero and work the silver and gold mines as soon as he can drive Santa Anna out of the country. . . . Will you honor me by writing me a line or two directed to 'Brownsville Texas care of King & Kennedy.'"[62]

On 29 October 1854, Wheat addressed a second letter to Quitman, describing the revolution then in progress in northern Mexico: "I arrived here on the 20th Oct & found Gov. Garza & Capistran the two leaders in this revolution on this side of the river with 350 men. They fought handsomely at Victoria & also above Matamoros, were victorious in a field fight above Matamoros, but were obliged to evacuate Victoria on account of the failure of their ammunition. The revolution is now in status quo for the want of Artillery, powder, & the silver sinews of war. . . . I am going up to see Carvajal in a day or two & shall then know definitely whether anything is soon to be done & if not I shall leave on the next steamer for New Orleans."[63]

Eager to find additional evidence in the matter of *Carvajal et al. v. the United States,* a "long and tedious" investigation on the matter of neutrality violations by Carvajal and his men was completed on 21 October 1854. The investigation was conducted by F. J. Parker, U.S. commissioner at

Brownsville, Texas. After "some sixty witnesses, as we understand, were examined, embracing some of the first men of the place, but from none was information of a character that would have led to the conviction of the accused elicited." Commissioner Parker concluded the hearing with a decision that there was insufficient evidence to sustain the indictments brought against Carvajal and his associates. Parker himself had been indicted for violation of the neutrality laws of the United States. The *Galveston News,* an admitted advocate for all "liberation movements," cast more doubts on the evidence against the Carvajal filibusters by noting that the Parker hearing had uncovered one affidavit having been sworn to by an illiterate woman who had no idea of what the neutrality laws were and that she had falsely accused several of the defendants of equipping an army in this country to invade Mexico, when in fact these defendants were not in the United States at that time.[64]

In a note of protest of 12 December 1854 to the U.S. State Department, from Mexican minister Juan N. Almonte, the minister expressed the continued frustration of his government over the failure to punish Carvajal: "The authorities of the United States of America, on the line of the Rio Bravo, not only do not prevent the Mexican territory from being invaded and attacked by armed people coming from those very states, but that when the latter are pursued by Mexican troops, they are sheltered on the American side."[65]

Carvajal's invasions of Mexico had far-reaching effects on the negotiation of an important treaty between that country and the United States. Robert P. Letcher, U.S. minister to Mexico, had been actively attempting to negotiate a treaty concerning the transit rights of American citizens across the Isthmus of Tehuantepec. In a 29 October 1851 communication to Washington, D.C., soon after Carvajal's attack on Matamoras, Letcher complained that progress on the treaty had been negated by Carvajal's incursion into Mexico. The opinion expressed in Mexico, according to Letcher, was: "Why grant privileges . . . to people whose object is to rob us of the whole of our country."[66]

After a late February 1852 meeting between Letcher and José F. Ramírez, minister of foreign affairs to Mexico, Letcher wrote to Washington, expressing pessimism regarding the Mexican ratification of the treaty to allow U.S. transit rights across the isthmus. Letcher reported that the treaty would be rejected due to the "intense prejudice against everything connected with American interests." He considered the anti-American feelings to have been the result of Carvajal's third invasion of Mexico from the United States, leading a force reported to consist of 480 Americans: "No member of the Government and no member of Congress, has the courage to intimate an opinion in favor of the Treaty."[67]

By 1855, Carvajal and his family were living in exile in Piedras Négras, across the Rio Grande from Eagle Pass, Texas. The reason for this change in residence from Camargo is unknown, but it is suspected that his filibustering activities in Tamaulipas during 1851 and 1852 had made him subject to arrest in that state. In October 1855 a gang of adventurers led by Texas Ranger James Hugh Callahan invaded Piedras Négras from across the Rio Grande, claiming to be in hot pursuit of a war party of Indians.[68] The invaders were in fact slave hunters, hoping to recover the many fugitives from Texas who had claimed refuge in Mexico. The invaders were met with an attack from a large party of Seminole Indians south of Piedras Négras that drove the Callahan party back into the city. To cover their retreat across the Rio Grande to sanctuary in the United States, the gang torched Piedras Négras. Carvajal now ironically became a victim of filibuster violence, as his residence was burned to the ground in the resulting fire.

José María then filed a claim for damages against the U.S. government, in which he stated that he was a citizen of Mexico, his house had been burned, and he and his family were forced to flee to the woods, and "wandered three days exposed to death under the tomahawk of the barbarous Indians." He claimed damages that totaled $21,792, which were disallowed by a U.S. government reparations commission convened to investigate the claims of Mexican citizens for the damages created by Callahan and his men.[69]

But political changes were afoot in Mexico, and the Liberal Party was to arise again, next under the leadership of Benito Juárez. Carvajal, the lifelong Liberal, was soon to find his political ideals in ascendancy, and his support of Juárez would result in amnesty for his former filibustering activities and a subsequent appointment to leadership positions in the Mexican government.

NINE

The War of the Reform in Mexico and the Southern Confederacy in the United States

The second Boabdil El Chico.

JOSÉ MARÍA DE JESÚS CARVAJAL,
description of himself after his failure to capture Matamoros,
quote taken from Ford's "Memoirs," p. 928

The mercurial nature of Mexican politics was soon to change the status of José María Carvajal from that of a fugitive to the military governor of Tamaulipas. By 1852 the Centralist government of Mexico, again led by Antonio López de Santa Anna, had become oppressive and corrupt. State and local governments were powerless, and all the important offices of the Central government were offered up as political plums to the president's cronies. The press was censored, and enemies of the government were imprisoned or exiled. The ever-suffering people of Mexico continued to grudgingly permit these excesses until Santa Anna committed the one unpardonable sin: selling Mexican lands to the United States.

In 1854 the United States acquired the Gadsden Purchase from Santa Anna's government, over the angry shouts of protest by Mexican citizens. The Republic of Mexico ceded a strip of land in the region south of the Gila River in present-day Arizona to the United States for the sum of ten million dollars. A revolt broke out in Guerrero that same year, and amidst the fighting, the new Plan of Ayutla appeared on 1 March 1854. This plan was to replace Santa Anna with a new Liberal government. By 15 August 1855, Santa Anna's government crumbled under Liberal military victories and the deposed tyrant slipped out of Mexico City into exile. Moderate Ignacio Comonfort was elected president of Mexico, while Benito Juárez assumed the role of second in command as minister of justice.

By 1857 a new Liberal constitution for Mexico had been approved that promised sweeping reforms. It guaranteed such civil rights as freedom of speech, press, petition, and assembly for the people, as well as a free public education for children. But the new constitution centered on disabling the entrenched powers of the military and the Catholic Church, those bulwarks of support for the Conservatives. For crimes against civilians the military would hereafter be tried in civil courts, rather than in military tribunals, and the army's size was to be drastically reduced. The new constitution no longer specified Catholicism as Mexico's official religion. Clergy accused of civil crimes were no longer permitted to be tried in ecclesiastical courts; rather, they were bound over for trial in civil courts. The constitution required the Catholic Church to divest itself of its vast land holdings by public sale, but it allowed the church to retain the proceeds of such sales.

Conservative backlash was almost immediate, and the stage was set for a Conservative-Liberal civil war that would come to be known as the War of the Reform. After a failed coup against his government, in which Comonfort was himself a conspirator, he went into exile, and the reins of power were passed to Juárez. Two governments now vied for control in Mexico: the Conservatives under the leadership of Miguel Miramón, centered in Mexico City, and the Liberals, who supported the constitution of 1857, under Juárez in Veracruz. Carvajal, ever sympathetic to the Liberals of Mexico, aligned himself with Juárez. His filibustering activities in northern Mexico, dating as far back as 1838, were all based on well-grounded Liberal ideals and could easily have been forgiven by Juárez, who forgave many others for much greater sins against the Republic of Mexico. During these chaotic times in Mexico, complete records were not kept, but it is felt that José María offered substantial support to the Juárez faction.

The first two years of the war went badly for the Liberals due to the vast number of trained military officers who opposed them, but by October 1861 the last of the smoldering embers of the revolution had been stamped out, and key Conservative figures—such as Miramón, Leonardo Márquez, and Tomás Mejía—had fled into exile but would soon return to Mexico to create a more serious crisis for the national government.[1] José María was rewarded for his services by the victorious Liberals with his appointment as military governor of Tamaulipas. In fewer than five years Carvajal had gone from the status of a fugitive to holding the highest position in that state's government.

The year 1859 found Carvajal residing in Matamoros, where his authority, influence, and persuasive powers saved the city of Brownsville from destruction. General David E. Twiggs, commander of the 8th Military District, which included Texas, was beset by the perennial problem of massive Indian raids then focused in North Texas, while the border between Mexico and Texas remained in a relatively peaceful state. Texas, notoriously neglected in the past by the U.S. government, was as usual undermanned with troops. To solve his immediate problem, Twiggs was allowed by the army command, in early February 1859, to abandon Fort Brown in Brownsville and Fort Ringgold in Rio Grande City. The troops from these two garrisons were shifted to North Texas to aid in quelling Indian disturbances. But the absence of the military along the border from Rio Grande City to Brownsville became an open invitation to the lawless element to take control.

Among those responding to this invitation was one Juan "Cheno" Cortina. Cortina was an influential leader of Tejanos living on the border at the center of opposition to Anglo political control of the government. A feeling of resentment smoldered between the Hispanic and Anglo populations of the lower Rio Grande Valley that had been nurtured by a long history of troubled relations. Only a spark would be required to ignite a violent reaction between Anglos and Tejanos, and that spark came in the person of the hot-tempered, red-headed Cheno Cortina.

On the evening of 28 September 1859, while most Brownsville citizens crossed the river to join a Mexican celebration in Matamoros, Cortina and his men captured Brownsville. In the battle for control of the city five citizens were killed and the prisoners in the city jail had been set free. The Brownsville raiders, according to a statement by a Brownsville citizen, were not interested in plunder, only in the murder of Cortina's enemies. Those enemies included the men who had volunteered to accompany the

Cameron County sheriff on an earlier expedition to arrest Cortina as well as those persons who had witnessed Cortina's earlier crimes.[2]

Later in the evening, as the liquor began to flow among the raiders, Cortina expressed his intent to complete his act of vengeance by burning Brownsville. At the request of many of the leading citizens of Brownsville, a delegation of Matamoros officials agreed to cross the river for a parley with Cortina. A party of the leading citizens of Brownsville and Matamoros—led by José María Carvajal and including Colonel Miguel Tijerina, Colonel Macedonio Capistrán, Don Agapito Longoria, Don Bartolo, and Don Manuel Treviño (the Mexican consul in Brownsville)—met with Cortina in Brownsville. The persuasive powers of Carvajal and the pleadings of Cortina's cousin, Tijerina, prevailed on Cortina to leave Brownsville before any further damage could be done. Tijerina took Cortina's horse by the reins and personally led the fiery redhead out of Brownsville.[3]

The raid caused panic to erupt in Brownsville. Frightened American citizens streamed across the river to the homes of relatives in Matamoros seeking protection. Without the U.S. Army garrison at Fort Brown, the city lay bare to further attacks from Mexican bandits and marauding Indians. A note requesting aid was sent from the sheriff of Cameron County to Mexican officials in Matamoros. Carvajal responded immediately by sending an armed company of the Mexican National Guard to protect the Brownsville citizens from further harm.[4] A citizen of Brownsville speaking for the city wrote: "We feel somewhat humiliated at the necessity of calling on the Mexican authorities for protection."[5]

Carvajal's policy of cooperation with the citizens of Brownsville was based on his feeling that the U.S. government might single out Matamoros for vengeance, blaming that city for the acts of Cortina's raiders.[6] Brownsville businessman and rancher Mifflin Kenedy set about to organize Brownsville citizens into a local militia, but no arms were available. Again, General Carvajal responded and through the office of the commander of the National Guard, he loaned Brownsville militia twenty-five muskets and about seventy Mississippi rifles.[7] But the services of the Brownsville militia were not needed, as U.S. military forces, under the command of Major Samuel Heintzelman, were quickly returned to the Rio Grande, where they linked up with a state force of Texas Rangers, commanded by

Colonel John S. Ford, to protect Brownsville. This combined force decisively defeated Cortina's forces near Rio Grande City on 27 December 1859, driving the remnants to sanctuary in Mexico.

Major Heintzelman crossed the Rio Grande to Matamoros to pay a social call on General Carvajal on 12 December and offered this glimpse of the general: "He received us politely & speaks English well. He was educated in Kentucky. We were pleased with our visit. He is not tall & a little stout. He leaves in a few days for Victoria—as to take the field in favor of the Liberal Government. He told us a treaty had been ratified between our governments & appeared to be delighted with it. He wore a black silk cap."[8]

Carvajal had been busily organizing troops to oppose the Conservative forces located then in Ciudad Victoria, Tamaulipas. Heintzelman reported on 17 December that "Gen. Carvajal left yesterday. He told me that his force was 700 men. Mendes says he counted them Sunday when they went to church & he did not make 400."[9] Carvajal's forces were combined with those of José Silvestre Aramberri, a Liberal who actively supported Benito Juárez. Aramberri had served for two months as military governor of Nuevo León before being driven from power by Carvajal's archenemy, Santiago Vidaurri. Carvajal's and Aramberri's forces did not leave Matamoros on 17 December, for on the next day Heintzelman met with them in Matamoros, where he was able to review their troops: "We stopped at Gen. Allanberry's [Aramberri] quarters & took a glass of wine. The troops were on parade & the general showed us their arms & new rifled canon. They have new minie muskets. He has about 700 men & leaves to-day or tomorrow for Victoria. He says he delayed to dine with us yesterday."[10]

Without Carvajal and his strong force of Liberals in Matamoros, the Conservative segment of the population, mostly the merchants and the clergy, felt more freedom to express their opinions. On 14 January 1860, Heintzelman reported that "I heard that Matamoros had pronounced against the Liberals & that Gen. Woll was after Carvajal."[11] But a week later Heintzelman wrote: "There has been no pronunciam[i]ento in Matamoros. Carvajal wrote to let two companies of volunteers cross over. They had a town meeting & refused. This is probably the foundation of the report."[12]

After being driven into Mexico by U.S. forces, Cortina and his men continued to engage in large-scale rustling operations north of the river. In a bold move to rid the border of Cortina's presence, U.S. forces requested permission to enter Mexico with two companies of men and attack Cortina's forces on their home grounds. Carvajal, at the urging of his old friend John S. Ford, had written General Guadalupe García, commanding the Mexican National Guard along the border, to seek approval of the request, which Heintzelman reported had been denied.[13] But by March 1860, Carvajal had prevailed, and General García grudgingly sanctioned the crossing of U.S. forces into Mexico to attack Cortina.

When word was received that Cortina and his men were camped at La Mesa, about four miles south of the Rio Grande, U.S. forces crossed into Mexico and struck the little village on 18 March in the predawn hours. Instead of confronting Cortina, the forces mistakenly attacked a unit of the Mexican National Guard. The blunder resulted in excoriating criticism from the press of both countries. Ford, who participated in the raid, could only comment that "we have played Old Scratch, whipped the Guardia National, wounded a woman, and killed a mule."[14]

There may have been some substance to rumors about the *pronunciamiento* (pronouncement) in Matamoros against the Liberal cause. Heintzelman reported on 28 January 1860 that "some letter Carvajal wrote to Gen. Guadalupe Garcia to make a forced loan, or fine of $100,000 on some there in Matamoros, who pronounced the other day & send them to Victoria is to come out in the Matamoros paper. He was to call on Ford for aid if necessary."[15] Carvajal, well known for his attempts to extort extravagant contributions for the Liberal cause from the Conservative-leaning merchants of Matamoros, had created staunch foes among the leading citizens of the city. But the Juárez government intervened in an effort to win over their opponents. On the next day Heintzelman heard, from across the river, "the blowing of bugles & beating of drums in Matamoros. I suppose it a pronunciam[i]ento, but at breakfast could hear nothing of it. I have just learned that the express sent to Juarez has returned & brought the information that he disapproved of Gen. Carvajal's orders about the $100,000 & arrest of certain citizens he wished sent to him under Major Ford. They had great rejoicing."[16]

There has been no further information found on Carvajal's march to Victoria, nor on any of his other efforts to aid Juárez's Liberal cause in its triumph over the Conservatives. In 1861 the Liberal faction took over the reins of power and became the legal government of the Republic of Mexico. Carvajal was awarded for his services by being appointed military governor of Tamaulipas from 26 September 1864 until April 1865 and again from March until 20 August 1866. North of the Rio Grande, Texas seceded from the Union in February 1861, becoming one of the Confederate States of America. Colonel John S. Ford was placed in command of Confederate forces in the Rio Grande Valley of Texas.

The victorious Liberal Party, under Juárez's leadership, had resumed popular elections in Tamaulipas. The race for governor that year resulted in the election of Jesús de la Serna in the fall of 1861. After a careful study of the returns, the Juárez government certified de la Serna as the winner. The opposing candidate, Cipriano Guerrero, was not willing to accept this decision and pronounced against de la Serna. Guerrero received the support of General Guadalupe García, military commander of Matamoros and leader of the Crinolinos Party, while de la Serna sought out and received the support of José María Carvajal, leader of the rival Rojos Party. The stage was thus set for a mini civil war in Tamaulipas between the forces of de la Serna/Carvajal and Guerrero/García.[17]

The editor of the *Fort Brown Flag* met with General Carvajal in December 1861 and found him to be "a very intelligent gentleman" who spoke "English like a book." Carvajal, the old states' rights Liberal, spoke of his "intimacy" with the Confederate cause in the United States, mentioning that his two sons were at this time protecting a "Southern school" from Northern invasion, referring to his two sons, José María and Antonio, who were then students at Bethany College in Virginia.[18] The editor later visited the forces of General García, reporting that the general was confident and denied any possibility of failure. García, "an agreeable gentleman and most popular officer," was reported to head an army of from eight hundred to twelve hundred men "who manifest an earnest disposition to fight until the bitter end."[19] The situation was tense in Matamoros in anticipation of another armed struggle, and commerce had basically come to a standstill. "The lately flourishing city looks like a graveyard. . . . It is dangerous to approach the town in any direction, for fear of the flying bullets."[20]

General García, knowing of the friendship between Colonel Ford and

General Carvajal, persuaded Ford to visit Carvajal's camp as a bearer of propositions between the two warring factions with the hope of heading off armed hostilities. After the delivery of the García message to his close friend and Masonic brother, Carvajal asked Ford for his advice on tactics to use in the upcoming attack on Matamoros. Remembering the tragic failure of Carvajal's forces to launch an all-out attack on that city during the Merchants War, Ford suggested that Carvajal "go in, make the fight, apparently desperate and you will win. You will lose fewer men by that course than you would be dilly dallying, fooling around, and half fighting." During the upcoming attack on Matamoros, Carvajal was to ignore Ford's advice a second time.[21]

Carvajal and his Rojos, camped above Brownsville, moved close to the Matamoros crossings on the river by November 1861. Colonel Ford, who had declared Confederate neutrality in the conflict, made a halfhearted attempt to disperse Carvajal's army, but by the early morning of 20 November the residents of Brownsville were awakened by the sounds of a battle across the river in Matamoros. During the night the Rojos army had crossed the Rio Grande and with a "lively charge" had thrown themselves against the defenders of Matamoros, estimated to be about five hundred cavalrymen and hundreds of foot soldiers. To one Brownsville resident, it sounded as if "three thousand muskets had all exploded at once." The Rojos, shouting "'Viva Peña!,' 'Viva Treviño!,' and 'Viva Carvajal!,'" were answered by the shouts of the Crinolinos: "'Viva García!,' 'Viva Capistrán!,' and 'Death to the traitors.'"[22] Confederate authorities in Brownsville seized the ferries, allowing only Carvajal's casualties to return to Brownsville. The Rojos's siege of Matamoros was to continue, as a piece-meal effort, for ninety-three days until finally relieved by an act of Juárez.[23]

The news that a triumvirate of European powers—Great Britain, France, and Spain—were planning to invade Mexico and seize the customs houses on the east coast to collect debts owed them had forced Juárez into action. To break the Matamoros stalemate, Juárez declared martial law in Tamaulipas, appointing Santiago Vidaurri, Carvajal's nemesis, state military commander. Vidaurri ordered Colonel Julián Quiroga to advance on Matamoras from Monterey with six hundred infantry to lift the stalemate.

Quiroga neared Matamoros by March 1862, and Carvajal's Rojos army, now vastly outnumbered, sought sanctuary by crossing the Rio Grande into Texas. Confederate authorities allowed Carvajal's army to return but confiscated all of the Rojos's small arms and their two pieces of artillery.[24] A smiling José María put a good face on his failure to capture Matamoros by declaring to his friends that he was "the second Boabdil El Chico."[25]

The size of Vidaurri's army—two thousand troops in Matamoros, one thousand in Tampico, and three thousand at Ciudad Victoria—did not deter General Carvajal, who immediately began preparations for another incursion south of the river. In an effort to regain the Rojos's impounded arms, Jesús de la Serna dispatched a message to Confederate forces north of the Bravo, which he signed as "Governor of the State of Tamaulipas," requesting the return of the confiscated arms to Matamoros. He argued that the arms were the property of the State of Tamaulipas, and as its head, he should receive the arms. A week later de la Serna dispatched a second note, gently commenting that no response to his earlier letter had been received. Within another week Colonel Ford received an official letter from Santiago Vidaurri, the Juárez-appointed "Military Commander of Tamaulipas," announcing that Manuel Treviño, Mexican consul in Brownsville and a de la Serna partisan, was "discontinued" from that position. As for the confiscated arms, Vidaurri asked Ford to "order the delivery to Col. Quiroga of the arms you may have taken from the soldiers that made a vandalic war against Heroic Matamoros . . . which are the property of the State of Tamaulipas."

General Carvajal entered the contest for possession of the confiscated arms in a letter to Ford in which he described the terms agreed to by Ford's predecessor, Colonel Luckett: "The Col. stated that those arms and two pieces of artillery belonging to the State of Tamaulipas represented by Gov. Serna, and by me his representative in the Military Department, were only envisioned a temporary deposit to be returned when properly call for by us." Carvajal requested the delivery of the arms "as soon as possible" to his "agent," Mr. Andres Treviño. Ford complied with Carvajal's request and turned the arms over to Treviño, who would in turn return them to Carvajal's Rojos. But Carvajal did not reissue the arms to his forces while in South Texas, the men marched "apparently unarmed" but had with them "arms in carts which accompany them" still representing a menace to Tamaulipas.

Quiroga, commanding the Mexican "Army of the Line of the Bravo," corresponded with Ford on 11 March 1862 to request that he, "with the forces in my command to pass to the left side of the Bravos," attack Carvajal's forces in Texas. He reminded Ford of the recent time "when Brownsville was threatened by Cortinas, who was not only pursued by our forces," but that the government of Mexico had "permitted the forces under your [Ford's] command to pursue him upon our territory."

By late March, Ford dispatched a Confederate force, under the command of Captain John Littleton, to the area across the river from Reynosa to investigate complaints from Quiroga that Carvajal had concentrated his forces there to cross the river and invade the city. Littleton reported on 1 April 1862 that he found Carvajal's army, consisting of about a hundred men, "but no arms." Littleton reported that Carvajal's purpose for being there was to see that the men of his army who wanted to return to their homes in Mexico be allowed to cross in safety, but apparently Carvajal also had other plans. Carvajal invaded Mexico again in April 1862, in an unsuccessful attack on Reynosa. Rumors again abounded that Carvajal was being aided by a sympathetic Confederate leader: Colonel John S. Ford. The rumors had some substance, especially since the attacking Rojos forces were armed with two distinctive rifled cannons, supposedly the same ones confiscated by Confederate forces earlier in the year.[26]

Vidaurri had run to the end of his patience in dealing with Carvajal and, citing as a precedence the American expedition that had received permission to cross the Rio Grande in pursuit of Cortina in 1860, requested permission to cross the Rio Grande into Texas in pursuit of Carvajal's forces. Ford continued to hedge in support of his old friend by denying Vidaurri's request for a hot-pursuit agreement. Vidaurri then played his trump card on 4 April 1862 by raising the import duty on cotton, previously duty free, to two cents per pound. Border merchants and Confederate authorities howled in dismay, but Vidaurri maintained that he needed to raise additional revenue to support the Mexican troops now required on the border to guard against Carvajal's forces.[27] To the blockaded Southern Confederacy, trade with northern Mexico represented essentially the only source for arms, ammunition, medicines, and the many other items required to supply an army. The main item of export for the South was cotton, and by placing an import duty on a commodity that had previously been allowed in Mexico without tariff duty, Vidaurri's action was bound to open the eyes of Texas and the entire South.

By late April 1862 the Confederate government responded to Vidaurri's newly ordered import tax. Colonel Ford received an order from his superior, General Henry McCulloch, to arrest José María Carvajal as soon as possible and turn him over to Colonel Quiroga in Matamoros. If carried out, the order meant certain death for Carvajal, who would be placed against the nearest wall in Matamoros and executed by a firing squad. Ford, torn between his duty to his country and his friendship for the "little general," erred in favor of friendship. He informed José María, his Masonic brother, of the arrest order, permitting him to escape the country. As punishment for disobeying the order to deliver Carvajal, Ford was relieved of his position as commander of Confederate forces on the Rio Grande by Confederate authorities in San Antonio. On 2 June 1862, Ford was reassigned to the most despised job in Texas: commander of the conscript program.

Carvajal disappeared from the Texas-Mexico border, destined to battle a new threat to the Liberal Juárez government of Mexico: the French imperialists.[28]

TEN

French Intervention

Never was a man more solicitous to do his duty
and serve his country.

LEW WALLACE,
describing José María de Jesús Carvajal,
in a March 1865 letter

The Republic of Mexico had historically been a debtor nation that balanced its yearly deficits with loans from France, Great Britain, Spain, and the United States. The Mexican federal government relied on its state governments to collect most of its internal taxes, but gross inefficiency and corruption in the system had caused only a small trickle of that revenue to reach federal coffers. The bulk of the Mexican government's revenue was generated by the taxing of imported and exported goods, creating a downward spiral in the nation's economic health. High import duties imposed on foreign goods resulted in exorbitant domestic prices choking off consumer demand, decreasing the volume of imports. As import duties were raised to offset the loss of import volume, demand again fell. Similarly, export taxes made Mexican products too expensive in the foreign markets to compete with goods manufactured by other countries.

By 1861, with the end of the War of the Reform, the treasury of the victorious Juárez government was depleted, and Mexico was over its head in debt to the four most powerful nations in the world. The system for the collection of internal revenues had completely collapsed by this time, and customs receipts that had been pledged to pay earlier debts were not available to meet current expenses. By 17 July 1861 the Mexican Congress took the only step possible to save the government by passing legislation for a two-year suspension on the payment of all domestic and foreign debts. The governments of France, Great Britain, and Spain met in London on 31 October 1861 to decide on a unified plan of action to collect their overdue debts. The three great powers agreed on an armed intervention into Mexico to coerce that country into repayment, but Great Britain insisted that the powers "bind themselves not to seek for themselves, in the employment of coercive measures foreseen by the present convention, any acquisition of territory, or any peculiar advantage, and not to exercise in the subsequent affairs of Mexico any influence of a character to impair the right of the Mexican nation to choose and freely to constitute the form of its own government."

But Napoleon III, the ambitious emperor of France, had other ideas about Mexico and would use this excuse for military intervention as a way to gain a toehold into the country. He had set in motion a covert plan to replace the Liberal Juárez government with a monarchy that would extend the French empire into the Western Hemisphere. Several influential Mexican Conservatives, still unwilling to turn the country over to the Liberals after the War of the Reform, had petitioned Napoleon III to place a monarch at the head of Mexican government. With the United States embroiled in its own civil war, French diplomats felt that the Monroe Doctrine would not be invoked as an excuse by the United States to come to the aid of Mexico. But what France needed was an excuse for intervention in Mexico, and the debt crisis offered just what was needed. The Mexican debt to France, while quite large, was exacerbated by French claims that the Juárez government also owed the debts incurred by the Conservatives during the War of the Reform. But Juárez had warned foreign powers as early as 1859 that the constitutional government would not assume any debts incurred by the Conservatives, and he thus refused to acknowledge this portion of French claims.

By January 1862 the forces of France, Great Britain, and Spain landed unopposed in Veracruz and had taken over the customs house. But by April 1862, Great Britain and Spain, sensing that France had imperial designs on Mexico and would not honor the provisions of the tripartite intervention agreement, withdrew their troops. On 9 April, using the excuse that Mexico had refused to pay its debt to France, France commenced hostilities against the Republic of Mexico, initiating the most crit-ically important struggle for its survival as a republic.

José María Carvajal, fresh from his narrow escape on the Texas border from Governor Santiago Vidaurri, traveled to Mexico City to place himself in the services of Benito Juárez and the Liberal cause. Juárez was recruiting an army to resist the French and appointed Carvajal to command a brigade of infantry. Carvajal's brigade, and that of O'Horan, were soon ordered off to suppress a small remnant of Conservative forces at Atlixco and Izúcar that supported the French intervention. Both brigades missed the oppor-tunity to participate in a signal Mexican victory against the French, led by General Ignacio Zaragoza, a Mexican officer who had been born in Texas. Modestly explaining his brilliant victory against the French on 5 May 1862 at Puebla, General Zaragoza stated that he "might have defeated the enemy completely in a victory that would have immortalized its name, with the additional troops from those two brigades under his direct command."[1]

By 1863 the French had steadily progressed in their military campaign to seize Mexico. Juárez and his government had been driven from Mexico City to begin the long retreat that would end in Chihuahua. The French soon occupied most of the principal cities of Mexico, but the Juáristas retained their popularity with the lower and middle classes of Mexico. Guerrilla bands, loyal to Juárez, controlled the countryside, choking off the transit of French military supplies, attacking small French garrisons, and collecting tribute from merchant caravans moving on the roads. This mode of warfare was very familiar to Carvajal, having received his baptism in hit-and-run tactics during the Mexican-American War. Imperialist colonel Manuel Llorente was the first to feel the sting of Carvajal's guerrilla forces. Putting together a band of about twelve hundred men, mostly from the shattered commands of other Mexican forces, General Carvajal success-fully defended the port city of Tuxpan against Llorente's forces. From there Carvajal threatened Tampico, now in French hands, and controlled virtually all of the roads surrounding that city.[2]

Carvajal's harassing guerrilla tactics soon caused the French to dispatch an expedition, under the command of imperialist colonel Charle Dupin, to exterminate guerrilla forces occupying the Huastecan area of Mexico. Dupin's forces advanced cautiously against Carvajal, not knowing what perils they might be facing. Carvajal was a master of the countryside, knowing every goat trail that crisscrossed the Huasteca and possessing the respect and resources of the Indian population of the three states whose boundaries sliced through that region.

Carvajal, at the rank of general of the Liberal forces, was leading the battalion "Fieles de Tamaulipas," consisting of four hundred men and two pieces of artillery, in a campaign against the "traitors," Mexican forces that had sided with the imperialists. He joined up with the brigade of General Francisco Gonzáles Pavón, assuming command of the combined force, to drive insurgents from the coastal city of Tuxpan. In control of that city, Carvajal was successful in depriving French forces of the port, which was to be used for landing supplies. Carvajal then moved against the traitors occupying the town of Tamapache but was held up by an ambush of his forces on the San Lorenzo Road. It was there that Carvajal's scouts discovered an imperialist force of 450 infantry and cavalry with two pieces of artillery bearing down on them.

Dupin, leading this expedition, had been commanded to link up with the traitors and attack the Carvajal battalion. Carvajal reacted by moving on a double-quick march to interpose his force between those of the imperialists and the traitors. Carvajal's little band of irregulars was finally cornered in the village of San Bartolo, assuming defensive positions in the village church and walled cemetery. French regulars and Mexican irregular forces charged Carvajal's position unsuccessfully on two attacks but were repulsed. One source stated that Carvajal himself mounted the walls of San Bartolo, firing with his Sharps repeating carbine, but it is doubtful that a man with only one good arm could manage such a ponderous firearm. The attackers regrouped for a third charge, and after bringing their artillery to bear on Carvajal's defensive position, overran the church and cemetery, but Carvajal and a portion of his forces managed to escape capture.[3]

Carvajal's actions during the battle came under the close scrutiny of his political enemy, Juan "Cheno" Cortina. In a report to the Ministry of War and Marine of 2 May 1864, Cortina stated that

it looks like the cause of this defeat was due to the lack of foresight and caution by Carvajal. The withdrawal of this chief of combat was so disorderly that no power could achieve the reassembly of his force. At Tancamegui, he reassembled the remnants of his force which consisted of no more than 40 men. The rest did not want to continue under the orders of a Chief for which they had no sympathy. . . . Gen. Carvajal is found now in Miquihuana, and at such time tries to acquire orders to raise new forces, the Government will regret turning over these presents, as it would be a misfortune for destiny to copy another disaster to waste in this way in a few hours that which the Government struggles so many days of hard work to organize and armaments that are so much needed.

But editor Jesús De León Toral, who could see the true intent of this acid-dipped correspondence, commented that "the hard pressed and patriotic Gen. Jose M. Carvajal, tireless warrior for the Republic, who was defeated after a long and bloody combat in the place of San Antonio, belonging to the Huasteca, Veracruzana, against imperialists reinforced by a gang of contraguerrillas of Col. Dupin, but without losing heart for such a failure and despite the bad opinion by several of the republican leaders that was undeserved, decided again to fight for the independence of Mexico."[4]

Carvajal regrouped his forces near Ciudad Victoria, centering his activities near Soto La Marina as he had done during the Mexican-American War. His forces, on 31 October 1864, mauled an imperialist column near Victoria. But Colonel Dupin's forces continued their relentless pursuit, capturing Carvajal's home at Soto La Marina and ten pieces of rifled artillery. With his forces decimated and without arms or ammunition, Carvajal moved his remaining troops into hiding in the wilds of the San Carlos Mountains.[5]

From his mountain hideout Carvajal dispatched Ramírez Arellano to meet with the Juárez government, then in residence in Chihuahua. Carvajal sought permission to request aid from the U.S. government, then engaged in a civil war. Arellano was successful on his mission, returning with a commission from Juárez, dated 12 November 1864. The document empowered Carvajal to enlist up to ten thousand foreign citizens in the Liberal cause and purchase up to forty thousand guns and three thousand assorted arms, pledging the income of the State of Tamaulipas as the source of capital.[6]

Carvajal did not act immediately on the commission, apparently feeling that his authority to solicit aid was not broad enough in scope. He was also personally destitute of funds, not having the money to travel outside of Mexico. But unscrupulous Mexicans with money were then abroad in the United States negotiating arms contracts with U.S. merchants. A secret deal was uncovered in 1865 whereby a certain Mexican "patriot" had proposed to buy muskets for five dollars from American arms dealers and sell them for fifteen dollars to the Mexicans. In a letter of 15 June 1865, discussing this proposal, Juárez reiterated that only Carvajal had a commission to act in the United States and that "if the Yankees put any trust in the promises and arrangements of Ortega, they will make fools of themselves."[7]

Meanwhile, back in Matamoros, the capture of that city by the imperialists became imminent by September 1864. A French force that had landed at Bagdad advanced on the city from the east while a force led by General Tomás Mejía approached from the south. Cortina's outnumbered irregular army controlled Matamoros at this time, but the opportunistic redhead was not committed to either side in the struggle for Mexican independence. After some negotiations Cortina surrendered Matamoros, without blood shed, on two terms: that imperialist forces accept his services and that of his army, and that Matamoros be garrisoned only by Mexican troops. Both requests were granted and Matamoros was turned over to imperialist troops under the command of Mejía on 29 September 1864. A portion of Mejía's Matamoros garrison consisted of freebooters and men recruited in Mexico from the remnants of disaffected Conservative units.[8]

José María Carvajal was soon to return from the San Carlos Mountains to embark on a mission for the Juárez government. In early 1865 a secret meeting was held in Washington, D.C., between General Lew Wallace, President Abraham Lincoln, and Secretary of War Edmond Stanton. With the American Civil War nearing a climax, the time had come for the United States to consider a more aggressive stance in the struggle between the Liberal forces of Benito Juárez and the French imperialists. Fearing that aid to Mexican Liberals might draw France into the American Civil War on the Confederate side, the U.S. government had maintained a strict policy of neutrality during earlier phases of the Civil War. Secretary of State William Seward strictly enforced the U.S. Neutrality Act of 1818, severely punishing all violators. But a new day was dawning, and as a result of this meeting, General Wallace was dispatched on a mission to Brazos Santiago, a barrier island off the coast of South Texas, then occupied by Union troops. Once there, Wallace was ordered to contact the "nearest reliable representative" of the Liberal government of Mexico having the authority to purchase arms on credit.

Upon arriving in South Texas in March 1865, Wallace dispatched a messenger into Mexico to summon General Carvajal for a meeting. Liberal forces at this time were in sad straits, with the Juárez government operating in Chihuahua, the last state capital not under French control. Carvajal's force had dwindled to about three hundred men destitute of any firearms who were hiding in the mountains near Ciudad Victoria. The force was in such a need for armaments that Carvajal had been exercising his troops in the use of bows and arrows.[9]

José María traveled to Brazos Santiago for the meeting, crossing French lines disguised as a "Texas horse-buyer." After first greetings to Wallace, Carvajal presented documents from Juárez, certifying him as a "commissioner with high powers." Wallace was impressed with Carvajal: "Never was a man more solicitous to do his duty and serve his country. In all Mexico, probably, there was not another better qualified for the task intrusted [sic] him. . . . he talked and wrote English as if it had been his mother-tongue; he was American in tastes and ideas."[10] Wallace offered to transport Carvajal to Washington for a meeting with Lincoln and Stanton. But Carvajal was so impoverished that he frankly acknowledged that he had neither the finances nor the clothes for such an enterprise. Wallace offered both, drawing three hundred dollars from the Secret Service fund for Carvajal, and the two were soon on their way to the capital.[11]

José María's arrival in late March 1865 in Washington was cloaked in secrecy, known only in the U.S. government to President Lincoln, Secretary Stanton, and General Ulysses S. Grant. Mexican Minister Matías Romero wrote, on April 26, that Carvajal had arrived in Washington incognito, registering in a hotel as "Joseph Smith." Carvajal's correspondence to Wallace over the next few months would all be signed by that nom de guerre.[12] That same day Carvajal wrote Wallace, offering him a major general's commission in the Mexican army, cleverly adding that he would have "command of a corps of Americans." The acceptance of such a commission would place upon Wallace the burden of raising a corps of volunteer soldiers in the United States for service in Mexico and confronting Seward's strict enforcement of the Neutrality Act.

For his services Carvajal promised Wallace that in case of his death, the government of Mexico would "secure my [Wallace's] family beyond the chances of want." In addition, Carvajal promised to pay Wallace $100,000 if the Liberal cause prevailed, or $25,000 in case of failure within a year. Wallace hesitated to accept this generous offer, and Carvajal sweetened the deal by promising Wallace $100,000 regardless of the outcome of the Liberal cause. Wallace, then an officer in the Union army, was compelled to decline the Mexican commission due to a conflict of interest. Later, after the cash-strapped Wallace had resigned his U.S. military commission, he accepted Carvajal's offer.[13]

Carvajal had arrived in Washington just before Lincoln's assassination, an act that nullified all previous secret agreements between the Mexican Liberals and the late president and paralyzed the U.S. government for several months. After fruitless waiting for U.S. government action, in June 1865, Carvajal traveled to New York seeking private financial aid for the Liberal cause in Mexico. From there the naive and trusting Carvajal was eagerly pounced upon by a confidence man.

At a business meeting in Carvajal's room at the Union Place Hotel, Wallace first met the so-called U.S. entrepreneur Daniel Woodhouse. Woodhouse, whom Carvajal certified as "a perfect gentleman," was promoting the "United States, European, and West Virginia Land and Mining Company." As secretary for this company, he claimed to have a liquid capital of twenty million dollars and offered to issue Mexican Liberal bonds. In exchange for selling fifty million dollars in Mexican bonds at 40 percent of face value, secured by 106,800 acres of select mineral lands in Tamaulipas and San Luis Potosí and state and federal revenues of three million dollars, Woodhouse demanded a sales commission of 2,169,232 acres of land in the two states and railroad rights extending from Matamoros to San Luis Potosí.[14]

Not bothering to check Woodhouse's references, Wallace drew up the business arrangement, which made him president of the venture, and along with Carvajal became a signatory to the formal contract. The contract was forwarded to Mexican Minister Matías Romero, with Wallace's guarantee of Woodhouse's "known respectability." But Romero, a shrewd business-man, began his own investigation of Woodhouse and discovered that the land and mining company he represented was bogus, thus exposing the fraudulent scheme. Even the ever optimistic Carvajal was later forced to admit, when faced with the facts, that the land and mining company was "a fake." That Carvajal, operating in a foreign country and unaware of U.S. business practices, should fail to check Woodhouse's background is excus-able but that Wallace should do likewise is a sad commentary on the man.[15]

To exacerbate matters, the good-hearted but somewhat gullible Carvajal had offered aid to Margarita Juárez, wife of Benito Juárez, then living in exile in New York. Discovering that Señora Juárez was living in poverty, Carvajal issued her warrants for twenty thousand dollars against Juárez's salary, secured by the bonds offered by Woodhouse. President Juárez, angered that his family had unwittingly been drawn into a shady dealing, wrote his wife to immediately return all warrants to José María. Juárez then ordered all of Carvajal's subsequent financial dealings to be placed under the supervision of Don Matías Romero.[16]

A humiliated Carvajal, writing to Wallace on 22 August 1865, declared that "Woodhouse is certainly a *counterfeit*, and has used within us a system of fraud sufficient to send him to the Penitentiary—His object has been to cheat us in a gigantic style and then laugh at me and my Govt. . . . I shall employ a good lawyer and *force* company to respectability and *responsibil-ity*, so that I can have a guarantee, or *break this contract*—They pretend now to be sensible in their duty. . . . Sturm is pressing them tightly, and I think they are beginning to see the elephant. I have good friends assisting me."[17]

At the behest of Wallace, Herman Sturm, an Indiana manufacturer of military supplies, had come to Carvajal's aid, furnishing both legal assis-tance in breaking the Woodhouse contract and in the funding of arms to Mexico. In return, Carvajal signed a contract on 1 May 1865 with Sturm that empowered the latter as "Agent of the Mexican Republic, for the pur-chase and shipment of all material necessary for the prosecution of the war against the French." Carvajal had Sturm commissioned as a brigadier gen-eral in the Liberal army, promising him from ten thousand to twenty thousand dollars for his services to Mexico.[18] Sturm notified Woodhouse that unless the contract was nullified, he would be arrested for fraud, and after some legal wrangling, the Carvajal contract was nullified.

With a recommendation from Sturm, Jonathan N. Tifft, representing John W. Corlies & Company of New York, agreed in August to issue bonds to support Juárez's Liberal army. But Minister Romero was very leery of the new arrangement. He and Carvajal came into conflict over the agreement, the ever eager Carvajal arguing that Tifft could furnish the means to liberate Matamoros within ten days. But Romero continued to demur, finally consenting on September 11. The agreement provided that Corlies & Company would loan thirty million dollars in exchange for seven and a half million dollars in Mexican bonds, one hundred square leagues of land, five unexploited mines, and free land for colonists.

José María was wildly optimistic about the arrangement, issuing Wallace a draft for twenty-five thousand dollars, payable in seven months, for his part in putting the deal together. Tifft reported to Wallace that "Carvajal is a new man."[19] The bonds were offered for sale to the public by October 1865. However, Mexican bonds were hard to sell. The majority opinion among bankers and financiers was one of sympathy for the Liberal cause, but overwhelming suspicion existed of the Mexican ability or will to repay its debt. Most asked, "Why should we take a Mexican bond? We doubt the Mexican faith; we have no assurance that if Maximilian were driven away the Mexicans could manage their resources so as to meet promptly the interest or principal on their bonds. The inducements offered don't compensate for the risks."[20]

However, with some persuasion by Wallace and Sturm, who himself heavily invested in the bonds, a modest number were sold in the western states. But by and large, the bond sale was a failure. By the end of the year only $936,150 of the bonds had been sold. In the meantime Wallace had resigned his U.S. Army commission and accepted the Mexican commission, promising to work full time for the Liberal cause.[21] But it was Sturm who put together the deal that sold Mexican bonds. Most munitions manufacturers had been left with a large surplus of goods at the close of the American Civil War and were eager to clear their large inventories. Sturm convinced arms makers and dealers to accept Mexican bonds for arms purchases in lieu of cash. The deal was considered speculative by the arms dealers, but there was now no other market available for weapons.[22] With a $1,520,00 draft written by Carvajal on Corlies & Company, arms and munitions were purchased by Sturm and sent to New York for shipment to Mexico.[23]

A joyous José María, savoring the prospects of a Mexican Republic free from the French, addressed his metered verses, written in Spanish, to Wallace on 16 December 1865:

VICTORY FINALLY

Chorus
Now victory finally
Crowns the nation,
And on land and sea is free
the flag from equalization.
Let us make it float
In the confines of the world,
Singing without ceasing
Finally, victory, finally

I.

Anxious we await
the dawn of peace,
The hour in which the war
Covers up its face.
The reveilles announce it to us,
Let the clarion salute it,
The soldiers return,
Finally, victory, finally.

II.

The heroes who conquered
The perfidious French,
Find in their path
garlands at their feet!
They forget their vigils
And their thousand tribulations,
And to their hearths they return
Finally, victory, finally.

III.

Oh children! Oh women!
Look at the conquerer,
Make of his return
a festival!
Make float in the wind
As it floated in the combat,
The banner of Hidalgo,
Finally, victory, finally.[24]

Wallace went to New York to supervise shipping details, and Carvajal was sent to Brazos Santiago to reconcile the squabbling Liberal forces in northern Mexico under one banner. But Carvajal's task was not easy. He had confided to Wallace in an 18 May 1865 letter that "the State of Nuevo Leon will not cooperate with Cortina, but they are doing so spontaneously with my officers—I hope that Gen Grant will not recognize the traitor and bandit Cortina and order the delivery of the three rifled cannon. Cortina . . . cant be trusted in *any capacity*—The people will not trust him, and besides he is no officer—My boys have done right not to form with him, I have him where I want him, between two fires, if he dont obey, and if he does obey, he can amuse the enemy—He is no general, and would not as such be an acquisition to my cause."[25] Sturm retained three ships to sail from New York to South Texas: the *J. W. Everman,* the *Suwanee,* and the *General Sheridan.* The *Everman* and *Suwanee* were to carry the arms and ammunition, and the *General Sheridan,* a gunboat, was sent as a gift to the Juárez government.

Extreme secrecy had to be employed in loading the ships, lest they be confiscated by the U.S. government for violation of the Neutrality Act. The *Everman* was dispatched on 16 July 1866 with Wallace on board, followed soon by the *Sheridan.* The *Sheridan* had been disarmed, to circumvent the neutrality laws, but her deck guns and munitions were to follow later, aboard the *Suwanee.* That ship left New York after the departure of the *Everman* and soon afterward foundered in a storm off the coast of North Carolina on 4 December 1866 and sank, losing a large shipment of Liberal arms and the deck mounts for the *Sheridan.* The cargo of the *Suwanee* had not been insured and was a total loss to the Liberal army. Wallace, a passenger aboard the *Everman*, reached Matamoros with the remainder of his cargo on 10 August 1866.[26]

The occupation of Matamoros by the French had continued on throughout 1865, but by early 1866 the fortunes of the imperialists in Mexico had changed. With the American Civil War at an end, the government in Washington, D.C., began to adopt a more militant attitude toward the French intervention in Mexico. Diplomatic pressure was applied to the government of Napoleon III and arms were being supplied to the Juáristas in secret by the U.S. government, in violation of the country's own neutrality laws.

General Philip Sheridan was now poised on the Texas border with an army of more than thirty thousand troops awaiting orders to invade Mexico on the side of the Liberals. The political climate in Europe was now uneasy over the efforts of Otto von Bismarck to unify Germany. Most important, Mexico refused to be conquered, and the campaign in Mexico had turned into a stalemate that required ever more amounts of French money and men. By early 1866, Napoleon III decided to abandon his hopes for an empire in Mexico and began to return troops to France, leaving Maximilian, the Hapsburg who had assumed the throne of Mexico, and his Mexican allies to fend for themselves as best they could.[27]

In Matamoros, General Tomás Mejía was beset with financial problems. He had proved to be an able and fair administrator of Matamoros, not requiring forced loans from the merchants of that city, relying instead on import duties to support his army. But Liberal irregular forces controlled all the roads from Matamoros to the interior of Mexico and had shut off all Matamoros trade with the interior of the country. By May 1866, with no sources of revenue remaining, Mejía was compelled to request a loan from the merchants of Matamoros. Mejía did not favor this action but knew that unless his men were paid, he would not be able to control them and that they might begin large-scale looting of the city.[28]

Matamoros merchants at that time were cash poor, their assets tied up in merchandise that could not reach its intended markets. After a meeting between Mejía and the merchants of Matamoros, it was decided that a convoy of wagons bearing merchandise from Matamoros would be sent under heavy military escort to the eager markets of Monterey. The proceeds from these sales would then furnish the cash needed for a loan to the imperialist garrison in Matamoros. The military escort supplied by Mejía was to be two regiments of European troops and more than fifteen hundred Mexican cavalry troopers.

The convoy left Matamoros on 6 June 1866, but ten days later it was captured by the Liberals near Camargo, in the famous battle of Santa Gertrudis, known in Mexico as "El Convoy." A Juárista force led by General Mariano Escobedo attacked the European escort in a frontal assault, while the Mexican cavalry contingent escorting the wagons abruptly turned on the European escort, attacking it from the flanks. Colonel Servando Canales of the Liberal army had secretly contacted the Mexican imperialist cavalry escort before the battle and convinced them to switch their allegiance to the Juárista side. The Plain of Santa Gertrudis that day was covered with "boots, shoes, woolens, silks, and satins," while Escobedo's victorious forces "were refreshing themselves with wondrous wines and brandies; preserved meats and other delicacies; and smoking the finest cigars."[29]

Sheridan, commanding the Military District of Texas in 1866, had been ordered by Grant to monitor the situation in Mexico very closely and to seek, if possible, an opportunity to invade Mexico on the side of the Juárez Liberals. Sheridan had placed the 4th Corps at Victoria and San Antonio, Texas, and the 25th Corps at Brownsville, both poised to enter Mexico. Knowing of the Liberal army's critical need for arms, Sheridan, acting on the orders of a sympathetic government in Washington, was able to covertly supply Juárez forces with more than thirty thousand muskets from the Baton Rouge Arsenal during the summer and fall of 1866, in compassionate disregard for the U.S. Neutrality Act of 1818.

Sheridan was concerned about the lack of unity in the command structure of the Mexican Army of the North. Three Mexican armies, more or less aligned with the Liberals, were then in the field: the armies of Mariano Escobedo, Servando Canales, and Juan Cortina. Seeking to unite them under a single leader, Sheridan requested an interview with José María Carvajal to determine his qualifications for that position of leadership. Carvajal reported to him in New Orleans; Sheridan later wrote that Carvajal "did not impress me very favorably. He was old and cranky, yet as he seemed anxious to do his best, I sent him over to Brownsville, with credentials, authorizing him to cross over into Mexico."[30]

Carvajal had only been in Brownsville for a short while after the imperialist military disaster at Santa Gertrudis, making arrangements for the warehousing of the shipment of arms from New York, when Mejía began seeking a Liberal Mexican leader to whom he could surrender Matamoros. José María, representing himself as the proper Liberal authority, rushed across the river to meet with Mejía. By 22 June 1866 surrender negotiations were complete and Mejía handed over the city to José María Carvajal.[31] The terms of surrender were ratified with a document signed by "General of Division José María J. Carvajal, Governor and Military Commandant of the State of Tamaulipas." The articles of surrender were controversial, especially:

> *Article 1.* General Mejía is to deliver up the Plaza of Matamoros within forty-eight hours to the Citizen General Juan de la Garza, commanding the division operating against Matamoros. . . .
>
> *Article 3.* General Mejía shall be permitted to withdraw with the troops of his division, unmolested, by the road to Bagdad, with two rounds of ammunition.
>
> *Article 4.* The lives, property, and interests of the citizens are guaranteed, and they shall not be molested for their previous political conduct or opinions.[32]

Sheridan believed that Carvajal had seized power in Matamoros by virtue of the letter of approval and other credentials that he had supplied; he correctly predicted that Carvajal's preemptive action would create much dissention among the forces of Juan Cortina and Servando Canales, who had been active in attacks on Mejía's forces.[33] Imperialist forces were allowed to decamp Matamoros with their arms, marching to the village of Bagdad, where the steamboat *Antonia*, a vessel owned by the company of Kenedy and King, had contracted to transport them to Veracruz.[34]

Carvajal, the new governor of newly liberated Matamoros, was not long in finding controversy at his doorstep, in the guise of the Catholic clergy who served the city's churches. Benito Juárez had long struggled to reduce the church's power in Mexico. The famous Ley Juárez (which required clerics to be tried in civil courts) and the constitution of 1857, drafted by the Liberal Party (which seized many of the lands owned by the Catholic Church), had caused Juárez to be considered by many as an enemy of the church. These church restrictions written into the constitution of 1857 had in fact been a major cause of the War of the Reform.

The Conservative Party, backed by the church and the military, had lost this war to the Liberals by 1861 but still harbored great bitterness against the Juárez party. Many of Mexico's Conservatives looked upon the French intervention, in that same year, as a second opportunity to overthrow the new constitution. Many Mexicans flocked to the banner of the imperialists, and the French clerics residing in Mexico were no exception. From the pulpit many clerics delivered anti-Liberal and pro-French homilies to their congregations, acts viewed as treasonous by the Liberals. Juárez countered the clerics with the decree of 30 August 1862, which included the following clauses:

> *Article 1:* Priests of any cult who, abusing their ministry, excite hate or disrespect for our laws, our government, or its rights, will be punished by three years' imprisonment or deportation. . . .
>
> *Article 3:* Priests of all cults are forbidden from wearing their vestments or any other distinguishing garment outside of their churches. . . . All violators will be punished with fines of ten to one hundred pesos or imprisonment from fifteen to sixty days.[35]

Governor Carvajal, attempting to carry out the mandates of the constitution of 1857, had ordered each French priest in Matamoros to "give up his church and parish; to make an inventory of the sacred vessels and other articles, and to deliver the keys of the church to the intruder." This intruder was none other than the Reverend Zertuche, an aging native-born Mexican and a colonel in the Mexican army whom Governor Carvajal had brought from Tampico and appointed to be parish priest of Matamoros. The French priests of Matamoros—Fathers Olivier, Vignolle, Jaffres, and Clos—eager for martyrdom and possible sainthood, refused all points of the Carvajal order and were imprisoned. From across the river in Brownsville, Father P. F. Parisot came to pay a visit to the imprisoned priests. The prisoners were in cells without beds, and "strict orders" had been issued to deprive "the prisoners of food and drink" until they should submit to Carvajal's demands. Just how strictly these orders were obeyed can be measured by Reverend Parisot's actions: he quickly had delivered to each prisoner a lunch contained in a basket that included a "bottle of good wine."

With righteous indignation, Reverend Parisot demanded and received an interview with the Protestant governor. The following dialogue is reported to have taken place:

CARVAJAL: When we arrived near the city, I was informed that the greatest enemies to our cause were the Priests and they have considerable influence over the people. . . . My reasons are justifiable, sir, for the priests of this place are imbued with monarchical principles and on many occasions they have preached from the pulpit against our government and the cause we advocate.

REV. PARISOT: I may assure Your Excellency that the priests have been maligned and have never uttered a single word from the pulpit against your cause.

CARVAJAL: Again, your priests are all Frenchmen and I wish to replace them by a Mexican Priest, whom I wish to appoint Parish Priest of Matamoros. He is favorable to our cause and is a very respectable old man and has the grade of Colonel in the Mexican Army.

REV. PARISOT: O General, the fact of being a Colonel is a poor recommendation for being appointed Parish Priest; moreover, my dear sir, the Bishop alone has the power of appointing Parish Priests.

This spirited interchange continued on for "over an hour." Finally the wily priest persuaded Carvajal to relent on most of his demands, settling only for delivery of the keys to the churches. Parisot, with a guile that would do credit to any attorney practicing before the bar, promised "delivery of keys to you [Carvajal] I shall take upon myself the obligation of having them delivered to you." The good father delivered keys all right, but with a priestly distinction, he returned to the prison with keys "of a passage-way running alongside the church" and an order for the prisoners' release by an unwitting Carvajal. The freed prisoners made for the river crossings to Brownsville at once. Half an hour after their crossing, orders were given to guard the crossings and rearrest the fathers, but they had escaped Matamoros.[36]

Carvajal had been active in Brownsville previous to Mejía's surrender of Matamoros, soliciting loans from the Brownsville merchants for arms, ammunitions, and supplies for the Liberal army. His success in this venture is documented by a certificate presented by José Manuel Jafre, representing the firm of Kenedy and King, dated 26 April 1870, to the Joint Claims Commission of the United States of America and the Republic of Mexico, listing the following claims:

Freight on Munitions of War, to Tampico	$10,000
Voucher from Headquarters, cash	10,000
Purchase of steamboat *Chicana*	30,000
formerly known as "Col. Holcomb"	
Goods and merchandise	26,032.90
Draft of Major Gen. Carvajal to King and Kenedy	10,000

The ten-thousand-dollar voucher was the charge by Kenedy and King to convert the *Chicana* from a river steamer to a "gunboat," used on the Rio Grande by Liberal forces.[37]

Now in control of Matamoros, Carvajal began to exact exorbitant forced loans from the city's imperialist-leaning merchants. During first two months of Liberal occupation, nearly four hundred thousand dollars was reportedly raised by forced loans and confiscations. Many foreign merchants unwilling to pay Carvajal's demands liquidated their business interests and moved across the river to Brownsville. The Matamoros merchant Jeremiah Galván alone was assessed ten thousand dollars in the form of a forced loan.[38]

John S. Ford, living at that time in Brownsville, approved of Carvajal's actions governing Matamoros. Ford noted that Carvajal had began at once to restore the republican form of government, to recruit soldiers, to appoint officers, and to raise funds from the city's residents. In fact, Carvajal was recruiting soldiers for the Liberal army from both sides of the river. He invited Ford to serve in the army of the Republic of Mexico by offering him a commission at the rank of brigadier general. Ford accepted the commission, recruiting a command that consisted mostly of former Confederate soldiers. Carvajal placed great confidence in his "American" troops—in fact, more than he placed in his Mexican troops, despite Ford's warning against any preferential treatment for American troops. As a result, Mexican soldiers of the garrison behaved in a rather unfriendly manner toward Ford's men. Such actions, Ford predicted, would cause political problems for the new governor, and such trouble was not long in coming.[39]

Other problems began to surface as well. General Carvajal's actions in drafting terms of surrender for the French garrison at Matamoros soon came under criticism. In a correspondence from General Mariano Escobedo, commanding the Liberal Northern Army Corps, Carvajal's actions were discussed:

> When I reached this place [Matamoros], . . . I could have annulled the stipulations between the traitor Mejía and General Garza, as the latter had no power to negotiate with a traitor who had done so much harm to the nation, . . . I wrote to the Governor General that I was displeased with the act, for General Garza and Carvajal came from abroad to Mexico, and had no right to let Mejía off, helping him away and securing him from danger. . . . If General Garza and Carvajal had not contributed to Mejía's evasion he might have got away alone, without a soldier, for I was marching upon the town. Now he can go on with the war; and the blood of our soldiers, shed on the battlefield in defense of our country will be sterile, in its results. In fine, Citizen Minister, when the traitor Mejía was in a bad fix, after the glorious victory of Santa Gertrudis, two Mexican Generals, living in the United States of the North, went over into Mexico and assisted him to get away.[40]

General Santiago Tapia, quartermaster of the Army of the North, sided with General Escobedo in the matter. In remarks addressed to Escobedo on 25 June 1866, Tapia wrote: "It was General Garza's duty to let you [Escobedo] decide upon the proposals made by the traitor Mejia. . . . Gen. Garza allowed Mejía to triumph unexpectedly by getting off with his troops, arms and ammunition; and so the traitor escaped, and will probably go to Maximilian and make him believe it was by strategy he got away, instead of by an error of General Garza and his aids [sic]."[41]

An official reprimand was sent to José María Carvajal from the Ministry of War and Marine on 4 August 1866, which read in part:

> Instead of collecting troops to prevent the escape of the traitors, you entered into negotiations with them and helped them to escape with the

honors of war, and giving them guarantees that only the Supreme Government could grant. . . . Therefore it has been determined to decree: First, the capitulation made by you on the 22nd of June, through your commissioner, Juan José de la Garza, with Don Tomas Mejía, Chief of the Matamoros garrison, is hereby declared null and void and of no force, because those who made it, on the part of the republican government, had not the proper authority.

Second, Therefore both you and Juan José de la Garza, who are responsible for the act, shall be subject to trial, you answering for the capitulation, and Juan José de la Garza in part for the same, and for other misconduct during this war.[42]

By 7 August 1866, Lerdo de Tejado, minister of relations and government, had appointed General of Brigade Santiago Tapia governor of Tamaulipas to replace José María Carvajal, who had been acting in that capacity without the proper authority of the Juárez government.[43]

In a final act of protest against Governor Carvajal, the military garrison at Matamoros pronounced against him in favor of Servando Canales on 12 August 1866, charging Carvajal with not paying the Matamoros garrison and for leadership that was "feeble and indecisive."[44] On that same day Canales's men staged a bloodless revolution that drove José María from office in Matamoros to sanctuary across the river to Brownsville. Ford related that on this day, as he proceeded to Carvajal's office, he noticed several demonstrations of protest against Carvajal, enough to convince him that "a revolution was pending." At Carvajal's office he met General Lew Wallace and informed him of his concerns. Wallace had only recently arrived in Matamoros with the arms shipment. Only a few minutes later Carvajal came dashing down the stairs, and as he passed Ford, he announced that a revolution had begun. He asked that Ford assemble his troops at Fort Paredes. But before anything else could be accomplished, the forces of Servando Canales had captured Matamoros without firing a shot. Ford pronounced the revolution a "peculiar affair," especially since Carvajal had raised and educated Servando Canales.[45]

A horrified Wallace, unaccustomed to the unsettled nature of Mexican politics of that time wrote: "A successful revolution fomented by General Canales (an Imperialist) took place. The governor [Carvajal] was driven to

Brownsville (Texas) literally at the lance's point. . . . For about two hours I was a prisoner, in some danger, not knowing my doom. . . . The revolt was certainly disgraceful. It was conceived and executed by the thieves, bandits, and outlaws who have congregated by hundreds in Matamoros."[46]

Wallace had recovered his composure somewhat a week later, and writing from Brownsville, recast his views on the Matamoros mini-revolution: "General Carvajal had to run for his life. I remained behind to take care of his family, and make terms for his two boys. In the town not a shot was fired, not a person hurt, yet, the revolution was complete. General Carvajal went out, his adopted son, and (as he has since proved) his true friend [Servando Canales] went in."[47] Describing the overthrow of Carvajal from office, Servando Canales was proud "that not one gun was fired" to accomplish the act and even more elated that "I was immediately chosen by popular will to replace Carvajal."[48] One of the first acts of the new military governor was to confiscate the Wallace/Carvajal arms but soon, with an adequate explanation from Carvajal and Wallace, all of the armaments were transported to the American side of the Rio Grande, from where they were successfully issued to Liberal soldiers.

Summarizing his adventures in Matamoros, Wallace reported in a letter home that he was "very well" with the exception of his hands and face that are "swollen with mosquito bites" and feet and ankles "raw with flea-bites." He declared the "bloodless revolution" that he witnessed to be "the funniest affair I ever beheld." Wallace continued to support the Juárez government actively until 11 May 1867, when he concluded all dealings with the now legal government of Mexico, wishing only to be repaid for his investment of time and money, writing: "From the beginning to the end he [Wallace] paid his own way without the receipt of the value of a claco." But Wallace had to wait his turn to be reimbursed by a government that was on the verge of insolvency. Wallace's claims were settled twenty years later by the government of Porfirio Díaz.[49]

Santiago Vidaurri, an old nemesis of José María, had turned traitor to the Liberal cause and was captured in Mexico City on 8 July 1867, during the last days of the imperialist resistance in Mexico. He was summarily sentenced to death before a firing squad and executed on that same day. One historian claims that Vidaurri was escorted to his execution site at the Plaza of Santo Domingo by none other than José María Carvajal.[50]

Carvajal, now feeling the weight of his sixty-two years filled with decades of campaigning for Liberal causes in Texas and Mexico, retired to his ranch in 1870. The ranch was located on the Rio Grande in Mexico, some thirty-three miles below Rio Grande City, due south of the settlement of Havana, on a tract of land known locally as "Porción Carvajal."[51] The aged general would from time to time travel from his ranch across the Rio Grande to Hidalgo, then county seat of Hidalgo County, to serve as a translator for the district court when in session, but he had by and large retired from any other public service. But Carvajal had not lost his love for adventure and intrigue, especially if those acts were against an old nemesis such as Juan Cortina. In a letter to John S. Ford, Carvajal discussed the prospects for a new campaign against Cortina:

> The favorable opportunity may pass, and not return. Cortina is evidently making his peace with the revolution, and will *fall on his feet*. I will always *protest* against such an event.
>
> If some steps are not taken to make a move as proposed, Cortina will succeed in entering into and commating [*sic*] an unholy alliance. I *cannot* act without proper backing, it is too late in life to fight 10 and 20 to one I must have a fair chance.

In 1872, Carvajal returned to live in Soto La Marina, Tamaulipas, on the property owned by his wife. He died there suddenly on 19 August 1874, and thus passed one of the giants of Texas and northern Mexico. Perhaps it should be reported in passing that his death seemed to be as his life was: filled with intrigue. His doctor, Constancio González, felt that Carvajal had died too suddenly, hinting perhaps that he may have been poisoned.[52]

ELEVEN

Summary and Conclusions

José María Carvajal was born in 1809 in the bustling village of San Antonio de Béxar, and as a lad he attracted the attention of Stephen F. Austin, who was impressed by Carvajal's keen intellect. Austin arranged to have José María sent to Kentucky, where the young man, curious about English and the Anglo ways, could satisfy that curiosity. Carvajal lived for five years in the home of the noted theologian Alexander Campbell, one of the founders of the Church of Christ. Carvajal attended college at the institution that was the forerunner of present-day Bethany College. The experience left a deep impression on José María, who would write to his mother: "I have renounced the doctrines of the Church of Rome," signing his letter in the Anglo style as "Mr. Joseph M. J. Carbajal." A Protestant he became and a Protestant he would remain for the balance of his life. When at the head of an army besieging Matamoros, Carvajal met with city delegates to negotiate a possible surrender. But when the Catholic clergy present in the delegation discovered that José María was not of their faith, they recoiled in horror, proclaiming to all that Carvajal was not a "buen cristiano," and the city would resist rather than surrender to an "heretico."

During his stay in the United States, Carvajal had indeed achieved his objective of learning English. An observer of one of Carvajal's speeches would later write that his English was "fluent and being free of any offensive idiom or provincialism in accent or expression." Carvajal's acquired knowledge of English and the Anglo ways, coupled with his native Spanish, placed him in an ideal position to be a leader among the peoples living in the bicultural society that flourished along the Rio Bravo. But more than language skills would be required. Of greater value were the traits of personal bravery and fidelity to friends, both of which Carvajal possessed. In

1839, during the battle of Alto Limpio, Texas mercenaries in the employ of the Federalist army became surrounded in a ravine by Centralist attackers and underwent a terrific artillery bombardment. While the remainder of the Federalist army, the Mexican Division under the leadership of Antonio Canales, was content to stand by as spectators in the slaughter, Carvajal organized a group of volunteers that counterattacked the Centralists, saving the Texans from death. Major Richard Roman, one of the trapped mercenaries that day fighting for his life, was to later write: "No Mexicans being injured, none having joined the fight except Zapata and Carbahal, who both behaved exceedingly well, the latter having an arm broken in the charge." Carvajal had received a musket ball in his left arm, which as a result was paralyzed. Thereafter, he suspended the useless arm from a colorful silk bandanna placed around his neck that he wore as a badge of honor among his many Anglo and Mexican friends.

My favorite incident regarding the bravery of the diminutive José María occurred in 1835, when as a fugitive from the Mexican military, he captured a courier bearing secret messages from General Martín Perfecto de Cos and Colonel Domingo de Ugartechea and proceeded with them to the Texas village of San Felipe de Austin. Once there, as a large crowd of colonists gathered about him, Carvajal mounted a stump and read the explosive contents of the courier's messages aloud in his own inimitable style, while angry colonists muttered oaths of revenge against the tyrannical government of Santa Anna.

If any should still doubt Carvajal's leadership skills, I offer one final example. During the Merchants War, Carvajal had assembled an army consisting in part of some of the most wild and undisciplined Anglo mercenaries to be found in the entire United States. He maintained remarkable control and discipline over these ragtag soldiers, strictly enforcing orders against the looting of civilian homes. One of these men, the gigantic six foot four inch, 275-pound artillerist Chatham Roberdeau Wheat, delighted in Carvajal, whom he referred to as "our youthful general." It must have been some sight to see Wheat bending over with cupped ear to hear Carvajal's orders during the din of battle.

Carvajal returned to Texas in 1830, where Stephen F. Austin trained him to be a land surveyor; he went on to survey thousands of acres of land in Robertson's Colony. One of my great surprises while researching this book was realizing that it was quite possible that José María (who surveyed vast tracts of land in Robertson's Colony) and my great-great-grandfather, Joseph Bell Chance (who was deputy surveyor of Robertson's Colony) were acquaintances.

But Carvajal was soon destined to assume a more influential role in Texas history by entering the seesaw world of Mexican politics as a Liberal. As such, he was an adherent of the constitution of 1824, believing that all political power resided in the several states of the Republic of Mexico, which were united by a weak Central government, a form of government akin to the Articles of Confederation that first bound together the thirteen colonies of the United States. Carvajal saw that the peoples of Mexico were oppressed by the excesses of the military and the Catholic Church. He decried the maintenance of a large standing army requiring vast amounts of state revenues whose only use was to suppress dissent among the civilian population. Those in the military accused of crimes against civilians were not tried in civilian courts but rather in special military tribunals. Catholic clergy were likewise shielded from legal proceedings, being tried in ecclesiastical courts for crimes against the populace. Carvajal supported land reform and believed that the enormous tracts of land owned in mortmain by the Catholic Church should be seized by the government and sold to private interests. But it would be many years later, with the ascendancy of Benito Juárez and the Liberal Party, that these steps would be instituted.

In 1834, when Antonio López de Santa Anna seized dictatorial control of the government of Mexico, Carvajal became his outspoken opponent. Elected as a deputy to the state legislature of Coahuila y Tejas, Carvajal worked to raise funds for the establishment of a state militia to oppose the Central government. The defiant legislative session of 1835 was closed by Centralist General Cos at the point of a bayonet, however, and Carvajal returned to Texas as a fugitive sought by the military government there. Two years later, when rebellion in Texas occurred, Carvajal and many other Hispanics in Texas who opposed Santa Anna but wished to prevent the dismemberment of Mexico were faced with a thorny decision. In the polarizing atmosphere of revolution, they faced the unlikely alternatives of either declaring for Texas independence or supporting the tyrannical gov-

ernment of Santa Anna. Carvajal and many of his fellow Hispanics did neither, remaining on the sidelines as neutrals. The question of support for
Texas independence split many Hispanic families, including the Carvajal
family. José María's brother, Mariano, elected for the former alternative,
was a signatory to the Goliad Declaration of Independence, and joined the
command of Colonel James Fannin in the Texas army as a cavalry officer.
Mariano was captured, along with the entire Fannin command, and executed by the Mexican military on Palm Sunday 1836.

Once Texas independence had been sustained by the battle of San
Jacinto and the capture of Santa Anna, Hispanic families in Texas that had
remained neutral in the struggle now became suspect, because of their lack
of action, of being traitors. The Carvajal family and many others were
driven from their Texas homes; José María finally took up residence in
Mexico, where he was to live for the remainder of his life, proclaiming himself ever thereafter to be "a good Mexican."

With the demand of a return to the constitution of 1824, and bolstered
by the success of the Texas Revolution, Federalists in northern Mexico
launched insurrections aimed at separating the Republic's northern states
to form the so-called Republic of the Rio Grande. José Maria, now not
opposed to the partition of Mexico as he was in 1836, joined the cause. But
by 1840 a powerful Centralist army, led by Mariano Arista, crushed the
rebellion in northern Mexico. Carvajal and others were forgiven for their
part in the rebellion, as General Arista generously granted the defeated
rebels amnesty. Carvajal returned to his peaceful pursuits as a surveyor in
Camargo but would later take up arms again against the repressive conservative Central government of Mexico.

With the annexation of Texas to the United States in 1846, Carvajal fore-
saw the onset of a war to fulfill the philosophy of Manifest Destiny, a con-
cept quite popular in the United States at the time. While he remained a
foe of the oppressive Central government of Mexico, he reasoned that the
struggle between Federalists and Centralists was an internal matter, and
that all Mexicans should put aside their differences for the time being and
join ranks to oppose the United States.

During the Mexican-American War, Carvajal commanded a brigade of
irregulars who fought a hit-and-run guerrilla campaign against U.S. forces

occupying northern Mexico. Such a type of warfare is usually without mercy, but even his North American opponents had to admit that Carvajal waged a war without excesses: one opponent would remark that "Carvajal is known to possess great control over his troops being a gentleman." The experience he gained as a guerrilla warrior in northern Mexico would later be employed successfully against French imperialist forces.

The conclusion of the Mexican-American War found Carvajal living in the little village of Camargo, situated about three miles south of the confluence of the Rio Grande and the Rio San Juan. In 1851 he launched a series of incursions into northern Mexico from across the Rio Grande with the old dream in mind of separating the northern states of Mexico from the oppressive Central government to form the so-called Republic of the Sierra Madre. Carvajal pronounced against the Central government with his Plan de La Loba, which enumerated the many grievances of the people of the north against their government. Carvajal pointed out that the Central government had ignored repeated petitions from the north, failed to protect the citizens from the repeated raids of bands of marauding Indians, and would not allow free trade with the United States. Carvajal demanded that Mexican soldiers, described as being "pernicious, oppressive, and useless," who were quartered in private homes be removed from the border. The plan further demanded the protection of all civil and property rights for citizens, proportional representation, and the direct election of all representatives.

But a revolution needs an army to enforce its demands, which in turn requires abundant financing and competent soldiers. In the acquisition of the latter two, Carvajal compromised the lofty ideals of the Plan de La Loba. His funding was obtained from U.S. merchants along the border, whose commerce with Mexico had shrunk due to the newly imposed destructive Mexican import schedules. With the promise of lowered tariffs on the areas of northern Mexico that he would control, Carvajal gained the financial support he needed from merchants, who cared only for their profits, not the social reforms promised by the plan.

Most of the Mexican citizens who swarmed to Carvajal's banner had never shouldered a musket, much less understood the intricacies of a military evolution. To obtain the competent soldiers he needed, Carvajal resorted to the practice of hiring U.S. mercenaries, many of whom had soldiered in Mexico during the late war. When Carvajal mustered his army for the first time, suspicious Mexican observers noted that the ranks appeared to look "muy agringado," men moreover led by a Protestant Mexican who by dint of his Anglo customs and dress also appeared "agringado." Although many of the Mexicans of the north hated the Centralist government, they hated only one thing more intensely: armed Americans in their country. By resorting to these extremes, Carvajal had lost his most important weapon: the support of the people of the north. His military defeats at Matamoros in 1851 and again outside of Camargo in 1852 were simply a postscript to his greatest defeat: the loss of the hearts and minds of his fellow citizens.

Carvajal's armed incursions into Mexico from the United States served as a severe embarrassment to the government in Washington, D.C., and pointed out the failure of the federal government to establish control over its newly acquired territory south of the Nueces River. Token army garrisons at Forts Brown and Ringgold stood by impotently to watch Carvajal's army cross and recross the Rio Grande with impunity. No federal marshals had been appointed for this region to enforce federal laws, and no federal courts had convened there to establish some modicum of civil order over the unruly populace. U.S. Army officers were ordered to arrest Carvajal's civilian mercenaries, but many doubted that they possessed the authority to arrest a civilian without the express order of a federal civil magistrate. The U.S. military code holds junior officers legally responsible for executing an illegal order, and two young officers who had refused to arrest the mercenaries were arrested for disobedience and court-martialed at Fort Ringgold. The trial of these officers represents a unique chapter in U.S. military history, and the legal precedents developed still apply to the operations of the modern military.

To develop the newly acquired California territory, the United States eagerly sought a route for travelers to the West Coast that avoided either the circuitous water route around Cape Horn, or the perilous overland route across the midcontinent. U.S. diplomats were in the process of completing a treaty with the Republic of Mexico for the transit rights of American citizens across the Isthmus of Tehuantepec when Carvajal initiated his incursions into Mexico. Progress on the treaty was immediately halted; U.S. diplomats in Mexico reported a climate in which there was "intense prejudice against everything connected with American interests. . . . No member of the Government and no member of the Congress, has the courage to intimate an opinion in favor of the Treaty."

Carvajal and his followers were indicted by a federal grand jury for violation of the Neutrality Act of 1818 and were tried in 1854 in Galveston, Texas, a city that was a hotbed of sympathy for Manifest Destiny. The investigation and research needed to adequately develop the government's case against Carvajal was never allowed to be funded by the equally sympathetic administration of Franklin Pierce. The federal judge quickly dismissed the proceedings against Carvajal and his followers.

The rise of Benito Juárez and the political philosophy of his Liberal Party brought support from Carvajal, who commanded a brigade of infantry fielded to support the Liberal cause against the Conservatives, a coalition of the disaffected military and clergy, during the internecine War of the Reform in Mexico. The success of the Liberal cause solidified the power of the Juárez government and placed José María, who had been pardoned by his fellow Liberals for his role in the Merchants War, as the military governor of Tamaulipas.

Carvajal's last service to the Republic of Mexico occurred during the time of the French intervention in Mexico. After fighting a guerrilla war against the French in the Huasteca region of Mexico, Carvajal's thread-bare guerrilla band, without arms or money, retreated into the wilds of the San Carlos Mountains to regroup. There Carvajal received a commission from President Juárez to journey to the United States in an effort to raise financial support for the bankrupt Juárez government, now on the verge of a final defeat by the French military.

Accompanied by Lew Wallace, the famous novelist who wrote *Ben Hur,* Carvajal traveled to the U.S. financial capital of New York to sell Mexican bonds. There the diminutive revolutionary fell prey to a confidence man who immediately set about, with glorious promises, to swindle Carvajal and thereby the Republic of Mexico. Without the valuable service of Herman Sturm, an Indiana capitalist, the naive Carvajal would have failed in his mission to the United States. Sturm successfully extricated Carvajal from the bogus contract and authored a successful method for the purchase of American arms for the Juáristas. The arms, smuggled to Mexico, aided in the ousting of the French from Mexico and the reaffirmation of the Liberal government.

An aging Carvajal, now no longer able to take up arms and campaign in the field, retired to his ranch, Porción Carvajal. In 1872 an inquiry to take the field again in support of Liberal causes brought this admission from Carvajal: "I cannot act without proper backing, it is too late in life to fight 10 and 20 to one I must have a fair chance." Carvajal soon returned to Soto La Marina to live on his wife's estate, where he died on 19 August 1874.

Several years ago, when I embarked on the project to write on José María Carvajal, a knowing friend commented that he approved of my efforts but asked, "Where will you find enough information to write a biography of Carvajal?" After years of plowing through libraries, books, and miles of microfilm, I have finally come to appreciate this person's concern and develop an understanding of why there are so few primary materials. José María Carvajal, as a revolutionary and guerrilla fighter, spent more than forty years eluding his enemies. Always on the move, he had to be vigilant not to leave behind any letter or document that might shed some light on his activities. Several of his homes, including his famous castle, were ransacked and burned by pursuers eager to find his whereabouts. Although he had extensive correspondence with the leaders of his time, few records remain, save those found in newspapers and official documents. Even a large oil painting made of him has been lost, taken from a public school in Victoria, Texas, in 1936 as a part of the Texas Centennial Commemoration, and never returned. Except for an engraving of him that appeared in *Harper's Weekly* in 1865, where he appears as an aged man, only a snapshot from the lost painting remains of the young Carvajal to give us some insight into the fiery and charismatic nature of this man whose life influenced that of so many others. When describing the determination of the United States to place a man on the Moon, John F. Kennedy said, "We go there not because it is easy, we go there because it is difficult."

My task in attempting to capture the essence of the man is a little like trying to piece together a beautiful vase from its broken shards after it has been dropped from the mantle. Thus I continued in the necessary arduous research efforts until completion. It is my hope that the life I have constructed from the shards discovered in the historical records and archives somehow favors this remarkable man. It is important to resurrect José María Carvajal from historical oblivion because of what he stood for. He represents the taproot of the civil rights movement for Hispanics that began to gain sway in the 1960s and has now made such great forward strides in our society. Early in his life he expressed his concern for the betterment of Hispanic people and hoped someday to "bring that excellent people out of this bondage and degradation both Political and Spiritual." Throughout his active life Carvajal strived to bring about those changes, fighting for a society that would be ruled by representative government and in which all persons would enjoy equality before the law. I think that if he could see the gains that have taken place since his death, he would be quite pleased.

Demographers tell us that within the next decade or two, the majority of surnames in Texas will be Hispanic. What are we going to tell these young persons and those yet to be born about the history of Texas? The traditional histories have marginalized the role of Hispanics, and only those who have taken the effort to scratch beneath the surface know better. Texas history needs to be rewritten to include the important roles played by such Hispanics as José María Carvajal in the social evolution of Texas and northern Mexico. Carvajal's courage, intelligence, and vision serve as a role model for young people on the power of what one person can do to effect change.

Chronology

1808   Napoleon forces King Charles IV and his son, King Ferdinand VII of Spain, to abdicate.

1809   José María de Jesús Carvajal is born in San Antonio de Béxar.

1810   Cortes de Cadiz is convened to rule Spain; Father Miguel Hidalgo raises the *grito* cry of revolution in Mexico.

1812   Cortes de Cadiz draws up a liberal constitution for Spain; the Gutiérrez-Magee filibusters enter Texas.

1813   The Gutiérrez-Magee army captures San Antonio de Béxar; Governor Manuel María de Salcedo is murdered.

1814   The Gutiérrez-Magee army is routed by Spanish Royalist forces at the battle of the Medina; Joaquín de Arredondo occupies San Antonio de Béxar.

1821   Empresario Stephen F. Austin brings Anglo-Saxon colonists to Texas; Mexico gains its independence from Spain.

1823   Carvajal travels to the United States for schooling.

1824   Mexico adopts a liberal constitution.

1833   Mexican Conservatives rise to power in Mexico.

1835   Antonio López de Santa Anna abrogates the constitution of 1824 and seizes the government of Mexico; the military government of Texas issues an arrest warrant for Carvajal; Carvajal is captured in the act of smuggling arms to rebellious Texans; Mexican troops are driven from Texas.

1836   Santa Anna enters Texas to put down the revolution; the Alamo falls; Santa Anna is defeated at San Jacinto and captured by victorious Texans; Carvajal is driven out of Texas into exile.

1838   Carvajal participates in the Federalist Wars of Mexico.

1840   The independent Republic of the Rio Grande is proclaimed; the Federalist rebellion in northern Mexico is put down.

1846   The opening battles of the Mexican-American War begin; Carvajal leads a brigade against U.S. forces in northern Mexico.

1848   The Treaty of Guadalupe Hidalgo ends the Mexican-American War.

1851   Carvajal issues a *pronunciamiento* against the Conservative Mexican Central government; Carvajal leads a filibuster army into northern Mexico and lays siege to Matamoros; the independent Republic of the Sierra Madre is proclaimed.

1852   Carvajal's army is defeated near Camargo; Carvajal is indicted by a U.S. federal grand jury for violation of the Neutrality Act.

1854   Carvajal's indictment is ruled defective by a federal judge in Galveston, Texas.

1857   Mexico adopts a Liberal constitution.

1858   Benito Juárez assumes the provisional presidency of Mexico; the War of the Reform begins; Carvajal sides with the Juárez Liberals.

1861   Carvajal is appointed military governor of Tamaulipas; he challenges the results of the gubernatorial election with an armed rebellion.

1862   France, Great Britain, and Spain land troops at Veracruz to enforce the collection of debts Mexico owes; France moves to establish a monarchy in Mexico; Carvajal commands a brigade in central Mexico to resist the French incursion.

1864   Carvajal's battalion is defeated by French imperialists commanded by Colonel Charle Dupin at San Bertólillo; Maximilian assumes the throne of Mexico.

1865   Carvajal enters into a plot with Lew Wallace to smuggle arms to the Juáristas.

1866   Carvajal accepts the imperialists' surrender of Matamoros; he is overthrown as the military governor of Matamoros by a garrison coup; France abandons its plans for an imperialist Mexican government.

1867   Benito Juárez returns to power; Maximilian is executed by the Mexican government.

1874   Carvajal dies at Soto La Marina, Tamaulipas.

Distribution of Army Forces in Texas

The Report of Colonel W. G. Freeman's Inspection

of the Army Posts in Texas

Colonel W. G. Freeman's report of 1853 lists the following manpower at each garrison:

Post	Location	Inspected	Personnel
Fort Ewell	On Nueces River where road from San Antonio to Laredo crosses river	6/11/53	Regt. of Mounted Rifles: Co. E 48 men Co. G 59 men Co. I 38 men
Fort Merrill	60 miles NW Corpus on Nueces River	6/21/53	Regt. of Mounted Rifles: Co. E 13 men
Fort Brown	Brownsville	7/2/53	4th Regt. Art.: Co. B 52 men Co. K 51 men
Camp at Edinburg	present-day Hidalgo	7/11/53	Regt. of Mounted Rifles: Co. C 43 men
Ringgold Barracks	Rio Grande City	7/14/53	Regt. of Mounted Rifles: Co. B 43 men 7th Regt. Inf.: Co. A 49 men Co. I 51 men
Camp at Redmond's Ranche	6½ mi N of Guerrero, Mex.	7/18/53	Regt. of Mounted Rifles: Co. F 69 men

(continued)

Post	Location	Inspected	Personnel
Fort McIntosh	Laredo	7/22/53	7th Regt. Inf.: Co. B 46 men Co. G 42 men
Fort Duncan	Eagle Pass	7/27/53	1st Regt. Inf.: Co. D 36 men Co. F 28 men
Fort Clark	present-day Bracketville	8/1/53	1st Regt. Inf.: Co. C 29 men Co. I 27 men
Fort Inge	on Leona River 3 mi from source	8/4/53	Regt. of Mounted Rifles: Co. D lost recd. Co. H lost recd.
Camp near Fort Inge	½ mi SE of fort	8/4/53	3rd Regt. Inf.: Co. A 58 men
Fort Martin Scott	Fredericksburg	8/13/53	8th Regt. Inf.: Co. unknown 16 men
Fort Mason	Mason	8/15/53	2nd Regt. Dragoons Co. A Co. G total 138 men
Fort McKavett	on San Saba River 2 mi from source	8/19/53	8th Regt. Inf.: Co. B 34 men Co. D 40 men Co. E 35 men Co. F 46 men Co. H 30 men
Fort Terrett	N fork of Llano River 200 yds S of head springs	8/21/53	1st Regt. Inf.: Co. A 30 men Co. E 39 men Co. H 28 men Co. K 27 men
Fort Chadbourne	120 mi NW of Fort Mason	8/27/53	8th Regt. Inf.: Co. A 40 men Co. C 38 men Co. G 42 men Co. I 38 men Co. K 41 men

Post	Location	Inspected	Personnel
Fort Phantom Hill	59 mi NE of Fort Chadbourne	8/30/53	5th Regt. Inf.: Co. B 47 men Co. C 37 men Co. E 48 men Co. G 46 men Co. K 41 men
Fort Belknap	137 mi from Fort Graham	9/3/53	5th Regt. Inf.: Co. A 48 men Co. D 42 men Co. F 48 men Co. H 49 men Co. I 45 men
Fort Worth	S side Trinity River, mouth of Clear Fork	9/7/53	2nd Regt. Dragoons Co. B 60 men
Fort Graham	40 mi N Waco 150 mi SE Fort Belknap	9/10/53	2nd Regt. Dragoons Co. C 41 men Co. F 44 men
Fort Croghan	present-day Burnet	9/16/53	abandoned

Notes

1. Austin, quoted in Fehrenbach, 142, 152.

2. Carvajal, quoted in the letter "A True Mexican to Messrs. Johnson, Baker & Givens," 18 July 1835, Papers of Samuel May Williams, Rosenberg Library.

CHAPTER ONE: *The Early Life and Education of José María de Jesús Carvajal*

1. Menchaca, 1–19; for Navarro's historical writings, see McDonald and Matovina, 44–58, 63–68, 87; Faulk, 10–11, 33; Almaráz, 4–6, 11, 179–82; Jarratt, 5–46; and Castillo Crimm, 126, 138.

2. Huson, *Refugio*, vol. 1, 118, 387; Tyler et al., "Jose Luciano Navarro," in *Handbook of Texas,* vol. 4, 955–56; Lea, vol. 1, 83; and Chabot, 32–35. José Luciano Navarro was a San Antonio jeweler and silversmith. Upon the death of Gertrudis de Carvajal, José María Carvajal's mother, Navarro was appointed to administer her estate. In 1839, he wrote José María Carvajal a letter of introduction to the president of the Republic of Texas, Mirabeau B. Lamar. At that time Carvajal was on a diplomatic mission seeking aid for the revolutionary movement sweeping northern Mexico.

3. Nance, *After San Jacinto,* 240–41. The *Colorado Gazette and Advertiser* of 11 January 1840 reported that a band of forty Cherokees were believed to have murdered all members of a traveling party consisting of Colonel Littleberry Hawkins and six Mexicans. The crime occurred on 29 October 1839, a few miles below Reynosa. Hawkins was serving in the Federalist army at that time and traveling in a party with Colonel José María Carvajal and other officers of the Federalist army.

4. Hawkins to Austin, in Barker, *Annual Report 1919,* 917–22.

5. "Alexander Campbell," in *Dictionary of American Biography,* vol. 3, 446–48.

6. Ibid., 467–68.

7. Cobb, letter to the author, 13 July 1999.

8. Carvajal to his mother, in Barker, *Austin Papers,* vol. 2, part 1, 921.

9. Lott and Fenwick, 60.

10. Carvajal to his mother, in Barker, *Austin Papers,* vol. 2, part 1, 921.

11. Note to Austin, in ibid.; Huson, *Refugio,* vol. 1, 118.

12. Indexed in Austin Papers, transcript received by private communication, Center for American History, University of Texas, to author, 10 July 1999.

13. Oates, 203.

14. Austin, in Gulick and Winnie, *Lamar Papers,* vol. 5, 49.

15. Henson, *Bradburn,* 131–32; Tyler et al., "José Francisco Madero," in *Handbook of Texas,* vol. 4, 454; and Castillo Crimm, 136. José Francisco Madero was born in what is known today as the state of Chihuahua and attended the School of Mines in Mexico City, where he received the title of surveyor. In 1830 he was appointed Texas land commissioner by José María Viesca, the Federalist governor of Coahuila y Tejas, and traveled to Texas to issue land grants to colonists who had settled lands outside the jurisdiction of any existing empresario land grants. While in Texas, Madero organized the Municipality of Villa de la Santisima Trinidad de la Libertad, the present-day town of Liberty, Texas.

16. Alamán, in Resendez, 44.

17. Pitner, 9–11; Smart, 71; Fehrenbach, 146–47, 155; and Hanna and Hanna, 13–14.

18. Henson, *Bradburn,* 58–66.

19. McLean, 30.

20. Austin, in Resendez, 120–31, 138–48.

21. Morton, 80–82; Fehrenbach, 164–66.

22. Biblioteca Nacional de Antropología e Historia, Paquete 51-9-68, folios 117–20. Jack Jackson, of Austin, Texas, kindly furnished this letter from his research papers. Hubert Miller, professor emeritus, University of Texas–Pan American, provided the translation. Many thanks to both of these scholars.

23. Gulick and Winnie, vol. 4, part 2, 49.

24. Rose, 11; Tyler et al., "Martin de León," in *Handbook of Texas,* vol. 2, 571. The main street of Victoria, Texas—the Calle de los Diez Amigos—was named for the following ten founders of the city: Martín de León, Fernando de León, Valentín Garcia, Pedro Gallardo, Rafaél Manchola, Leonardo Manso,

J. M. J. Carvajal, Julián de la Garza, Plácido Benavides, and Silvestre de León. Martín de León was born in 1765 in Búrgos, Nuevo Santandér, which is today in the state of Tamaulipas. In 1795 he married Patrícia de la Garza. In 1805 he moved to Texas and took up ranching. He then joined the Republican cause to successfully drive the Spanish from Mexico. In 1824, Martín de León received a colonization grant from the Mexican government and settled forty-one families on the lower Guadalupe River, founding the town of Nuestra Señora Guadalupe de Jesús Victoria, the present city of Victoria. Martín de León died in 1833, leaving behind one of the most prominent families in Texas.

25. Castillo Crimm, 25; Hammett, 6.

26. Huson, *Refugio,* vol. 1, 439; Huson, "Iron Men," 43–44.

27. Lea, vol. 1, 46–48.

28. Austin, in Barker, *Austin Papers,* vol. 2, 745.

29. Davis, 341; Cox letter, as cited in Barker, *Austin Papers,* vol. 2, 761.

30. Castillo Crimm, 116; Fehrenbach, 178–80; and the Santa Anna quote appears in Crawford, xiv.

31. Henson, *Williams,* 63.

32. Ibid., 63–64; Vigness, 144.

33. Vigness, 144.

34. Ibid., 147.

35. Shearer, 26; the Travis quote appears in Gulick and Winnie, vol. 1, 204. A translation of state laws and decrees, found in Gammel, vol. 1, 111–465, was ordered published later by the secretary of state of the Republic of Texas in 1839. The translator is listed as "J. P. Kimball, M.D.," possibly not the work of Carvajal.

36. McLean, 50–51.

37. Ibid., 50; Henson, *Williams,* 65.

38. Barker, "Land Speculation," 82.

39. Ibid.

40. Austin, in McLean, 202.

41. Ibid., 278.

42. Letter, "Carvajal to Menchaca," 29 April 1835, Texas State Library, Box 2004/046, Bound Book B, 100. Thanks to Jack Jackson for calling this letter to my attention.

43. Chambers, in McLean, 75–76.

44. Ibid., 55.

45. Ibid.

46. Ibid., 59, 63.

47. Henson, *Williams,* 69.

48. Greene, 189–200. The struggle between the Federalist Mexican states of the north and the Centralist government had reached a stage of open rebellion by 1835. The state of Zacatecas had, by that date, recruited a militia. Fearing the potential use of any state militia against the Central government, a law was proposed to the Mexican National Congress that state forces be allowed only one militia man per five hundred population. The Central government issued an order directing the confiscation of all arms "in the hands of individuals not pertaining to the army." A Centralist army was then sent to "observe" the state of Zacatecas. The state legislature of Zacatecas responded by passing a decree "permitting the Governor to use all of the State Militia to repel any aggression." A Centralist army, under the personal command of Santa Anna, defeated state militia forces at the town of Guadalupe, near the city of Zacatecas on 11 May 1835. As a stern lesson to any other Mexican states that might be thinking of rebellion, Santa Anna reportedly executed hundreds of his captives and declared Zacatecas an open city. Centralist soldiers burned and destroyed private homes and abused the citizenry. Mexican historians, when they speak on the subject, condemn the so-called Rape of Zacatecas as a "foul blot on the fair history of Mexico," and they think it an incident "that is best forgotten." Santa Anna's actions against a rebelling state could not have failed to make a great impression on the colonists of Texas.

49. Henson, *Williams,* 62–76; Resendez, 163; and letter, "Carvajal to Menchaca." There is evidence that Carvajal was working in the legislature to create legislation favoring a trade of land for military service. Writing to his cousin Antonio Menchaca, Carvajal declared: "To the Cherokee, we shall give land enough to make them live happy, and so shall we to the isolated families—All the Texans shall find approbation."

50. Ugartecha, in McLean, 70.

51. Linn, 36–39; Shearer, 26; Tyler et al., "Plácido Benavides," in *Handbook of Texas,* vol. 1, 484; Barker, *Austin Papers,* vol. 3, 63; and Huson, "Iron Men," 4. Plácido Benavides married Agustina de León, Martín de León's daughter, in 1831 and settled on Placido Creek, which was so named in his honor. In 1832 and again in 1834 he was elected *alcalde* of Guadalupe Victória, present-day Victoria, Texas, and served as captain of the militia for the colony. In 1835 he joined the forces of George M. Collingsworth's Matagorda volunteers that drove the soldiers of General Cos out of Goliad on 9–10 October. The volunteers marched on to San Antonio, becoming part of a division that laid siege

to and later captured the city. Benavides died in exile, after being driven off his land, in 1837 at Opelousas, Louisiana.

52. Kerr, in McLean, 496.

53. Barr, 63.

54. "A True Mexican to Messrs. Johnson, Baker & Givins," 18 July 1835, Papers of Samuel May Williams, Rosenberg Library.

55. Nance, *After San Jacinto,* 143–44, 172.

56. McLean, 67.

57. Vigness, 155.

58. Henson, *Williams,* 76; Vigness, 159; and McLean, 67, 73.

CHAPTER TWO: *Revolution Comes to Texas*

1. Austin, cited in Jenkins, vol. 2, 32.

2. Fisher, cited in Jenkins, vol. 2, 315–16.

3. Tyler et al., "Peter Kerr," in *Handbook of Texas,* vol. 3, 1076–77; Shearer, 27; Jenkins, vol. 3, 218; Rose, 14, 111, 154; Dienst, part 1, 179–89; and Castillo Crimm, 156. Governor Henry Smith, of the provisional government of Texas, signed a bill into law on 27 November 1835 that issued letters of marque and reprisal for ships wishing to blockade the coast of Mexico and harass Mexican shipping. Among the first to receive a privateering commission was Ira R. Lewis and other owners of the schooner *William Robbins,* commanded by Captain William A. Hurd. The *William Robbins*—described as "being of some sixty tons burthen," of stout construction, and an ordinary sailer carrying four guns of small caliber—was purchased by the infant Republic of Texas Navy and rechristened *Liberty.*

4. Huson, *Refugio,* vol. 1, 237; Tyler et al., "Goliad Declaration of Independence," in *Handbook of Texas,* vol. 3., 218; and Shearer, 28. The Goliad Declaration of Independence was signed by ninety-one citizens of Goliad and ratified on 20 December 1835, preceding Stephen F. Austin's pronouncement of independence on 22 December 1835 and the Texas Declaration of Independence on 5 March 1836.

5. Linn, 184.

6. Certificate signed by Holland, Brenan, and Shackelford, so that heirs of M. Carvajal could collect his pay for army service; Davenport, 479.

7. Shearer, 28; Tyler et al., "Jose Maria Carvajal," in *Handbook of Texas,* vol. 1, 971.

8. Lamar and Rusk, cited in Nance, *After San Jacinto,* 10–17.

9. Jenkins, vol. 7, 232; Hammett, 60–63, 189–91. The Carvajal family made

attempts to recover some of their lands in Texas. Four undated letters from António Carvajal, the younger son of José María, to members of the de León family, then living in Victoria, Texas, requested aid in finding a competent attorney. The first letter, to Francisco de León, described the extent of the family holdings. The lands in question were located near the Natschitoches [*sic*] River, near the Trinity River in Polk County, and a site near the Guadalupe River in Victoria County that had been deeded to the elder Carvajal by grants authorized by the State of Coahuila y Tejas in 1833. These grants totaled some 48,885 acres. The Supreme Court of Texas, according to the younger Carvajal, had ruled these grants as valid. António claimed that he had not pursued litigation earlier "because my late dear brother, Joe [José María Jr.] held these vouchers in his hand, and for 12 years he never undertook anything in this connection." The second letter, directed to Alfonso de León of Victoria, Texas, indicated that the firm of Proctor and Vandenberg was under consideration to be retained. António asked his nephew to obtain letters of recommendation for the law firm from persons living in Victoria. The third letter from António to "My dear Nephew" expressed his frustrations in finding a lawyer to handle his case but mentioned that he had finally located a qualified Mexican attorney, with an office in San Antonio, to take the case. António confidently stated that "since this licentiate is a fellow countryman of ours he wouldn't handle a 'bum' lawsuit nor play us an evil turn. . . . There is not in existence a gringo lawyer in whom one can trust or depend—They are the greatest land-thieves on earth!" In his last letter António probed for answers to several questions prompted by his lawyer's requests for information: who sold those lands, who bought those lands, etc. Whether any of the Carvajal lands were eventually recovered by the family is unknown.

10. Catlett to Editor, *Arkansas* (Little Rock) *Gazette,* 26 August 1836, cited in Jenkins, vol. 7, 490.

11. Castillo Crimm, 163.

12. "Joseph M. Carvajal to L. Hawkins [Texas]," Power of Attorney, Notarial Records, pp. 176–200, St. Landry Parish, Louisiana.

13. Davenport, 496; Tyler et al., "Martin de Leon," in *Handbook of Texas,* vol. 2, 571.

14. Rose, 14–15, 106, 154–55; Castillo Crimm, 182.

CHAPTER THREE: *The Federalist Wars of Northern Mexico, 1839–1840*

1. Zorrilla and Salas, 75–77. Antonio Canales Rosillo was born in Monterey, Nuevo León, in 1802, the son of José Antonio Canales Treviño and

Josefa Rosillo. His first studies were in Monterey, but he moved to the Tamaulipas village of Camargo while still very young. The legislature of Tamaulipas confirmed his license to practice as an attorney in 1829. In Camargo he entered the civil militia, attaining the rank of colonel in 1839, and was promoted to the rank of general in 1842 for his actions in the city of Mier against the expedition of Texans. He distinguished himself in battles against the Comanches, the Lipans, and the Apaches that devastated northern Mexico for many years. From 1838 to 1840 he participated in a movement to form the so-called Republic of the Rio Grande. In 1851, Canales Rosillo acted decisively during the rebellion of La Loba, routing Carvajal's rebel forces at Paso del Zacate of the municipality of Camargo. Canales Rosillo was the governor of Tamaulipas briefly in 1851 and is thought to have died around 1852. His sons, Servando and Antonio, with the family names Canales Molano, were governors of Tamaulipas.

2. Shearer, 49.

3. Huson, "Iron Men," 66–70.

4. Ibid., 9, 18, 44, 47, 50, 60, 92, 109, 128, 129, 135; Nance, *After San Jacinto,* 142–88.

5. Nance, *After San Jacinto,* 207–17; Huson, "Iron Men," 27–28, 55, 87–112; and Nance, *After San Jacinto,* 146, 168, 172, 187, 192, 216, 249, 281, 304, 354–55, 359–61. José María González had served, before November 1835, as a colonel in the regular Mexican army. He was sympathetic to the cause of the Texas Revolution until it became clear that the Texans intended independence from Mexico, not a restoration of the constitution of 1824. González sided with the Federalist cause after a *pronunciamiento* against the Central government issued by Antonio Canales Rosillo in Guerrero on 5 November 1838. He commanded a cavalry unit in the revolutionary Federalist Army of the North. In the fall of 1839 he was a member of a party of Mexican Federalists, led by Juan Anaya, that visited President Mirabeau B. Lamar in Houston on a diplomatic mission. On April 1840, González returned to Texas, on a diplomatic mission led by Canales Rosillo to Austin, to meet again with Lamar.

6. Gulick and Winnie, vol. 6, 100–101; Nance, *After San Jacinto,* 227.

7. Huson, "Iron Men," 90–96; Gulick and Winnie, vol. 6, 137. Quote is found in Nance, *After San Jacinto,* 227.

8. Roman, cited in Davenport, 482.

9. Nance, *After San Jacinto,* 252–59; Huson, "Iron Men," 105–9.

10. Huson, "Iron Men," 126–27.

11. Carvajal's letter cited in ibid., 140–41; Nance, *After San Jacinto,* 279–307.

12. Letter, "George W. Hockley to Ashbel Smith," 1 June 1840, as found in Nance, *After San Jacinto,* 303.

13. Nance, *After San Jacinto,* 304–5.

14. *Brazos Courier,* 9 June 1840, as found in Nance, *After San Jacinto,* 307–8.

15. Huson, "Iron Men," 118–22.

16. Ibid., 157–92; Nance, *After San Jacinto,* 330–63.

17. Huson, "Iron Men," 193–98; Nance, *After San Jacinto,* 360–77.

CHAPTER FOUR: *The Mexican-American War in Northern Mexico*

1. J. M. Carvajal to Valentín Gómez Farías, 20 April 1845, Benson Latin American Collection, University of Texas.

2. Ibid.

3. "Miscellaneous Papers Concerning the Mexican War," the Justin Smith Papers, Benson Latin American Collection, University of Texas. I am indebted to Lic. Ahmed Valtier of Monterey, Nuevo León, for bringing these letters to my attention.

4. Ibid.

5. Ibid.

6. Clayton and Chance, 55.

7. The *American Flag* of Matamoros, Mexico, 4 July 1846.

8. *American Flag,* 24 July 1846.

9. *New Orleans Picayune,* Louisiana, 23 February 1847, hereafter abbreviated as *Picayune;* Chance, *Mexican War Diary,* 192–210.

10. Dobie; Linn, 322–24; Spurlin, 151, 190; Smith, *Chile con Carne,* 294; *American Flag,* 13 and 20 March 1847, 3 July 1847; and Chance, *The Coastal Bend Sun,* Corpus Christi, Texas, 13 June and 20 June 1998. General Taylor's quote appears in Chance, "South of the Border." In early 1847 a company of Texas Mounted Volunteers led by Mabry B. "Mustang" Gray entered the Rancho Guadalupe near Ramos, Nuevo León, and murdered twenty-four unarmed men. Mustang Gray was by that time well known in South Texas. South Texas historian John J. Linn described Gray as an "assassin" and a "moral monstrosity." This company of Texas Volunteers was referred to by Compton Smith, a soldier stationed in Monterey at the same time as the Texans, as a "gang of miscreants," who "in cold blood, murdered almost the entire male population of the rancho of Guadalupe,—where not a single weapon, offensive or defensive could be found!" Enraged by such an act of barbarity, Gen-

eral Zachary Taylor pressed an investigation to identify the culprits but was met by a wall of silence. He soon admitted that his investigation was a failure: "I could not possibly ascertain what individuals were concerned in this atrocious massacre." Gray's company was disbanded by 17 July 1847, and Gray was reported to have died in Camargo on 26 February 1848. His body was interred in Rio Grande City, probably in the old cemetery near the principal square, in an unmarked grave. The apparent lack of efforts by the U.S. Army to stem the murder, robbery, and rape of Mexican civilians by volunteer soldiers had a legal basis, as discussed in Chance, "South of the Border."

11. Letter, "A. Canales to . . . ," 4 April 1847, found in Gulick and Winnie, vol. 4, 167–68.

12. *American Flag,* 19 May 1847.

13. *Picayune,* 28 May 1847.

14. *Picayune,* 21 May 1847; Quaife, vol. 2, 253–57.

15. Quaife, vol. 2, 253–57; *American Flag,* 26 June 1847.

16. *American Flag,* 10 July 1847.

17. *American Flag,* 14 July 1847.

18. *American Flag,* 17 July 1847.

19. *American Flag,* 21 July 1847.

20. *American Flag,* 28 July 1847.

21. *Picayune,* 30 July 1847.

22. *Picayune,* 27 August 1847.

23. *American Flag,* 4 September 1847.

24. *American Flag,* 8 September 1847.

25. *Independente* (San Luis Potosí), 18 August 1847, found in *American Flag,* 8 September 1847.

26. *Independente,* 31 July 1847, found in *American Flag,* 8 September 1847.

27. The *Independente* letter was reprinted in *American Flag,* 31 July 1847.

28. Giddings, 335.

29. Garza Sáenz, 23–26, as translated by Al Ramírez of Edinburg, Texas.

30. Kelsey, 25.

31. Lott and Martínez, 150–52.

32. Tyler, *Vidaurri,* 1–26.

33. Lott and Martínez, 152.

34. Lott and Fenwick, 53–60; *El Mesteño,* 22–23.

35. Tyler, "Callahan Expedition of 1855," 580–82. On or near 29 September 1855, Ranger Captain James Hughes Callahan, leading a party of 115 men,

invaded Mexico. The party, claiming to be in hot pursuit of an Indian raiding party, crossed the Rio Grande below Eagle Pass, heading toward San Fernando de Rosas. It is thought that the true purpose of Callahan's raiding party was to capture the many fugitive Negro slaves living in this area and return them to the United States for a reward. Reward money offered at that time for the return of a slave to the United States was between two hundred and five hundred dollars. But the Texan raiders soon met a large combined force of Mexican soldiers and Seminoles and engaged them in battle. Greatly outnumbered, Callahan and his men retreated into the Mexican village of Piedras Négras, just across the river from Eagle Pass. With help from the U.S. Army garrison at Fort Duncan, Callahan's band retreated back across the Rio Grande after burning Piedras Négras. Ranger Callahan returned with neither Indians nor Negroes, but he and his men did manage to liberate "large amounts of produce, gold necklaces and chains, earrings, watches, rings, and other valuable articles including a silver-mounted Mexican saddle valued at approximately $100." The U.S. government paid a total of fifty thousand dollars in claims to the citizens of Piedras Négras in 1876 for the incident with no culpability attached to either Captain Callahan or any of his men for their destructive acts in Mexico.

36. Shearer, 68.

CHAPTER FIVE: *The Texas-Mexico Border in the Mid-Nineteenth Century*

1. Buchanan letter cited in Rippy, *United States and Mexico,* 70.

2. Shearer, 275.

3. Crimmins, vols. 51, 52, 53, 1948–50. For a detailed analysis, see the appendix to this book, "Distribution of Army Forces in Texas: The Report of Colonel W. G. Freeman's Inspection of the Army Posts in Texas."

4. *Picayune,* 25 November 1848.

5. *Corpus Christi Star,* 13 January 1849.

6. *Corpus Christi Star,* 23 June 1849; Montgomery, 138; and Olmsted, 298–99. Other writers saw the defect in sending infantry to confront mounted Indian raiding parties. Mrs. William L. Cazneau, nee Jane Storms, writing under the nom de plume of Cora Montgomery, from her home in Eagle Pass, Texas, noted that the Indians "rush down so suddenly upon their prey, and disappear with it so rapidly, that it requires an alert, light-armed, experienced woodsman, like themselves, to pursue them with any hope of success. Judge, then, of the sagacity of the Solomons at Washington in sending infantry to

suppress these wild horsemen of the wilderness!" Frederick Law Olmsted, visiting the frontier of Texas in 1857, observed that "in truth, the inefficiency of regular troops for Indian warfare needs no evidence. Wherever posted, they are the standing butt of the frontiersmen."

7. Ford, as quoted in Oates, 222.

8. Letter, "Gen. Brooke to Gov. Wood," 11 August 1849, Governor's Papers, Texas State Library, Austin, Texas.

9. Letter, "Gen. Brooke to Gov. Wood," 30 January 1850, Governor's Papers, Texas State Library, Austin, Texas.

10. *Reports of the Committee of Investigation,* 254–61, 302–3.

11. Quoted in Rippy, *United States and Mexico,* 80.

12. Letter, "Webster to Letcher," 18 August 1851; Manning, 89–91; and Shearer, 291.

13. Shearer, 294–95.

14. Ibid., 298.

15. Lott and Fenwick, 114; *Daily National Intelligencer,* 2 August 1848 (hereafter abbreviated as *National Intelligencer*). Yet another advertisement soliciting volunteers for the Sierra Madre Expedition appeared in a Washington, D.C., newspaper: "Buffalo Hunt on the Rio Grande.—All those desirous of joining in the buffalo hunt upon the Rio Grande next fall, are requested to send in their names and address to the Grand Scribe of the O. O. O., on or before the first day of September next. They will state the number of persons in each party, their equipments, &c. Rifles, muskets, or 'revolvers' must be furnished by each hunter. As the party may expect occasional attacks from the hostile Indians roaming in that section of the country, it is recommended that each party should be organized and drilled before meeting at the rendezvous. It is expected that many friendly Mexicans, skillful in the sport, and acquainted with the habits and haunts of the animal, will join the party. Due notice of the time of meeting and the rendezvous will be given through the public press."

16. *New Orleans Daily Delta,* 12 April 1848.

17. *Reports of the Committee of Investigation,* 211.

18. *New Orleans Daily Delta,* 30 September 1848; *Reports of the Committee of Investigation,* 211.

19. *Picayune,* 20 August 1848.

20. *Baltimore Patriot,* 14 August 1848, as reported in the *New Orleans Daily Delta,* 24 August 1848.

21. *New Orleans Daily Delta,* 27 August 1848.

22. *New Orleans Daily Delta,* 12 September 1848; private communication with secretary in City Hall, Mobile, Alabama, unknown date; Heitman, vol. 2, 59; Butler, 25, 108; Garrett, *Public Men in Alabama,* 92, 759–60; and Owen, 1085. Blanton McAlpin was quite likely the Brownsville "Buffalo Hunter," stirring up support for an incursion. A check with the City Hall of Mobile, Alabama, revealed that McAlpin was the mayor of that city from 1846 to 1847. During the Mexican-American War, he served at the rank of captain of volunteers, leading a company of Seibel's Battalion of Alabama Infantry, which served on garrison duty at Orizaba, in central Mexico. McAlpin's company was described as being "composed of the roughest elements in Mobile . . . mostly of Irish, Italians, and Spaniards." McAlpin served two terms in the Alabama State Legislature, in 1838 and 1841, and a term as mayor of Mobile. As a legislator he was remembered to be "a good working member, but weakened his influence by too much speechmaking . . . and once or twice he addressed empty benches." McAlpin later moved to California after his brief stay in South Texas.

23. *Charleston Courier,* 8 September 1848, as found in *Picayune,* 27 September 1848.

24. *Picayune,* 28 September 1848. General Memucan Hunt issued a plausible denial of his association with the Sierra Madre Expedition on this date: "We are informed by Gen. Hunt that he has no connection whatever with that movement, and that as a citizen of the South he is opposed to any additional acquisition of territory from Mexico."

25. *St. Louis Republican* article as cited in Heitman, vol. 1, 369; *Biographical and Historical Memoirs of Louisiana,* 75–76. Lewis Gustavus DeRussy graduated from the United States Military Academy in 1814 and was assigned to the 1st Artillery. By 1826 he had risen to the rank of major, serving as a paymaster. DeRussy was dropped from the service on 28 July 1842. During the Mexican War he raised the regiment of Louisiana Volunteers on December 1846. The regiment was assigned to garrison the Mexican city of Tampico and was mustered out of service on July 1848. During the war between the States he served as colonel of the 2nd Regiment of Louisiana Volunteers. DeRussy died on 17 December 1864.

26. *New Orleans Daily Delta,* 25 August 1848, as found in *Picayune,* 27 September 1848, citing a "Hartford, Connecticut" newspaper.

27. *National Intelligencer,* 22 August 1848. No mention is found of this meeting in Polk's diary.

28. *National Intelligencer,* 9 November 1848.

29. *National Intelligencer,* 7 October 1848.

30. Heitman, vol. 2, 45; Biographical and Historical *Memoirs of Louisiana,* 75–76; and *Corpus Christi Star,* 16 December 1848. Lorenzo A. Besançon served as a captain of volunteers in the Battalion of Louisiana Mounted Volunteers during the war with Mexico. The battalion was mustered into federal service on August 1847 and sent to Veracruz, serving as scouts. The battalion was mustered out of service on July 1848. After the fiasco at Corpus Christi, the *Star* reported that Besançon and a number of the "Ousel Owls" had sailed for the state of Yucatán to join the American regiment there fighting in a civil war raging in that state against the Centralists.

31. *Corpus Christi Star,* 12 September 1848, as found in *Picayune,* 23 September 1848.

32. *Corpus Christi Star,* 19 September 1848.

33. *Picayune,* 23 September 1848.

34. Ibid.

35. *Picayune,* 19 October 1848.

36. *Corpus Christi Star,* 14 November 1848.

37. Neale, as quoted in Chatfield, 14.

38. Schwarz, 7.

39. Erasmo Seguín, as quoted in ibid., 9.

40. Ibid., 17.

41. Ibid., 27–28; Olmsted, 508. Another typical newspaper advertisement of the time, seeking a runaway slave, gives insight into the wretched lives of blacks in slavery. Following the heading "Two Hundred Dollars Reward," the ad read: "Run Away or was stolen from the subscriber, about the 1st of December last, a negro man named BOSTON, aged about 31 or 32 years, black complexioned, about 5 feet 6 or 8 inches high, weighs about 150 lbs., has a delicate hand and foot for a negro, and is by profession a Methodist preacher—says a great deal about his religion. One hundred dollars reward will be paid for the delivery of said negro to me, or two hundred dollars for the negro and thief, if stolen, with evidence sufficient to convict the thief. Any information concerning said negro will be thankfully received." Schwarz, 47.

42. Green, 122–23.

43. Olmsted, 313, 472; Schwarz, 32, 37, 54; and Gammel, vol. 2, 46–47, 649–50, 950–51. The penalty for haboring a runaway Negro slave was harsh. An act of 15 January 1839 passed by the Congress of the Republic of Texas set

the punishment as a fine not less than five hundred or more than one thousand dollars and a term of imprisonment of not fewer than six months or more than one year. A subsequent act of 5 February 1841 reduced the penalty to a fine not to exceed five hundred dollars and a term of imprisonment not fewer than one month nor more than six calendar months. This same act empowered "any person" to "lawfully" apprehend a runaway slave, and this person was to receive a bounty of ten dollars for each slave from the lawful owner upon return of the runaway slave or slaves. But by 27 January 1844, a later act, evidently passed in response to an increased number of runaways, allowed a bounty of fifty dollars per returned runaway and a travel allowance of two dollars per thirty miles for travel expenses to return the slave to its legal owner.

44. Ford, as quoted in Oates, 196.

45. Ibid.

46. Information on the Freethinkers was made available to me by William Paul Burrier Sr. of Leakey, Texas, who generously shared portions of his unpublished manuscript on that subject. These brave settlers established an underground railroad from San Antonio to Eagle Pass, Texas. Many slaves escaped to freedom in Mexico thanks to their clandestine efforts.

47. Cazneau, as quoted in Montgomery, 138.

48. Olmsted, 327.

49. Ibid., 329.

50. Barker, "Land Speculation," 76–95; Hawkins, *Watrous,* 10–14; and Henson, *Williams,* 87, 89, 95–96.

51. *Who's Who in America,* 198; *Picayune,* 9, 10, and 11 December 1845, 20 December 1846; Chance, *The Mexican War Journal of Captain Franklin Smith,* 81–82; *American Flag,* 7 and 9 June 1847; and Coker, 93. Rice Garland was a prominent congressman, judge, and attorney from Louisiana. He practiced law in Brownsville, Texas, from 1846 to 1861, the year he died. Judge Garland was indicted for forgery while serving as associate justice of the Louisiana Supreme Court on or about 11 December 1845. By 16 December, New Orleans was rocked by the rumor that Judge Garland had fled the city to Havana, Cuba, evidently to escape prosecution. By 20 December 1846 the editor of the *New Orleans Picayune* noted that "by an advertisement in the Matamoros Flag, I see that Rice Garland is about opening a law office and land agency at this place and Matamoros, intending to pursue the legal profession in the courts of Texas." Helen Chapman, in a letter to her mother of 10 December 1848, singled out Rice Garland as an example of immoral life styles

found on the border: "There is, as in all new countries, I suppose, a curious order of things, peculiarly so here perhaps, because men who are banished by crime from the United States can live across the river and still carry on business here. You may have heard of Judge Garland, a gentleman of great learning, high standings and talents, who committed a forgery in Louisiana. He is living in Matamoros, with his mistress as his wife, by whom he has five children."

52. Miller's letter, as cited in Robertson, 75–76.

53. Ibid., 76–77.

54. Bell's letter, as cited in ibid., 77.

55. Dugan, 270.

56. Ibid., 275.

57. Rusk, as quoted in ibid., 279–80.

58. *Texas State Gazette,* 30 March 1850, as found in Dugan, 277.

59. Clay, as quoted in ibid., 280.

60. Rusk, as quoted in ibid., 286.

61. *American Flag,* 6 February 1850, as found in ibid., 284.

62. *Texas State Gazette,* 6 April 1850, as found in ibid., 286–87.

63. Kearney and Knopp, 16, 68; Hawkins, *Watrous,* 31.

64. *American Flag,* 14 June 1848.

65. Hawkins, *Watrous,* 31; Kearney and Knopp, 68.

66. Dugan, 275; Hawkins, *Watrous,* 31. Brownsville, Texas, was seen in a negative light by one traveler to that city in 1848, who wrote: "Brownsville is one of those little places like thousands of others in our Southern states; little work and large profits give an undue share of leisure without education or refinement, consequently drinking-houses and billiards with the etc. are abundant. The river here is narrow and rapid, and crossed by two ferry-boats swung on hawsers in the old-fashioned way stretching from bank to bank in the great 'Rio Grande del Norte.' They do a thriving business, as Matamoros contains many Mexicans who do both a wholesale and retail 'running business,' that is, smuggling." Audubon, 53.

67. Neale, as quoted in Chatfield, 14.

68. Stambaugh and Stambaugh, 103.

69. *American Flag,* 31 July 1846.

70. *American Flag,* 1 October 1846.

71. Smith, *War with Mexico,* vol. 2, 261–62.

72. *American Flag,* 2 June 1847.

73. *American Flag,* 30 June 1847.

74. *American Flag,* 25 August 1847.

75. Ibid.

76. *American Flag,* 17 November 1847.

77. *American Flag,* 1 July 1848.

78. Domenech, 327; Shearer, 29–33; and Rippy, *United States and Mexico,* 88.

79. Letter, "P. W. Humphries, Agt QM Dept., to Maj. George Deas," 1 December 1849, copy in Papers of Gov. P. H. Bell, Texas State Library, Austin, Texas. Thanks to Dunnaly Brice, archivist at the library, who brought this letter to my attention. He has been very helpful throughout this study.

80. Letter, "Hill to Father," 4 February 1852, Papers of A. P. Hill, Virginia Historical Society.

CHAPTER SIX: *The Merchants War*

1. *Picayune,* 17 August 1851; Moretta, "Carvajal," 11; Consular Dispatches from Matamoros, National Archives, Department of State Series, microfilm, M281, 12 rolls, November 1851.

2. *Picayune,* 3 September 1851.

3. *Picayune,* 15 September 1851.

4. The *Nueces Valley* (Corpus Christi), 7 September 1851, as reported in the *Texas State Gazette,* 4 and 11 October 1851. Also see Dufour. Chatham Roberdeau "Rob" Wheat was born on 10 February 1826, the eldest son of John Thomas and Selina Blair Patten Wheat, in Alexandria, Virginia. Rob was a giant of a man, filling out a six foot four inch frame with a weight that could soar to as much as 275 pounds. During the Mexican War he joined the 1st Tennessee Mounted Regiment at the rank of assistant second lieutenant, serving both in northern and central Mexico. In April 1850, Wheat joined the filibustering forces of Narciso López in an invasion of the Spanish island of Cuba. After barely escaping capture and death, Wheat returned to New Orleans, where he was indicted by a federal grand jury for violation of U.S. neutrality laws, but the charges were dismissed. By fall 1851, New Orleans newspapers hinted of plans for a revolution in northern Mexico, and Rob Wheat was soon under way to South Texas, to join the army of José María Carvajal.

5. Manning, doc. 3831, 97.

6. *Picayune,* 30 September 1851; Oates, 196; and Zorilla and Salas, "El Plan de La Loba," 541. The signatories to the Plan of La Loba were José María Canales, José María González Cuéllar, Rafael Uribe, Julián Villarreal, Juan Benavídes Garza, Félix Flores, Juan Flores Buentello, Antonio Ochoa, Manuel

Flores, José María Leal, Gabriél Sáenz, Vicente Gutiérrez, Jesús García, Tomás Benavídes, Dionisio Guerra, Félix Lindo, Francisco Sáenz, Antonio Telek, Pedro Díaz, Antonio Barrera, José Ma. Uribe, and Apolinar Amezquita.

7. *Picayune,* 30 September 1851.

8. *Picayune,* 3 January 1852; *Picayune,* 19 June 1849; Caruso, 152–58. As the American army advanced up the National Highway to Mexico City in 1847, General William Worth, serving as military governor of the city of Puebla, was first introduced to Manuel Domínguez. One of the citizens pointed out Domínguez, then in the city, as a robber who should be put in jail. Worth arrested Domínguez, but after a subsequent conversation offered Domínguez employment as a U.S. government courier. Domínguez performed well in this capacity, catching the eye of Colonel Ethan Allen Hitchcock, who had taken note of Domínguez's dubious abilities. Hitchcock negotiated a monetary arrangement with Domínguez, considered by many to be a bandit leader of central Mexico, to allow American travelers to pass on the highways from Puebla to Veracruz without being robbed. After briefly employing Domínguez and five of his men to scout the countryside as spies, Hitchcock united Domínguez and his men into the famous Mexican Spy Company. The Mexican Spy Company, under the leadership of now colonel Manuel Domínguez, was able to furnish valuable information to U.S. forces that prevented the ambush of several supply trains making the trek from Veracruz to Puebla. During the height of the U.S. campaign in central Mexico, Domínguez's Spy Company was increased to five companies, staffed by Mexicans released from prison. With the end of the war Domínguez, now branded a traitor in Mexico, fled to New Orleans with his family, where he was living in poverty in 1849. After this date Domínguez relocated to the lower Rio Grande Valley of Texas, where he was implicated in smuggling, robbery, and horse-stealing incursions into Mexico.

9. Graf, vol. 1, 323.

10. *Picayune,* 6 December 1851.

11. Ibid.

12. De la Rosa, as cited in Manning, doc. 4038, 412.

13. *Picayune,* 30 September 1851; Shearer, 43.

14. *Picayune,* 7 October 1851.

15. Graf, vol. 1, 327.

16. Ibid., 328.

17. Oates; Sowell, 399, 814. The muster roll for Ford's Ranger Company

has not been found. Based on Ford's "Memoirs," a list of Ranger names has been compiled. Those with the letter "C" after their names were certain to have been a part of Carvajal's Liberator Army: "1st. Lieut. Andrew J. Walker (C); 2nd. Lieut. Malcijah B. Highsmith; Orderly Sgt. David M. Level (C); Surgeon, Philip N. Luckett; Guide, Roque Mauricio; bugler, Mat Nolan; Privates: Jack Sharpe, Alpheus D. Neal, Milt May, Andrew Hayhurst, Robert Adams, David Steele, Ed Stevens, Jose Morales, Mr. Hardy, August Harmuth, Warren Lyons, Alfred Wheeler, Wallace McNeil, John E. Wilson (C), Volney Rountree (C), Jim Carr, Alf Tom, Jim Wilkinson, ? Leech, Jack Spencer, Sam Duncan, Plas McCurly (C)." A. J. Sowell gives a partial list of the men of Ford's company: "Andrew Jackson Walker, Lieut., Robert Rankin, Vol. Roundtree, David Steele, John Walker, Andrew Gatliff, Marvin McNeill, Albert Gallatin,—Brown, Baker Barton, William Lackey, James Carr, Alf Tom, Warren Lyons, and a German whose name was something like Mille. John E. Wilson, David Steele, Charles Wiedenmiller, John Dickens, James Wilson (John's brother), Ed. Stevens, Jack Taylor, Jack Spencer, Andrew Wheeler, D. M. Level, Robert Rankin,—Good." Sowell states that John E. Wilson went in 1852 on an expedition into Mexico under Carvajal and was badly wounded by a bullet in the arm during one of the battles.

18. Oates, 204; Shearer, 43.

19. Manning, doc. 4039, 413.

20. Papers of John Grant Tod, 1830–78, Rosenberg Library, Galveston, Texas; Manning, de la Rosa to Crittenden, 23 October 1851, 415–17. John Grant Tod was born in Kentucky in 1808. He served as a midshipman in both the U.S. Navy and the Mexican Navy before 1837, when he moved to Texas. During 1851 it was widely reported that a "Captain" Tod had organized about seventy discharged troops from Fort Duncan, in Eagle Pass, Texas, for service with Carvajal's army. The unit was reported to have marched to Lampazos, Mexico, and from there continued on to join up with Carvajal. However, nothing more was heard of their activities, or of the activities of the mysterious "Captain" Tod, who was not indicted by a federal grand jury at Brownsville.

21. *Picayune,* 21 October 1851; private communication with Mr. Joe Ponce, Edinburg, Texas.

22. *Picayune,* 23 October 1851.

23. Manning, doc. 4040, footnote, 414.

24. *Picayune,* 30 October 1851; Oates, 197.

25. Kearney and Knopp, 96.

26. *Picayune,* 18 November 1851.

27. Chapman, as quoted in Coker, 265.

28. *Picayune,* 28 October and 4 November 1851.

29. *Washington Union,* 15 November 1851.

30. Oates, 198.

31. Chapman, as quoted in Coker, 266.

32. *Picayune,* 4 November 1851.

33. Chapman, as quoted in Coker, 264.

34. *Picayune,* 3 November 1851. Kelley, 112. The *Mentoria* was a sidewheeler of 106 tons built in Cincinnati, Ohio, in 1845. She was purchased by the U.S. Quartermaster Department for use on the Rio Grande during the Mexican War and later sold at auction to M. Kenedy & Company. The *Mentoria* was used by Kenedy and King to transport freight from Brazos Santiago to the mouth of the Rio Grande via the Gulf of Mexico.

35. *Picayune*20 3 November 1851.

36. Oates, 196.

37. Spurlin, 137, 167; Oates, 200–201; and Sowell, 814–27. John E. "Black Tan" Wilson was born in Wilson County, Tennessee, on 6 July 1828, coming to Texas with his family in 1832. On 23 August 1849, Wilson joined the Ranger company of John S. Ford, stationed in South Texas between Brownsville and San Patricio. Ford's Ranger company was disbanded in September 1851, and Wilson was one of those who followed Ford into Mexico to enlist in Carvajal's Liberator Army. Sowell related that "Mr. Wilson went on an expedition into Mexico under Carabahal [*sic*], mostly Mexicans, and they had a battle in which he was badly wounded in the arm by a bullet." Sowell, 814–27.

38. *Picayune,* 4 November 1851.

39. Ford, as quoted in Oates, 198–99. Tyler et al., *Handbook of Texas,* 517; Thompson, *Mexican Texans,* 13–15; and Oates, 199. John Leal Haynes was born on 3 July 1821 in Bedford County, Virginia. He served in the volunteer service at the rank of lieutenant during the Mexican War. After the war he returned to the Texas-Mexico border, settling in the towns of Camargo, Tamaulipas, and Rio Grande City, Texas. Haynes served on the staff of Carvajal's Liberator Army, at the rank of colonel. In 1850 he served as county clerk of Starr County and was elected to the state legislature from Starr County (1857–61). During the American Civil War, Haynes became an officer in the Union 1st Texas Cavalry, led by E. J. Davis. He was promoted to the rank of

colonel, leading the 2nd Texas Cavalry (U.S.), and later leading the consolidated regiment formed from these two regiments in 1864. He lived in Austin from 1865 to 1868, serving as an internal revenue collector. Subsequently, he was appointed collector of customs in Galveston from 1869 to 1870, and he served in the same position at Brownsville from 1872 to 1884.

40. Oates, 199.

41. Domenech, 333–34.

42. *Picayune,* 4 November 1851; Oates, 200.

43. *Picayune,* 3 November 1851; Oates, 200.

44. *Picayune,* 3 November 1851; Consular Dispatches from Matamoros, 7 October 1851; and Amberson, McAllen, and McAllen, 138. The census of 1850 lists F. R. Gracesqui as a clerk, twenty-two years of age, and born in France. He owned real estate valued at eight hundred dollars.

45. *Picayune,* 3 November 1851.

46. *Picayune,* 4 November 1851; *Washington Union,* 15 November 1851.

47. *Picayune,* 3 November 1851.

48. Dufour, 65.

49. *Picayune,* 3 November 1851.

50. *Texas State Gazette,* 26 June 1852; Ford, as quoted in Oates, 201.

51. Tyler et al., *Handbook of Texas,* vol. 6, 793; Nance, *Attack and Counterattack,* 597, 630; and Oates, 197–98, 201–2. Andrew Jackson "Andy" Walker was born in Alabama in 1822, coming to Texas in 1830. During the Mexican War he joined the notorious Mabry B. "Mustang" Gray's Company of Mounted Volunteers and served with the U.S. Army in northern Mexico until 17 July 1847. He joined John S. Ford's Ranger Company in February 1850 as a guide and was promoted to the rank of lieutenant for his successful actions against Comanche raiders on 25 January 1851. Walker was one of the men from Ford's disbanded Ranger Company who joined Carvajal's forces in October 1851, participating in the Siege of Matamoros, where he commanded the rear guard during Carvajal's retreat from that city. Carvajal promoted Walker to the rank of major for his gallantry during the action at Cerralvo.

52. Portilla, as quoted in Oates, 202.

53. *Picayune,* 18 November 1851; Dufour, 66.

54. *Picayune,* 15 November 1851.

55. *Picayune,* 1 December 1851.

56. Kearney and Knopp, 95; Shearer, 49; and Moretta, "Carvajal," 11–12.

57. Manning, doc. 4045, 426–32.

58. *Rio Bravo* article as quoted in Oates, 202.

59. As recollected by Ford, quoted in Oates, 203–5.

60. Kearney and Knopp, 97.

61. *Picayune*, 18 November 1851 and 19 December 1851; letter to author from Professor Robert E. May, 13 August 1999; May, "Young American Males," 875; letter from Sandra Ragonese, the Historical Society of Pennsylvania, to author, 3 August 2000; Peskin, 172; and *National Intelligencer*, 15 November 1851. The *National Intelligencer* identified McMicken as "adjutant general of the auxiliaries, and stirs with his energy as much as he did the Cuban cause." During the Mexican-American War, McMicken had followed Colonel Geary's Pennsylvania Regiment to Mexico. Geary described McMicken as "accompanying the army, who by his appeals to the State and National pride of the men, contributed much to the enthusiasm of the regiment." From what Sergeant Thomas Barclay recorded in his diary, it is evident that McMicken took an active part in the fighting. As the American Army, fresh from the capture of the Chapultepec Castle, advanced along the Cosme Causeway toward the gates of Mexico City, Barclay chanced to see McMicken: "We had also the pleasure of meeting Capt. Montgomery and Maj. McMiken in the Castle, two Pennsylvanians who were among the first that entered Chapultepec." The Pennsylvania Census of 1850 lists J. S. McMicken as an attorney, twenty-seven years of age, and having been born in Pennsylvania. By 1856, McMicken had become known as a mercenary. Captain John Casey, writing a terse entry in his diary on 21 May 1856 from Fort Brooke, where he was stationed: "Filibuster McMicken of Phil. here."

62. *Picayune*, 24 December 1851.

63. Wheat, as quoted in Dufour, 67.

64. Mulroy, 69; *Picayune*, 6 December 1851.

65. *Picayune*, 19 December 1851.

66. *Galveston Journal*, 20 November 1852; McReynolds, 167, 169, 175, 194, 225, 251, 281; biography of Wild Cat taken from Mahone; Porter, "Seminole in Mexico, 1850–1861," 153–68; Porter, "Hawkins Negroes Go to Mexico," 55–58; Porter, "Wildcat's Death and Burial," 41–43; and Olmsted, 314–55. Wild Cat or Coacoochee was a noted leader of the Seminole Indians in Florida. He was one of the organizers of resistance to the Anglo settlement of Florida that resulted in the Seminole Wars from 1837 to 1841. The Seminoles conducted a hit-and-run warfare against small parties of travelers and isolated army posts. By November 1841, Wild Cat and his followers surrendered under

terms that included a bonus payment for resettlement and the right to retain their black slaves. The Indians were transported from their ancestral homes in Florida to a reservation near Fort Gibson, Arkansas. Unhappy with the lands given to the Seminoles, Wild Cat negotiated a plan for an Indian and Negro colony in Mexico, where the Indians could live in freedom. The Mexican government, eager to keep Comanche raiding parties out of their country, granted lands in the state of Coahuila to the Seminoles, Kickapoos, and free blacks in 1852. The lands were located south of Eagle Pass, Texas, at Musquiz, and Nacimiento, near the headwaters of the Rio Sabinas, on lands that straddled the traditional route of Comanche raiding parties into Mexico. Wild Cat served the Mexican authorities as a scout, being commissioned as a colonel in the Mexican Army. While on a scouting mission against the Comanches in 1857, Wild Cat contracted smallpox and died near Musquiz.

67. *Picayune,* 24 December 1851.

68. Ibid.

69. *Picayune,* 3 January 1852.

70. *Picayune,* 24 December 1851.

71. Oates, 201.

72. Ibid.

73. Note from Everett appears in *Picayune,* 23 December 1851, 3 and 28 January 1852; *Picayune,* 30 November 1847; and Heitman, vol. 2, 47. The Lieutenant Chinn killed in the attack on Cerralvo, Mexico, is thought to be Christopher C. Chinn, who served as a first lieutenant in Company B, the "Marshall Relief Guards," of the 2nd Volunteer Infantry Regiment of Mississippi, during the Mexican War. Thanks to Grady Howell of Madison, Mississippi, for this information.

74. *Picayune,* 3 January 1852.

CHAPTER SEVEN: *Defeat at Camargo*

1. Fenwick, 27–37.

2. As seen in *Picayune,* 3 January 1852.

3. Returns from Fort Ringgold; Returns from Fort Brown; Heitman, vol. 1. John Gibbon, of the 4th Artillery, was cited for gallantry and meritorious service at the battles of Antietam, Fredericksburg, Spottsylvania, and in the capture of Petersburg. William Warren Chapman, of the 2nd Artillery, was cited for gallantry at the battle of Buena Vista. For more information on Chapman and his wife, Helen, see Coker. Julius Peter Garesche, of the 4th Artillery, was

born in Cuba. He was killed during the battle of Murfreesboro while leading a counterattack against Confederate forces. Henry Macomb Whiting, of the 4th Artillery, was cited for meritorious conduct at the battle of Buena Vista. Robert Selden Garnett, of the 4th Artillery, graduated from West Point in 1841. He was cited for meritorious conduct in the battles of Monterey and Buena Vista. Brigadier General Garnett, of the Confederate States Army, was killed in action at Carricks Ford, Virginia. Joseph Abel Haskin, of the 1st Artillery, was cited for gallantry at the battles of Cerro Gordo and Chapulte-pec. Henry Hill was the brother of Confederate general A. P. Hill and served as a paymaster. Daniel Huston, of the 8th Infantry, was cited for gallantry at the battle of Wilsons Creek, Missouri, and the siege of Vicksburg. Joseph Hatch LaMotte, of the 1st Infantry, was cited for gallant conduct in the Battle of Monterey. Gabriel Rene Paul, of the 7th Infantry, was cited for gallantry at the battle of Chapultepec and again during the Civil War at the battle of Get-tysburg. Henry Prince, of the 4th Infantry, was cited for meritorious conduct at the battles of Contreras, Churubusco, and Molino del Rey. During the Civil War he was again cited for actions in the battle of Cedar Mountain, Virginia. William Edgar Prince, of the 1st Infantry, was cited for gallantry at the battle of Santa Cruz de Rosales, Mexico. Rufus Saxton, of the 3rd Artillery, was awarded the Congressional Medal of Honor for distinguished gallantry in the defense of Harper's Ferry, Virginia. Egbert Ludovickus Viele was a member of the 7th Infantry. His wife, Teresa, wrote an interesting account of army life. See Viele.

4. *Picayune,* 24 October 1851.

5. Letter, "Dear Ellen," 27 September 1851, La Motte–Coppinger Family Papers, Missouri Historical Society.

6. Ibid.

7. Letter, "My Dear Wife," 25 October 1851, ibid.

8. Letter, "My Dear Wife," 25 November 1851, ibid.

9. Letter, "My Dear Wife," 22 December 1851, ibid.

10. *Galveston Journal,* 13 June 1853; 1850 Census for Texas; Tyler et al., "John C. Watrous," *Handbook of Texas,* vol. 6, 848; and Hawkins, *Watrous,* 41, 67. John Charles Watrous moved to Texas in 1837 and set up a practice that specialized in land speculation. In 1846 he was appointed the first federal judge for the newly formed state of Texas. The new court met on 5 December 1846 for its first session in Galveston, Texas. On 20 March 1848 the state legislature passed a resolution requesting "John C. Watrous to resign his office," charging

Watrous with "remaining but a small part of the time within his district," and more seriously that Watrous while in office aided and assisted certain individuals in an attempt to fasten upon this state one of the most "stupendous frauds ever perpetrated upon any country or any people." But a federal grand jury, convened in 1848, concluded that Judge Watrous was not guilty of the charges specified in the legislative resolution. On 15 January 1852, Texas congressman Volney Howard submitted an impeachment memorial to the U.S. Congress charging that Judge Watrous, "since his appointment and while absent from his district, . . . has exercised the profession or employment of counsel and has been so engaged in the practice of law," an act declared as a "high misdemeanor"—an impeachable offense. Hearings on the Watrous matter were held before the Senate Judiciary Committee started in spring 1852, but the Howard memorial failed to be reported out of committee. The impeachment resolution was brought up again in December 1858 and defeated. In 1860 yet another impeachment resolution was introduced by Congressman A. J. Hamilton. On this occasion the judiciary committee reported in favor of impeachment, but the full House of Representatives refused to consider the matter. The 1861 term of the Federal District Court in Texas was started by Judge Watrous and concluded by Judge William P. Hill, appointed by the Confederate Congress. Judge Watrous resumed his position on the bench of the Federal District Court on 7 May 1866, but declining health forced his resignation in 1870. Chatfield, 14; Hawkins, *Watrous,* 41. The Census of 1850 lists John P. Putegnat as a merchant, forty years of age, born in France. He owned real estate valued at $2500. Putegnat established and was the owner of the Botica del Lion, a drugstore located on the corner of Elizabeth and Twelfth Streets in Brownsville, Texas. This *botica* was the site of the first session of the Federal District Court for the Eastern District of Texas, to be held in Brownsville, under the gavel of Judge John Charles Watrous. A sketch of the Botica del Lion can be found in Hawkins, *Watrous,* 41.

11. Letter, "Hill to Father," 4 February 1852, Papers of A. P. Hill, Virginia Historical Society.

12. Oates, 385–98; Heitman, vol. 1. Ambrose Powell Hill of the 1st Artillery graduated from West Point in 1847. Hill rose to the rank of lieutenant general in the Confederate States Army and was killed on 2 April 1865 at the battle of Five Forks. James E. Slaughter joined the army in 1847, serving in the Regiment of Voltiguers. He rose to the rank of brigadier general in the Confederate States Army.

13. *Picayune,* 14 January 1852.

14. "Trial of Garnett," 5; Heitman, vol. 1. Persifor Frazer Smith was appointed colonel of the Regiment of Mounted Rifles in 1846 and cited for gallantry at the battles of Monterey, Contreras, and Churubusco. William Selby Harney joined the service in 1818 and was assigned to the 1st Infantry at the rank of second lieutenant. He was cited for gallantry in several successive engagements with the hostile Indians in Florida and again for his actions in the battle of Cerro Gordo.

15. "Trial of Garnett," 5–6.

16. *Picayune,* 3 January 1852.

17. Ibid.

18. *Picayune,* 31 January 1852.

19. *Picayune,* 26 December 1851; Kelley, 108. The *Corvette* was a sidewheeler of 149 tons, built in Brownsville, Pennsylvania, in 1846. It was purchased by the U.S. Quartermaster Department for use on the river during the Mexican War.

20. "Trial of Garnett," 9.

21. *Picayune,* 24 December 1851.

22. Ibid.

23. Ibid.

24. *Picayune,* 16 February 1852.

25. *Picayune,* 18 February 1852; Moretta, *Ballinger,* 53.

26. Tyler et al., *Handbook of Texas,* vol. 1, 360; Spurlin, 1. William Pitt Ballinger was born in Kentucky in 1825 and attended St. Mary's College in Bardstown, Kentucky. He moved to Galveston in 1843 to study law at the office of his uncle and was admitted to the bar in 1847. He served as a U.S. district attorney for eastern Texas from 1850 to 1854. The county seat of Runnels County is named in his memory.

27. Viele, 193.

28. *Picayune,* 15 February 1852.

29. *Picayune,* 16 and 18 February 1852.

30. *Picayune,* 18 February 1852; Kelley, 110. The *Grampus* was a sidewheeler of 221 tons, designed and built for the firm of Kenedy and King at Freedom, Pennsylvania, in 1850.

31. *Picayune,* 14 November 1851; letter from Helen Chapman to mother, 17 February 1852, Coker, 277–78.

32. Viele, 194.

33. *National Intelligencer,* 9 March 1852.

34. "Trial of Garnett," 3–4.

35. Ibid., 2.

36. Ibid., 4.

37. Letter, "Prince to Harney," 8 January 1852, Reports from the 8th Military District.

38. Letter, "La Motte to Harney," 23 January 1852, Reports from the 8th Military District.

39. Letter, "Viele to Harney," 7 February 1852, Reports from the 8th Military District. The letter from Governor P. H. Bell in the possession of Warren Adams was copied by Lieutenant Viele and attached to his report. The letter is as follows:

> Whereas I have been notified, by Marcellus Duval, agent of the Seminole Tribe of Indians, that a large number of negro slaves belonging to the said Indians have run or been decoyed off from their owners, and that many of them are believed to be at or near Eagle Pass, in the vicinity of the Rio Grande and whereas I have also been credibly informed, that many runaway negro slaves belonging to the citizens of Texas are at this time lurking in the same neighborhood I do therefore request the citizens of the State of Texas, her legal authorities and all others who may be disposed to do so to give whatever aid and facility may be in their power to Warren Adams Esq. or to whomsoever also may be the legally constituted agents of said Seminole Indians and others in the recovery, and safe keeping of said runaway negroes, so that they may be dealt with according to law." Moretta, "Carvajal," 12. U.S. District Attorney William Pitt Ballinger believed that Warren Adams was to lead a band of "runaway negroes . . . with the professed design of returning to Texas to help free other slaves after they had been sufficiently armed by Carvajal." Ibid. Perhaps this is the reason that Ballinger had Adams indicted by a federal grand jury.

40. Manning, doc. 4111, 556; Kelley, 112.

41. Letter, "Holabird to Prince," 21 February 1852, Reports from the 8th Military District.

42. *Picayune,* 8 March 1852; *National Intelligencer,* 17 March 1852.

43. *Picayune,* 8 March 1852.

44. Ibid.; *National Intelligencer,* 15 and 17 March 1852; and Domenech, 340. On 20 February 1852, as Carvajal's Liberator Army approached Camargo, they were struck by a powerful attack from the cavalry of Canales, whose

National Guard forces were defending the village. A large body of Carvajal's untried forces stampeded in panic. Leading the rush were the forces of Captain Núñez, who "were mostly, if not all, Mexicans; but in their progress took with them many Americans." This quote appeared in *Picayune,* 8 March 1852. Later, many of Carvajal's supporters blamed Núñez for the defeat at Camargo and believed that Núñez had conspired in some way with Canales and Ávalos to defeat Carvajal. To save his life from angry Liberators, Núñez passed over to Matamoros, surrendering to General Ávalos. He begged to be put in a place of safety from the Americans, and Ávalos obliged by placing him in prison. Ávalos then convened a court-martial and had Núñez condemned to death. Fearing that the sentence might actually be carried out, Núñez escaped from the makeshift prison, returning to the Brownsville side. The death sentence was sufficient proof to Núñez's many critics that he was not in league with either Ávalos or Canales, and he was restored to their good graces.

45. As reported in Viele, 195–211.

46. *National Intelligencer,* 17 March 1852.

47. *Picayune,* 8 March 1852.

48. *National Intelligencer,* 17 March 1852.

CHAPTER EIGHT: *The Indictment and Trial*
of José María de Jesús Carvajal and His Men

1. *Picayune,* 20 April 1853; Kelley, 113. Peter Dowd, the quartermaster for Carvajal's Liberator Army, was a resident of Rio Grande City, described as "an innocent and inoffensive man, and a mere tool of the others." Dowd was once the owner of the river steamer *Tom Kirkman,* which he offered for sale in 1849. The steamer was evidently purchased by Charles Stillman. Dowd was interred in the old cemetery at Rio Grande City.

2. Oates, 200. A. J. Mason is not listed in the census of 1850 and probably belonged to Ford's Ranger Company, as Ford referred to him as "Jo" Mason. Mason claimed to be the man that shot U.S. Consul J. F. Waddell during the attack on Matamoros. The wound was superficial, however—a buckshot in the cheek.

3. Coker, 112, 145, 236, 255. The census of 1850 lists R. N. Stansbury as a teacher, twenty-four years of age, born in Louisiana. Helen Chapman approved of Stansbury, writing in her diary on 5 February 1849 that "at last to my great joy, they have got a school started in Brownsville to be kept by a very excellent, and I should think, well educated young man, a member of the Methodist Church." Stansbury was engaged to Henrietta Chamberlain, who

would later become the wife of Richard King, but the engagement was "broken off forever" by 10 July 1851.

4. Alfred Norton was among the group of men camped on Mustang Island, near Corpus Christi, Texas, waiting for transportation to Cuba to participate in López's second filibustering attack on that island. Fortunately for him and the men of this group, no ship arrived, and they escaped the imprisonment and death sentences meted out by the Spanish, who captured all the members of the López expedition. A cannonball tore off one of Norton's arms during Carvajal's attack on Matamoros. Norton later served as a justice of the peace in the newly formed Starr County and led the dastardly raid on Reynosa. A passenger manifest of 21 June 1852 for the steamship S.S. *Prometheus* from New York to Graytown, Nicaragua, lists as one of its passengers a certain "Alfred Norton, age 40," as a U.S. citizen with occupation "miner." It appears that Norton had joined the filibustering expedition of William Walker in his plan to capture Nicaragua.

5. *Picayune,* 18 November 1851. The 1850 census lists R. H. Hord as a lawyer, twenty-nine years of age, and born in Virginia. He owned real estate valued at fifty thousand dollars. In a long letter of 15 November 1851, addressed to "His Excellency Millard Fillmore," and appearing in the Brownsville newspaper *Rio Bravo,* Hord complained about the resistance offered by federal officials and army officers to efforts by U.S. citizens to violate the territorial sovereignty of Mexico as a part of Carvajal's Army:

> The [revenue] collector, Mr. Rhea, is a well-disposed but weak man. Excited, agitated, and incapable of forming or acting on any definite plan. . . . His deputy in Brownsville, named Kingsbury, is as weak as Rhea, with less integrity, and with a mischievous and malicious disposition. He is a tool of foreign merchants. . . .
>
> Capt. Phelps sought to induce a part of them [troops under his command] to assail a boat of inoffending men, in which I was one of the passengers, by commanding Lieut. Cummings of the U.S. Army to fire upon us. This order was about to be executed, when the prompt and determined action of the men in the boat arrested it, by threatening to shoot in return. . . . He [Captain Phelps] insulted all who had occasion to cross the river either way, and whether singly or in companies of three or four unarmed persons, insisted upon their submission to the most humiliating espionage.
>
> . . . Capt. Phelps, warrants the conviction that he has acted more as

a partizan of the Central Government of Mexico than as an independent officer of the United States Army. During the whole of the troubles on this frontier, the American Consul, Mr. Waddell, has taken an active part in favor of the Central Government of Mexico, . . . forgetting altogether the duty he owed to his fellow countrymen, and the honor of his nation.

6. Tyler et al., *Handbook of Texas,* 696; Oates, 345; Manning, 101; and Spurlin, 191. Edward R. Hord was born in Virginia around 1827, coming to the Texas border in 1846. He served during the Mexican War, enlisting in the infamous Mabry B. "Mustang" Gray's Company of Texas Mounted Volunteers. Hord, a lawyer, was living in Rio Grande City in 1851 when asked by W. P. Ballinger, U.S. district attorney of Texas, to investigate an incident between U.S. and Mexican citizens that occurred at the Roma Crossing of the Rio Grande. But there was such a feeling of rivalry between the towns of Rio Grande City and Roma that citizens of the latter town refused to be deposed by Hord. In a letter addressed to Ballinger, they stated that "entertaining objections to the gentleman [Hord] appointed by Mr. Rhea, and particularly to any comments he might make on the conduct of our community, feel it our duty to decline the interrogatories which you solicited." This letter was signed by seventeen of the leading citizens of Roma. Captain Hord commanded the Brownsville Company of Carvajal's Liberation Army and was heavily involved in the attack on Matamoros. Hord was elected to the Fourth, Fifth, and Sixth Texas Legislatures (1851–56) from Starr County, serving his last term as a senator. He served as a delegate to the Secession Convention of 1861 from Starr County and later declined a commission as a major in the Texas Militia. Hord did serve the Confederacy on the Rio Grande as a colonel under John S. Ford, in Ford's Cavalry of the West. Hord represented Cameron County in the Confederate Tenth Legislature (1864–65).

7. *Papers of Jefferson Davis,* vol. 2, 124, 330–32, 374–76, vol. 3, 14; Oates, 196–205; *Picayune,* 9 March 1852 and 6 August 1853; Chance, *Doubleday,* 167–68, 171–72; and Asbury, 138–43. Joseph Davis Howell was born on 23 November 1824, the eldest son of William Burr and Margaret Kempe Howell. He was the namesake of Joseph E. Davis, older brother of Jefferson Davis, the elder Davis being a business partner of William Howell. During the Mexican War, Howell served in the 1st Mississippi Volunteer Regiment, the "Mississippi Rifles," commanded by Jefferson Davis. He participated in the capture of Monterey but was later discharged on 5 December 1846 for illness. The dis-

charge certificate described him as "six feet six inches high, fair complexion, black hair, black eyes, and by profession when mustered in a lawyer." He stayed in Mexico during the war, serving as a clerk in the quartermaster's depot in Camargo until July 1848. The Cameron County Census of 1850 records a "J. D. Howell, a lawyer of age 27, with property valued at $15,000," as residing in Brownsville. The 1857 New Orleans Directory listed Howell as a resident, where he continued to live until 1859. Howell mysteriously disappeared from family records past this date, and little else is known of his life or whereabouts. For insight into the character of Howell, see Chance, *Doubleday*.

8. Lott and Martinez, 140; Sweet and Knox, 159. The census of 1850 lists Robert C. Trimble as a surveyor, fifty years of age, born in Tennessee. Testimony given by Manuel María Uribe, in a 1904 case involving land ownership, mentions Trimble: "I knew El Capitán Colorado well. He is dead. His name was Robert C. Trimble. He was a surveyor. He surveyed the lower line of the grant from old San Ygnacio to the Toro Hill at the Sierrita." Little else can be found of this pioneer border surveyor, but if we are to believe the account of Alex Sweet and J. A. Knox, Robert Trimble was murdered south of San Antonio at some unknown date. Trimble had left San Antonio for his home on the Rio Frio, driving a wagon pulled by two mules. The mules, without the wagon, appeared some days later at his home, and searchers subsequently found Trimble's body, led by a circling flight of buzzards that marked the murder scene. Trimble's murderer, José Cordova, had taken the wagon to Mexico, but a dent in one of the wagon wheels left a distinctive trail in the dust, easy to follow by trackers. This well-marked trail led to the wagon and the home of Trimble's murderer.

9. Ramírez, "Everetts of South Texas"; Nance, *Attack and Counterattack,* 170, 176, 186, 188, 207, and "Muster Roll of Mobile Alabama Volunteers" in appendix; *Corpus Christi Gazette,* 8 January 1846; *Brownsville Herald,* 1 January 1947; and Nance, *Dare-Devils All,* 72, 209, 467–68. Jack Ross Everett, the youngest son of John Fagan and Sarah Hand Everett, was born on 10 March 1822 in Montgomery County, Alabama. On 1 April 1842, Jack Everett arrived in Texas, at Galveston, leading a company of fifty-five men, known as the Mobile Alabama Volunteers, who were mustered into the Republic of Texas Army for six month's duty. In 1845, Everett opened a sutler's store in Corpus Christi to serve the needs of the soldiers of General Zachary Taylor's army, then stationed there. During the war's early months a party of McCulloch's Texas Rangers, on a scouting party in Mexico, met Captain Jack and offered

this description of him: "A horseman rode into our camp, Jack Everitt [*sic*], . . . a young man who had been living some years in Mexico, trading. He was dressed like a Mexican, and spoke the language very well, and was employed in the quarter-master's department as interpreter and contractor. He was so well known throughout that part of the country (Mexico), that he was generally allowed to travel unmolested. He afterwards joined our company, as the army moved on, and fought with the Texians at the storming of Monterey." On 19 April 1847, Everett wed Antonia Flores, a resident of Mier, and settled there, opening up a store and a tavern. Everett reported guerrilla activities to the American army, then holding northern Mexico, saving many American supply trains from destruction. After the war Captain Jack settled on his wife's land, Rancho Buena Vista, just across the Rio Grande from Mier, to establish a general merchandising and commission business. He attempted to develop a city on the site of his ranch, referred to as "Everettville," but he could not lure any settlers to the wild country. Jack Everett disappeared in a mysterious manner, at about the time of the Civil War, while on a mission to transport two prisoners to jail.

10. *National Intelligencer,* 9 March 1852; *Texas State Gazette,* 13 March 1852; Consular Dispatches from Matamoros, undated. The census of 1850 lists E. B. Scarborough as a printer, twenty-seven years of age, born in Georgia, and R. E. W. Adams as a doctor, forty years of age, born in Maine.

11. Kearney and Knopp, 74, 92; *Picayune,* 17 March and 2 June 1852; *Picayune,* 24 March 1852; and Spellman, "Corpus Christi," 6–16.

12. Wheat, as cited in Dufour, 64, 68–69.

13. Ford, as quoted in Oates, 204; Papers of John A. Quitman. But Ford was not through with his filibustering ways. In a letter of 30 April 1854 from Hugh McLeod to General John A. Quitman and others, McLeod wrote: "Col John S. Ford, Editor of the State Times at Austin and formerly associated with almost every Ranger enterprise in the Republic and State of Texas. . . . I wrote him to know if he could give up his newspaper & at what loss, and recruit a force of 200 Rangers of the old set, Col. Ford has every qualification—experience—judgement—coolness—personal knowledge of the men who are fittest for the duty. . . . He is a cold water man. There is no man in Texas, better qualified to recruit & command the force you want." After consultation with Ford, McLeod drafted these thoughts to J. S. Thrasher on 31 May 1854: "You want from Texas some 300 of our old Rangers—which Ford can raise with funds, but not without—many of the best of them cant buy a pony, much less a

revolver." By 5 June 1854, Ford contacted Quitman from Austin to show progress in his recruiting efforts through the state: "Committees are now organized and at work in Galveston, Harris, Montgomery, Polk, Fort Bend, Washington, Bastrop, and Travis Counties." The plot to invade Cuba appeared to fail, probably for want of funds. But Ford's filibustering plans were, by 17 December 1854, focused on Mexico again. In a letter from Austin, of this date, addressed to "Comrade," he seems to suggest that a plot is under foot for another expedition to Mexico with Carvajal. The rumors reported in the press at that time of another Carvajal-led invasion of Mexico perhaps stemmed from Ford's recruiting activities. Ford wrote: "I have just returned from San Antonio, where all is right. Gen. Carvajal has not arrived. Texas will muster strong. They will not mis-understand us this time. I long to receive your greetings on the banks of the Rio Grande. Make my compliments to all good fellows and true."

14. *Picayune,* 2 June 1852.

15. "Trial of Garnett," 1, 4. Thirteen distinguished officers presided at the court-martial proceedings of Robert S. Garnett. These officers were: Brevet Brigadier General John Garland, Colonel 8th Infantry; Brevet Colonel Charles A. May, Captain 2nd Dragoons; Brevet Colonel William W. Loring, Lieutenant Colonel Mounted Riflemen; Brevet Lieutenant Colonel Thompson Morris, Major 1st Infantry; Brevet Lieutenant Colonel George Nauman, Captain 1st Artillery; Brevet Lieutenant Colonel James V. Bomford, Captain 8th Infantry; Brevet Lieutenant Colonel William Chapman, Captain 5th Infantry; Brevet Lieutenant Colonel Andrew Porter, Captain Mounted Riflemen; Brevet Major Pitcairn Morrison, Captain 8th Infantry; Brevet Major Henry H. Sibley, Captain 2nd Dragoons; Brevet Major Joseph A. Haskin, Captain 1st Artillery; Captain William E. Prince, Captain 1st Infantry; Captain Washington I. Newton, Captain 2nd Dragoons. First Lieutenant Frederick J. Denman, Adjutant 1st Infantry, was appointed advocate of the court.

16. Ibid., 5.

17. Ibid., 5–6.

18. Ibid., 14.

19. Ibid., 14.

20. Ibid., 15.

21. Ibid., 35. The findings of the court in the cases of Majors Paul and Garnett were submitted to headquarters of the 8th Military District for review and approval. The response by Persifor F. Smith, commanding the 8th Military District, demurred with the findings of the court: "I cannot come to the same con-

clusion as the court, as to Brevet Major Paul's guilt. He had a 'positive order' to disarm and disperse the 'avowed adherents of Carbajal,' whom he himself had reported as assembled in camps, and about to march; and he refused to obey this order." General Smith felt that the previous proclamations issued by President Millard Fillmore which called upon all civil and military officers to enforce the provisions of the Neutrality Act of 1818 were authority enough for the officers of Ringgold Barracks to arrest Carvajal and his forces. "The law being in force, ignorance of its provisions is no excuse for a breach of it, and the officer who refuses to obey an order as illegal, assumes the responsibility of being better informed of the law than he who issues the order . . . but as I have no doubt the court have given their decision with the conscientious desire of rendering justice, I will not place my opinion in active opposition to theirs. The sentence of the court is confirmed."

22. *Texas State Gazette,* 26 June 1852; Consular Dispatches from Matamoros, 16 June 1852.

23. Domenech, 336–46; *Galveston News,* 5 July 1852; *Texas State Gazette,* 26 June 1852.

24. That important prisoner was Captain Núñez, who had surrendered himself to Mexican authorities rather than face the wrath of Carvajal's followers.

25. Domenech, 347.

26. *Texas State Gazette,* 26 June 1852.

27. Domenech, 338.

28. Manning, doc. 4111, 556; *New Orleans Daily Delta,* 10 July 1850, as seen in Coker, 372; *Galveston Journal,* 22 May 1854. General Ávalos's love for the fair sex became his downfall. A female resident of Matamoros, known locally as the "Widow Garcia," became intimate with Ávalos. She departed Matamoros mysteriously in February 1850, traveling to Mobile, Alabama. *The Mobile Advertiser* reported shortly thereafter an account of a birth and subsequent infanticide of a male child by a Mexican lady, who was finally acquitted of all charges in the matter. Rumors swirled around the general and his "widow friend" that their first child had been born in the United States, in Alabama. Señora Garcia returned to Matamoros, but the status of her relationship with Ávalos is unknown. General Ávalos was reported to have been married on 5 February 1852, but not to Garcia. There was "great rejoicing in Matamoros" to celebrate the wedding. A correspondent reported that "his bride is said to be young, handsome, accomplished, and rich, while he is old and ugly, and a perfect Sambo in color." The couple were married by proxy and reportedly had never

seen each other until a few days before the wedding. But all was not well. The *Galveston Journal* reported that General Ávalos had been reduced to the ranks as a common soldier after being confirmed as a bigamist. His second wife was the daughter of General Sánchez, "a lady universally esteemed for her intelligence and virtue." This unhappy young lady was reported to have taken her own life with a pistol over the disgrace. General Ávalos was replaced by General Adrian Woll as commandant of Matamoros in late 1853.

29. *National Intelligencer,* 3 February 1853; Amberson, McAllen, and McAllen, 133–34; and Castillo Crimm, 115, 207.

30. *Texas State Sentinel,* 30 April 1853.

31. Manning, 555–62.

32. Shearer, 62–64; *Galveston Journal,* 13 June 1853.

33. Smith, as quoted in *Picayune,* 14 April 1853.

34. *Picayune,* 30 March, 4 and 12 April, and 6 August 1853; *National Intelligencer,* 12 April 1853; *Texas State Gazette,* 30 April 1852; and Shearer, 62.

35. Wright, 70–75.

36. *Picayune,* 17 March 1853; Shearer, 57; and Kelley, 108. The *Comanche* was a sternwheeler of 164 tons, built in Freedom, Pennsylvania, in 1850, and owned by M. Kenedy and Company; May, *Manifest Destiny's,* 117; and Moretta, *Ballinger,* 53.

37. *National Intelligencer,* 2 June 1853.

38. *Galveston Journal,* 13 June 1853.

39. Manning, doc. 4111, 558.

40. *Galveston Journal,* 2 May 1853; Hawkins, *Watrous,* 27; and Manning, 45–47.

41. The census of 1850 lists Elisha Basse as a lawyer, thirty years of age, and born in Maine. He owned real estate valued at fifty thousand dollars.

42. Chatfield, 14; Graf, vol. 2, 466, 635. The census of 1850 lists Frances J. Parker as a brickman, thirty years of age, born in Massachusetts. Parker was employed as assistant editor of the *Rio Bravo,* a newspaper founded to support the Republic of the Sierra Madre scheme, and served for a time as U.S. commissioner. He owned real estate valued at ten thousand dollars. Parker served as mayor of Brownsville, Texas, before 1876, was described by LeRoy P. Graf as a "lawyer," and was in partnership with another lawyer, W. G. Hale, in the ownership of the Santa Rosa Ranch.

43. Alfred Norton was indicted this second time for his raid on Reynosa.

44. Pingenot, vii, 61, 69–71. Jesse Sumpter, pioneer settler of Eagle Pass, Texas, referred to "Captain" Warren Adams as a "notorious slaver." Adams,

bolstered by a 17 September 1851 proclamation of Governor P. H. Bell that urged all citizens to assist such slavers as Adams in their attempts to recover runaway slaves, invaded Mexico. Taking advantage of the turmoil created in Mexico by Carvajal's invasion of that republic, Adams and seventeen of his followers rode from San Antonio to Eagle Pass. From there, they planned to cross the border and capture free Negroes living near Monclova Viejo. Alerted Mexican authorities managed to assemble a force of 150 armed men that met the Adams party near Villa de Nava and drove them back to the United States. But before Adams returned, he captured a family of Negroes living at Santa Rosa and returned to Texas with his booty. This invasion of Mexico was probably the reason for Adams's federal grand jury indictment. In all likelihood, Adams was not a member of Carvajal's army.

45. Chance, *Doubleday,* 276–78. The census of 1850 lists Joseph Moses as a merchant, twenty-six years of age, born in New York, owning real estate valued at ten thousand dollars. For some idea of the type of men to be found in Carvajal's Liberator Army, see an account of the duel between Moses and Walter Hickey in Chance, *Doubleday.*

46. Peter Dowd served as quartermaster of Carvajal's army.

47. Oates, 176, 181; Hughes, 170. Voltaire or Volney Roundtree, as Ford refers to him, was a member of Ford's Ranger Company, participating in the Indian battle at Arroyo Gato, above Laredo, in 1852. He was indicted for his part in the infamous raid on Reynosa, on 25 March 1853. As late as 1860, Roundtree was active on the border. During that year he joined John S. Ford's Rio Grande Squadron, formed to combat the raids on Texas by Cortina and his men from across the Rio Grande.

48. Howell's second indictment could have been a result of his participation in the Reynosa raid, but there is no evidence of his having been a member of that gang.

49. *National Intelligencer,* 6 August 1853.

50. Graf, vol. 1, chapter 6, 326.

51. *Picayune,* 13 May 1853.

52. *Picayune,* 16 May 1853.

53. *Picayune,* 3 May 1853; *Galveston Journal,* 14 July 1853; *National Intelligencer,* 18 July 1853; and the Carvajal quote appearing in *Indianola* [Texas] *Bulletin,* 8 April 1852. Accompanying José María at his hearing before the U.S. commissioner were his staff, Lieutenant Colonel A. D. Gonzáles, as well as his aide and military secretary, Colonel José M. Cabasos [Cavazos?], formerly in command of the Reynosa Squadron. Several other men also accompanied

Carvajal, including Don Ignacio Guerra, who was now an exile from his country for aiding the Liberation Army; Moretta, *Ballinger*, 54.

54. Stillman, 16. The census of 1850 lists Charles Stillman as a merchant, twenty-nine years of age, and born in Connecticut. He owned real estate valued at twenty-five thousand dollars.

55. Oates, 459. The King Ranch archivist, Lisa A. Neely, indicates that there is nothing to be found there about José María Carvajal, except possibly some minor business matters. The Papers of Miflin Kenedy have been sealed by the courts due to pending litigation and are not available for inspection by historians.

56. *The South-Western American*, Austin, Texas, 17 November 1852: Tyler, "Fugitive Slaves," 5–6; Viele, 192; and private communication, 9 July 1997, from James D. Ward, Grand Secretary, Masonic Grand Lodge Library and Museum of Texas, Waco. The first Masonic lodge meetings in South Texas were held on Brazos Island by American soldiers during the Mexican-American War. Little is known of its operations, but it was one of several Traveling Army Lodges then in existence that followed the movements of the army. The Rio Grande lodge was granted a dispensation on 26 February 1849 and set to work under the guidance of John C. Cleland as master. It was 23 January 1852 before Rio Grande Lodge No. 81 was officially granted to Hiram Chamberlain, W. W. Nelson, and E. B. Scarborough. The returns of this lodge indicate that several of the men prominent in the Carvajal invasions of Mexico, including Carvajal, were members. The names are listed in the order of appearance on the returns.

RETURNS OF THE RIO GRANDE LODGE NO. 81 MASONIC ORDER

1850

J. C. Cleland, J. E. Garey, H. L. Howlett, J. Edward Dougherty, L. B. Cain, S. Powers, E. Clements, W. Nelson, Elisha Basse, Jefferson Barthelow, T. B. Buchanan, ? A. Bell, P. Culver, O. H. Cunningham, J. M. J. Carvajal, H. Chamberlain, ? A. Cravens, Geo. Dye, Peter Dowd, Edward Downey, Budd H. Fry, Robt. H. Hord, Gerhard D. Kothman, ? Nickels, A. Glavaecke, M. H. Harrison, F. W. Latham, A. R. Mauck, W. L. Patterson, T. W. Slemmons, John T. Frith, E. B. Scarborough.

1851

S. Powers, J. Daugherty, W. W. Nelson, S. B. Cain, G. D. Kothman, M. S. Patterson, R. N. Stansbury, J. W. Waterhouse, Geo. Dye, ? Oliver,

J. Southwell, W. J. Alexander, J. Barthelow, E. Basse, ? Barton, ? A. Bell, A. P. Bennett, T. F. Brewer, ? L. Campbell, J. M. J. Carvajal, H. Chamberlain, R. E. Clements, O. H. Cunningham, P. Dowd, E. Downey, B. H. Fry, J. E. Garey, A. Glavecke, ? H. Harrison, W. H. Harrison, R. H. Hord, H. L. Howlett, T. B. King, F. W. Latham, D. H. Marks, Jonas Marks, ? Martin, A. R. Mauk, Benj. Moses, Jos. Moses, ? McCarthy, J. R. McFadin, H. O'Connor, ? J. Parker, ? S. Patterson, ? Nickels, E. Putegnat, ? Ravesi, E. B. Scarborough, D. H. Marks, F. J. Parker, Robt. Barton, D. Harrison, T. F. Brewer, R. B. Gage, E. M. Anderson, Wm. McCarthy, A. P. Burnett, J. P. Putegnat, T. B. King, O. C. Phelps, Geo. Krausse, H. O'Connor, J. Ravessi, J. Cliver, A. Werbiski, N. Mitchell, M. J. Alexander, J. S. Hixon, Jno Martin, Alfred Moses, Hy Weaver, M. Speyer, T. Slatter, J. L. Thompson, T. H. Harris, Chs Martin, J. L. Edmondson, Jonas Marks, Wm. Gross, W. L. Campbell, Benj Moses, J. P. McDonough, S. Kidder, Wm. Boardman, W. H. Harrison, W. S. Patterson, A. R. Mauk, F. W. Latham, T. W. Slemons, John Southwick, Jos. Moses.

57. de la Cova, 99.

58. Ibid., 100, Returns of the Rio Grande Lodge No. 81 Masonic Order.

59. *National Intelligencer,* 15 November 1854; Moretta, *Ballinger,* 57; May, *Manifest Destiny's,* 117–18; and *The Galveston News,* 7 November and 10 January 1854.

60. Rankin, *Twenty Years,* 39–40.

61. *National Intelligencer,* 2 December 1854.

62. Letter, "Dear General," 13 October 1854, John A. Quitman Papers, Mississippi Archives.

63. Letter, "C. R. Wheat to Dear General," 29 October 1854, Papers of John A. Quitman; short biography of Wheat taken from Dufour. With the failure of Carvajal's plans for the Republic of the Sierra Madre, Chatham Roberdeau "Rob" Wheat returned to New Orleans to resume the practice of law. But Wheat, yearning for a life of adventure, joined the forces of the filibuster William Walker in 1854. Walker's forces had invaded the Mexican state of Sonora, but Wheat arrived in California too late to join the battle. By 1855, Wheat had joined the forces of General Juan Alvarez, governor of the Mexican state of Guerrero, who led forces that opposed the rule of President Santa Anna. Wheat wrote to his mother that "Santa Anna is a doomed man . . . our motto is 'Mueran a tyranno [Mueran las tiranes]' and is worn on every man's

hat." The forces of General Álvarez and others drove Santa Anna from power in 1856, and General Wheat soon became bored with the inactivity of the army. In 1856, Wheat left New York with a party of forty men to travel to Nicaragua on a mission to reinforce William Walker, who had invaded that country and appointed himself president. But again, Wheat could not reach Walker's forces, which had been encircled, and were on the verge of surrender. Wheat then abandoned Walker's cause and returned to the United States. By 1859, Wheat returned to Mexico, under the command of General Álvarez, and took up residence in Acapulco. But Wheat remained restless for action and in 1860 journeyed to Italy to enroll in the forces of Giuseppi Garibaldi, then fighting in Sicily in a revolutionary effort to unite that country. With the election of Abraham Lincoln as president of the United States in November 1860, Wheat knew that civil war in the United States was inevitable, and he resigned his commission with Garibaldi after only two months, returning to the United States. Rob Wheat rushed to New Orleans, where he organized the 1st Special Battalion, known as the Louisiana Tigers. Wheat and his battalion saw action at First Manassas, where he was severely wounded by a ball passing through his chest. By the spring of 1862 the Louisiana Tigers were transferred to the command of General Thomas J. "Stonewall" Jackson, then located in Virginia's Shenandoah Valley. The Tigers, led by Major Rob Wheat, fought in the Battles of Front Royal, Winchester, and Port Republic. But Rob Wheat's luck ran out at Gaines Mill on 27 June 1862. Wheat, far in advance of his troops, was scouting Yankee positions when he was killed by a sharpshooter.

64. *National Intelligencer*, 15 November 1854.

65. Almonte, quoted in Manning, doc. 4205, 735–36.

66. Letcher, quoted in ibid., 421–23.

67. Ibid., 466–67; Rippy, "Diplomacy Regarding the Isthmus of Tehuantepec," 503–31. By 1847 it became apparent that the United States would possess California as a result of the Mexican War. To reach this new territory required either a harrowing overland trip or a sea passage around Cape Horn. Shorter isthmian routes were envisioned by means of transit across Panama, Nicaragua, and more important, across the Isthmus of Tehuantepec in southern Mexico. But the concession that would grant the United States right of passage met with violent opposition in Mexico, which had recently been carved up by the Treaty of Guadalupe Hidalgo. The Mexican press proclaimed: "The experiment with Texas should be enough" if the United States were given "a foothold in Tehuantepec," they would gobble up the remaining half of the

Republic of Mexico. By late 1852 the cash-poor Mexican government granted transit privileges to the Louisiana Tehuantepec Company, which set to work building a plank road across the isthmus. But the project was now of secondary importance to the U.S. government, who were using transit across Nicaragua and eyeing routes that would be constructed entirely within U.S. territory. By 1857 the plank road was completed and "experienced a brief season of apparent prosperity." A contract to carry the California mail across the isthmus resulted in a savings of twelve days' time. But the company floundered financially, and in spite of monetary infusions from loans, failed to meet its contract agreements with Mexico; the republic nullified the grant by 15 October 1866.

68. Tyler, "Callahan Expedition of 1855," 580–82.

69. Shearer, 68.

CHAPTER NINE: *The War of the Reform in Mexico and the Southern Confederacy in the United States*

1. The discussion of the rise of Juárez to power in Mexico can be found in Smart, 99–255, and in Pitner, 8–19, 99–100. The Zaragoza quote is found in Smart.

2. The situation on the border at this time can be found in Oates, albeit tinctured by John S. Ford's ego and selective memory. "Ford to Sam Houston," 29 December 1859, as found in Hughes, 167. John S. Ford believed that Cortina's forces were receiving support from the Mexican Conservative Party, headed by Miguel Miramón, who were then engaged with the Liberal Party of Benito Juárez in the War of the Reform that raged through Mexico from 1857 to 1860.

3. Graf, vol. 1, chapter 7, 383; Oates, 264; Stambaugh and Stambaugh, 105; and Ford, "Memoirs," 889.

4. Census of 1850, "Difficulties on Southwestern Frontier," hereafter known as DSF, "Citizens to Gov. Runnels," 12a, 22; *Reports of the Committee of Investigation*, 137–38; and Papers of Hiram Runnels, Archives Division, Texas State Library and Archives Commission, Austin, Texas, "Ford to Runnels," 2 June 1858. Ford expressed the opinion of many living on the frontier of Texas at that time when he wrote: "The Citizens of this State are entitled to protection and they ought to have it. The General Government have failed and refused to accord it. . . . There is no better principle established than, that when a Government fail or refuses to protect its citizens the ties of the alle-

giance are dissolved, and they have a perfect right to take care of themselves. In my opinion Texas has already had ample cause to sever her connection with the Union on this very head." This very issue would top the list of grievances expressed in the Articles of Secession framed fewer than three years later when Texas left the Union.

5. DSF, "Latham to Twiggs," 28 September 1859, 14a, 32.

6. DSF, anonymous, 10 October 1858, 24b, 40.

7. Graf, vol. 1, chapter 7, 385–87.

8. Heintzelman, as quoted in Thompson, *Fifty Miles,* 137.

9. Ibid., 148.

10. Ibid., 144.

11. Ibid., 175.

12. Ibid., 179.

13. Oates, 291.

14. Ford, as quoted in Oates, 291–94; Hughes, 173–74.

15. Heintzelman, as cited in Thompson, *Fifty Miles,* 182.

16. Ibid.

17. Tyler, *Vidaurri,* 61.

18. Ibid., 61–62; private communication, Bethany College.

19. Tyler, *Vidaurri,* 62.

20. Ibid.

21. Ford, "Memoirs," 928.

22. Tyler, *Vidaurri,* 63.

23. Ford, "Memoirs," 1006.

24. Tyler, *Vidaurri,* 70–71.

25. Ford, "Memoirs," 928, 1006. As defined in Merriam-Webster's Biographical Dictionary (1989), Boabdil, also known as Mohammed XI, was the last Moorish king of Granada (1486–92); he was expelled by Ferdinand and Isabella and later fled to Morocco.

26. Tyler, *Vidaurri,* 70; John S. Ford Confederate Military Papers, Haley Library.

27. Tyler, *Vidaurri,* 70–75; Daddysman, 43–58.

28. Hughes, 202–4, 206; Oates, 328–30; and Irby, 21.

CHAPTER TEN: *French Intervention*

1. Bazant, 85–90; Hanna and Hanna, 13–20, 23–24, 36, 43; Pitner, 10–16, 43–44; and Zaragoza, as quoted in Smart, 267.

2. Brown, "Guns over the Border," 93–96.

3. Ibid., 93–97; Toral, 266–68.

4. Toral, 269.

5. Brown, "Guns over the Border," 99; Toral, 265.

6. Brown, "Guns over the Border," 99–100.

7. Smart, 345. The "Ortego" referred to is quite likely Jesús Gonzáles Ortega, a Mexican Liberal and political rival of Benito Juárez.

8. Hughes, 230.

9. Wallace, 845.

10. Ibid., 869.

11. McKee, 95.

12. Ibid.

13. Ibid., 96; Wallace, 846, 869.

14. McKee, 98.

15. Ibid.

16. Smart, 338–39.

17. Letter, "Carvajal to Wallace," 22 August 1865, Wallace Papers, Indiana Historical Society.

18. Miller, "Herman Sturm," 4.

19. McKee, 99.

20. Wallace, 867.

21. McKee, 101–2.

22. Miller, "Herman Sturm," 8.

23. McKee, 99.

24. Letter, "Carvajal to Wallace," 16 December 1865, Wallace Papers. Translated by Eleanor Moore.

25. Letter, "Mr. Joseph Smith to Wallace," 18 May 1865, Wallace Papers.

26. Miller, "Herman Sturm," 9–11; Miller, "Lew Wallace," 46; and Brown, 174–77.

27. Meyer and Sherman, 397–99.

28. Private Collection of Enrique Guerra, Linn, Texas.

29. Ibid.

30. Sheridan, 210–20; Hanna and Hanna, 217. It is no surprise that Carvajal should be judged so harshly by General Philip Sheridan, as the former was a known associate of General Lew Wallace. Sheridan despised Wallace since the latter general's fiasco at the Battle of Shiloh, where he reported that his division had been "lost" and did not enter the struggle at all during the first

crucial day of the battle, despite the roar of cannon and musketry that could be heard for miles. Sheridan reported in the summer of 1865 to General U.S. Grant that Wallace with "some other sharks" had arrived in New Orleans, but Sheridan doubted "if they can do much good."

31. McKee, 103.

32. Private Collection of Enrique Guerra.

33. Sheridan, 220.

34. Private Collection of Enrique Guerra.

35. Ibid.; Meyer and Sherman, 390.

36. Parisot, 68–74.

37. Private Collection of Enrique Guerra.

38. Graf, summary vol., 117.

39. Ford, "Memoirs," 1216–18.

40. Private Collection of Enrique Guerra; Zorilla and Salas, *Diccionario Biográfico de Tamaulipas*, 140–41. Mariano Escobedo de la Peña was born in Labradores (now Galeana), Nuevo León in 1826, the son of Manuel de Escobedo and Rita de la Peña. He joined the military during the American invasion, participating in the defense of Monterey and the Battle of Buena Vista. In 1848 he became a sublieutenant in the National Guard, fighting in the many battles against Comanche and Lipan Indian parties who were raiding Mexico with frequency. In 1855, Escobedo joined the movement of Vidaurri that supported the Plan of Ayutla, participating with Juan Zuázua and others in the attack on Saltillo and the occupation of San Luis Potosí. During the War of Reform he sided with the Liberals and was considered by Benito Juárez as one of his most trusted allies. During the French intervention Escobedo served as a general of brigade in the battles of Acultzingo and Pueblo and in battles in Oaxaca, Puebla, Guerrero of Mexico, Querétaro, and Michoacán. In 1865, Escobedo reorganized the Army of the North, which would seize control of Nuevo León from the imperialists. He was triumphant in the battle of Santa Gertrudis on 16 June 1866, which decided the destiny of Matamoros and Monterey. He entered Monterey on 9 August 1866, then turned his army south to seal Maximilian's fate at the Siege of Querétaro. Escobedo was elected governor of San Luis Potosí, for a term from 1870 to 1874, and served as a senator from that state in 1875. He went into exile after the triumph of Porfirio Díaz with the rebellion of Tuxtepec.

41. Private Collection of Enrique Guerra.

42. Ibid.

43. Ibid.
44. Ibid.
45. Ford, "Memoirs," 1219.
46. Wallace, 871, 875.
47. Ibid., 875.
48. Private Collection of Enrique Guerra.
49. Wallace, 873–75; McKee, 112–14. Wallace returned to the United States in February 1867, on the verge of personal bankruptcy. In May 1867 he tendered his resignation of his commission in the Mexican army, writing to Minister Romero that "his means were about exhausted," and offered to settle his claim of $100,000 against the government of Mexico for $25,552.50. Romero responded by noting that Carvajal did not have the authority to employ Wallace and made a counter offer to settle for $10,000. Wallace journeyed to Washington the next year to negotiate a settlement with Minister Romero. The hot-headed Wallace, in a verbal exchange with Romero, offered to sell Carvajal's promissary note for $2,500. The shrewd Romero snapped up the deal, causing Wallace to lose the most important document needed to verify his claim for services rendered. But hard negotiations continued for a settlement, with Juárez himself writing that "$6,000 or $7,000 was enough." The Joint American and Mexican Claim Commission, set up by treaty in 1868, heard claims presented by Wallace for services to Mexico and ten years later rejected Wallace's claim. It agreed that Carvajal had exceeded his authority in promised funds to Wallace, found that "Wallace had performed no real service to Mexico," and as a final blow found that Wallace had abandoned his rights as an American citizen by serving as an officer in the Mexican army. With none other than a moral basis, the Mexican government in 1882 awarded Wallace $15,000 for his services. Hermann Sturm, whom Wallace had persuaded to aid the Liberal cause, also fared badly. Sturm finally received $42,500 in recompense from the Mexican government, less than one-third of his personal expenditures.
50. *El Mesteño,* January 2000; *San Antonio Express,* 4 March 2001. The earthly remains of Santiago Vidaurri were buried in Mexico City, but soon, under the direction of his son-in-law, Patricio Milmo, were reinterred on the sprawling forty-thousand-acre ranch on La Mesa de Los Catujanes, about fifty miles south of Laredo, Texas. There are no roads onto the mesa, which rises a thousand feet above the surrounding landscape, and can only be visited by a laborious climb up a burro trail known as the *cuesta de dolores.* Vidaurri's body was

placed in a chapel on the ranch there that was built to house his remains. A memorial service is conducted there annually to honor the ex-governor by the Milmo family of San Antonio and Monterey, who still own the ranch.

51. Ford, "Memoirs," 1222. Undated author interview with Robert Reyna, great-grandson of José María Carvajal.

52. Brown, "Guns over the Border," 185–86; John S. Ford Confederate Military Papers, Haley Library.

Bibliography

Almaráz, Félix D., Jr. *Tragic Cavalier: Governor Manuel Salcedo of Texas, 1808–1813*. Austin: University of Texas Press, 1971.

Amberson, Mary M., James A. McAllen, and Margaret H. McAllen. *I Would Rather Sleep in Texas*. Austin: Texas State Historical Association, 2003.

Asbury, Herbert. *The French Quarter*. New York: Alfred A. Knopf, 1936.

Audubon, John W. *Audubon's Western Journal: 1849–1850*. Ed. Frank Heywood Hodder. Glorieta, New Mexico: Rio Grande Press, 1969.

Barker, Eugene C. *The Austin Papers*. 3 vols. Austin: University of Texas Press, 1926.

———. *The Life of Stephen F. Austin: Founder of Texas, 1793–1836*. Dallas, Texas: Cokesbury Press, 1926.

———, ed. *Annual Report of the American Historical Association for the Year 1919: The Austin Papers*. 2 vols. and a supplement. Washington, D.C.: United States Printing Office, 1924.

———, ed. *Annual Report of the American Historical Association for the Year 1922: The Austin Papers*. 2 vols. and a supplement. Washington, D.C.: United States Printing Office, 1922.

Barr, Alwyn. *Texans in Revolt: The Battle for San Antonio, 1835*. Austin: University of Texas Press, 1990.

Bartlett, J. R. *Personal Narratives of Explorations and Incidents in Texas, N. Mexico, California, Sonora, and Chihuahua, Connected with the United States and Mexican Boundary Commission during the Years 1850, '51, '52, and '53*. Chicago: Rio Grande Press, 1965.

Bazant, Jan. *A Concise History of Mexico*. London: Cambridge University Press, 1977.

Benavídes, Ádan, Jr. *The Bexar Archives (1717–1836): A Name Guide*. Austin: University of Texas Press, 1989.

Biographical and Historical Memoirs of Louisiana. Vol. 1. Chicago: Goodspeed Publishing Company, 1892.

Brown, Charles H. *Agents of Manifest Destiny: The Lives and Times of the Filibusters.* Chapel Hill: University of North Carolina Press, 1980.

Burr, Anna R. *The Portrait of a Banker, James Stillman.* New York: Duffield Company, 1927.

Butler, Stephen R. *Alabama Volunteers in the Mexican War: A History and Annotated Roster.* Richardson, Texas: Descendents of Mexican War Veterans, 1996.

Campbell, Selina Huntington. *Home Life and Reminiscences of Alexander Campbell by His Wife.* St. Louis: John Burns, Publisher, c. 1882.

Caruso, A. Brooke. *The Mexican Spy Company: United States Covert Operations in Mexico, 1845–1848.* Jefferson, North Carolina: McFarland & Company, 1991.

Chabot, Frederick C. *With the Makers of San Antonio.* San Antonio, Texas: Artes Graficas, 1937.

Chance, Joseph E. *The Mexican War Journal of Captain Franklin Smith.* Jackson: University Press of Mississippi, 1991.

————. *My Life in the Old Army: The Reminiscences of Abner Doubleday.* Fort Worth: Texas Christian University Press, 1998.

Chatfield, W. H. *The Twin Cities: Brownsville, Texas, Matamoros, Mexico.* New Orleans: E. P. Brandao, 1893.

Clayton, Lawrence R., and Joseph E. Chance, eds. *The March to Monterrey: The Diary of Lt. Rankin Dilworth, U.S. Army.* El Paso: Texas Western Press, 1996.

Coakley, Robert W. *The Role of Federal Military Forces in Domestic Disorders, 1789–1878.* Washington, D.C.: Center for Military History, U.S. Army, 1988.

Coker, Caleb, ed. *The News from Brownsville: Helen Chapman's Letters from the Texas Military Frontier, 1848–1852.* Austin: Texas State Historical Association, 1992.

Crawford, Ann F., ed. *The Eagle: The Autobiography of Santa Anna.* Austin: State House Press, 1988.

Daddysman, James W. *The Matamoros Trade: Confederate Commerce, Diplomacy, and Intrigue.* Newark: University of Delaware Press, 1984.

Dávila, Rosaura A., and Oscar R. Saldaña. *Matamoros En La Guerra Con Los Estados Unidos.* Matamoros, Mexico: Ediciones Archivo Histórico Colección Matamoros, 1996.

Davis, William C. *Three Roads to the Alamo.* New York: Harper Collins, 1999.

de la Teja, Jesús F., ed. *A Revolution Remembered: The Memoirs and Selected Correspondence of Juan N. Seguín.* Austin: State House Press, 1991.

Domenech, Emmanuel. *Missionary Adventures in Texas and Mexico: A Personal Narrative of Six Years' Sojourn in Those Regions*. London: Longman, Brown, Green, Longmans, and Roberts, 1858.

Dufour, Charles L. *The Gentle Tiger: The Gallant Life of Roberdeau Wheat*. Baton Rouge: Louisiana State University Press, 1957.

Emory, William H. *Report on the United States and Mexican Boundary Survey*. Vol. 1. Austin: Texas State Historical Association, 1987.

Faulk, Odie E. *The Last Years of Spanish Texas: 1778–1821*. London: Mouton and Company, 1964.

Fehrenbach, T. R. *Lone Star: A History of Texas and Texans*. Cambridge: Da Capo Press, 2000.

Fenwick, Charles G. *The Neutrality Laws of the United States*. Washington, D.C.: Carnegie Endowment for International Peace, 1913.

Filisola, Vicente. *Evacuation of Texas*. Translated by George Lewis Hammeken. Waco,Texas: Texian Press, 1965.

———. *Memoirs for the History of the War in Texas*. Austin, Texas: Eakin Press, 1985.

Fisher, Lillian E. *The Background of the Revolution for Mexican Independence*. New York: Russel and Russel, 1971.

Gammel, H. P. N., comp. *The Laws of Texas, 1822–1897*. Vols. 1 and 2. Austin: Gammel Book Company, 1898.

Garrett, Julia K. *Green Flag over Texas: A Story of the Last Years of Spain in Texas*. Austin, Texas: Pemberton Press. Undated; probably 1939–1940.

Garrett, William. *Reminiscences of Public Men in Alabama, for Thirty Years*. Atlanta, Georgia: Plantation Publishing Company's Press, 1872.

Garza Sáenz, Ernesto. *Cronicas De Camargo*. Second edition. Victoria, Mexico: Instituto de Investigaciones Históricas Universidad Autónoma de Tamaulipas, 1998.

[Giddings, Luther.] *Sketches of the Campaign in Northern Mexico in Eighteen Hundred Forty-Six and Seven*. New York: George P. Putnam, 1853.

Green, Thomas J. *The Journal of the Texian Expedition Against Mier*. New York: Arno Press, 1973.

Gulick, Charles A., Jr., and Winnie Allen, eds. *The Papers of Mirabeau Buonaparte Lamar*. 6 vols. Austin, Texas: Von Boeckmann–Jones Company, 1924.

Hammett, A. B. J. *The Empresario: Don Martin De Leon*. Waco, Texas: Texian Press, 1973.

Hanna, Alfred J., and Kathryn A. Hanna. *Napoleon III and Mexico: American Triumph over Monarchy*. Chapel Hill: University of North Carolina Press, 1971.

Hart, John M. *Empire and Revolution: The Americans in Mexico Since the Civil War*. Berkeley: University of California Press, 2002.

Hawkins, Walace. *The Case of John C. Watrous: United States Judge for Texas*. Dallas, Texas: University Press in Dallas, 1950.

————. *El Sal del Rey*. Austin: Texas State Historical Association, 1947.

Heitman, Francis B. *Historical Register and Dictionary of the United States Army*. 2 vols. Washington, D.C.: United States Government Printing Office, 1903.

Henson, Margaret S. *Juan Davis Bradburn: A Reappraisal of the Mexican Commander of Anahuac*. College Station: Texas A&M Press, 1982.

————. *Samuel May Williams: Early Texas Entrepreneur*. College Station: Texas A&M Press, 1976.

Hughes, W. J. *Rebellious Ranger: Rip Ford and the Old Southwest*. Norman: University of Oklahoma Press, 1964.

Huson, Hobart. *Captain Phillip Dimitt's Commandancy of Goliad, 1835–1836*. Austin: Von Boeckmann–Jones Company, 1974.

————. *Refugio: A Comprehensive History of Refugio County from Aboriginal Times to 1953*. 2 vols. Woodsboro, Texas: Rooke Foundation, 1953.

Irby, James A. *Backdoor at Bagdad: The Civil War on the Rio Grande*. El Paso: Texas Western Press, 1977.

Jackson, Jack. *Almonte's Texas*. Austin: Texas State Historical Association, 2003.

Jackson, Ronald, Gary Teeples, and David Schaefermeyer. *Texas 1850 Census Index*. Bountiful, Utah: Accelerated Indexing Systems, 1976.

Jarratt, Rie. "Gutierrez de Lara," in *The Mexican Experience in Texas*. New York: Arno Press, 1976.

Jenkins, John H., ed. *The Papers of the Texas Revolution, 1835–1836*. 10 vols. Austin, Texas: Presidial Press, 1973.

Johnson, Allen. *Dictionary of American Biography*. Vol. 3. New York: Charles Scribners' Sons, 1929.

Kearney, Milo, and Anthony Knopp. *Boom and Bust: The Historical Cycles of Matamoros and Brownsville*. Austin, Texas: Eakin Press, 1991.

Kelley, Pat. *River of Lost Dreams: Navigation on the Rio Grande*. Lincoln: University of Nebraska Press, 1986.

Kelsey, Anna M. *Through the Years: Reminiscences of Pioneer Days on the Texas Border*. San Antonio, Texas: Naylor Company, n.d.

Lack, Paul. *The Texas Revolutionary Experience*. College Station: Texas A&M Press, 1992.

Lea, Tom. *The King Ranch*. 2 vols. Boston: Little, Brown and Company, 1957.

Linn, John J. *Reminiscences of Fifty Years in Texas.* New York: D. & J. Sadlier and Company, 1883.

Lott, Virgil N., and Mercurio Martinez. *The Kingdom of Zapata.* Austin, Texas: Eakin Press, n.d.

Lott, Virgil N., and Virginia M. Fenwick. *People and Plots on the Rio Grande.* San Antonio, Texas: Naylor Company, 1957.

Mahone, John K. *History of the Second Seminole War: 1835–1842.* Gainesville: University of Florida Press, 1967.

Manning, William R. *Diplomatic Correspondence of the United States: Inter-American Affairs, 1831–1866.* Vol. 9. Washington, D.C.: Carnegie International Endowment for Peace, 1937.

May, Robert E. *Manifest Destiny's Underworld: Filibustering in Antebellum America.* Chapel Hill: University of North Carolina Press, 2002.

McDonald, David R., and Timothy M. Matovina, eds. *Defending Mexican Valor in Texas: José Antonio Navarro's Historical Writings, 1853–1857.* Austin, Texas: State House Press, 1995.

McIntosh, James T. *The Papers of Jefferson Davis.* 11 vols. Baton Rouge: Louisiana State University Press, 1974.

McKee, Irving. *"Ben-Hur" Wallace: The Life of General Lew Wallace.* Berkeley: University of California Press, 1947.

McLean, Malcolm D., ed. *Papers Concerning Robertson's Colony in Texas.* Vol. 10. Arlington, Texas: UTA Press, 1983.

McReynolds, Edwin C. *The Seminoles.* Norman: University of Oklahoma Press, 1957.

Menchaca, Antonio. *Memoirs.* With an introduction by James P. Newcomb. San Antonio, Texas: Yanaguana Society, 1937.

Meyer, Michael C., and William L. Sherman. *The Course of Mexican History.* New York: Oxford University Press, 1987.

Montgomery, Cora [Mrs. William L. Cazneau]. *Eagle Pass, or Life on the Border.* Austin: Pemberton Press, 1966.

Mora-Torres, Juan. *The Making of the Mexican Border.* Austin: University of Texas Press, 2001.

Moretta, John A. *William Pitt Ballinger: Texas Lawyer, Southern Statesman, 1825–1888.* Austin: Texas State Historical Association, 2002.

Morton, Ohland. *Terán and Texas.* Austin: Texas State Historical Association, 1948.

Mulroy, Kevin. *Freedom on the Border.* Lubbock: Texas Tech Press, 1993.

Nance, Joseph M. *After San Jacinto: The Texas-Mexican Frontier, 1836–1841*. Austin: University of Texas Press, 1963.

———. *Attack and Counterattack: The Texas-Mexican Frontier, 1842*. Austin: University of Texas Press, 1964.

———. *Dare-Devils All: The Texan Mier Expedition, 1842–1844*. Austin, Texas: Eakin Press, 1998.

Oates, Stephen B., ed. *Rip Ford's Texas: By John Salmon Ford*. Austin: University of Texas Press, 1998.

Olmsted, Frederick Law. *A Journey Through Texas*. Austin: University of Texas Press, 1978.

Owen, Thomas. *History of Alabama and Dictionary of Alabama Biography*. 4 vols. Chicago: S. J. Clarke Publishing Company, 1921.

Owsley, Frank L. *King Cotton Diplomacy*. Chicago: University of Chicago Press, 1959.

Parisot, Rev. P. F. *The Reminiscences of a Texas Missionary*. San Antonio, Texas: Press of Johnson Bros. Printing Company, 1899.

Peskin, Allen, ed. *Volunteers: The Mexican War Journals of Private Richard Coulter and Sgt. Thomas Barclay, Company E, Second Pennsylvania Infantry*. Kent, Ohio: Kent State University Press, 1991.

Pierce, Frank C. *Texas' Last Frontier: A Brief History of the Rio Grande Valley of Texas*. Menasha, Wisconsin: Georg Banta Publishing Company, 1917.

Pingenot, Ben, ed. *Paso del Águila: A Chronicle of Frontier Days on the Texas Border as Recorded in the Memoirs of Jesse Sumpter*. Austin, Texas: Encino Press, 1969.

Pitner, Ernst. *Maximilian's Lieutenant: A Personal History of the Mexican Campaign, 1864–67*. Albuquerque: University of New Mexico Press, 1993.

Quaife, Milo M. *The Diary of James K. Polk*. Vol. 2. Chicago: University of Chicago Press, 1910.

Rankin, Melinda. *Texas in 1850*. Waco, Texas: Texian Press, 1966.

———. *Twenty Years Among the Mexicans: A Narrative of Missionary Labor*. Cincinnati, Ohio: Chase and Hall, Publishers, 1875.

Reports of the Committee of Investigation Sent in 1873 by the Mexican Government to the Frontier of Texas. New York: Baker and Godwin, Printers, 1875.

Rippy, J. Fred. *The United States and Mexico*. New York: Alfred A. Knopf, 1926.

Robertson, Brian. *Wild Horse Desert: The Heritage of South Texas*. Edinburg, Texas: New Santander Press, 1985.

Rose, Victor M. *Some Historical Facts in Regard to the Settlement of Victoria, Texas*. San Antonio, Texas: Lone Star Printing, 1961.

Santoni, Pedro. *Mexicans at Arms*. Fort Worth: Texas Christian University Press, 1996.

Schwarz, Rosalie. *Across the Rio to Freedom: U.S. Negroes in Mexico*. El Paso: Texas Western Press, 1975.

Sheridan, P. H. *Personal Memoirs of P. H. Sheridan*. Vol. 2. New York: Charles L. Webster and Company, 1888.

Smart, Charles A. *Viva Juárez: A Biography*. London: Eyre and Spottiswoode, 1964.

Smith, Compton. *Chile con Carne, or The Camp and Field*. New York: Miller and Curtis, 1857.

Smith, Justin. *The War with Mexico*. 2 vols. New York: Macmillan Company, 1919.

Sowell, A. J. *Early Settlers and Indian Fighters of Southwest Texas*. New York: Argosy-Antiquarian Limited, 1964.

Spellman, Paul N. *Forgotten Texas Leader: Hugh McLeod and the Texan Santa Fe Expedition*. College Station: Texas A&M University Press, 1999.

Spurlin, Charles D. *Texas Veterans in the Mexican War*. Nacogdoches, Texas: Erickson Publishing, 1984.

Stambaugh, J. Lee, and Lillian J. Stambaugh. *The Lower Rio Grande Valley of Texas*. Austin: Jenkins Publishing Company, 1974.

Stillman, Chauncey D. *Charles Stillman, 1810–1877*. New York: Published privately, 1956.

A Story of Texas Tropical Borderland: Valley By-Liners, Book II. Mission, Texas: Border Kingdom Press, 1978.

Stout, Joseph A. *The Liberators: Filibustering Expeditions into Mexico, 1848–1862*. Los Angeles: Westernlore Press, 1973.

Sweet, Alex E., and J. A. Knox. *On a Mexican Mustang Through Texas from the Gulf to the Rio Grande*. London: Chatto and Windus, Piccadilly, 1884.

Thompson, Jerry D. *Fifty Miles and a Fight: Major Samuel Peter Heintzelman's Journal of Texas and the Cortina War*. Austin: Texas State Historical Association, 1998.

———. *Juan Cortina and the Texas-Mexico Frontier*. El Paso: Texas Western Press, 1994.

———. *Mexican Texans in the Union Army*. El Paso: University of Texas at El Paso, 1986.

Tijerina, Andrés. *Tejanos and Texas Under the Mexican Flag, 1821–1836*. College Station: Texas A&M University Press, 1994.

Toral, Jesús De León. *Historia Documental Militar De La Intervencion Francesa En*

Mexico y El Denominado Segundo Imperio. Mexico City, Mexico: Secretaria De La Defensa Nacional, Departamento De Archivo, Correspondencia E Historia, Comision De Historia Militar, 1967.

Tyler, Ron, Douglas E. Barnett, and Roy R. Barkley, eds. *The New Handbook of Texas.* Austin: Texas State Historical Association, 1996.

Tyler, Ronnie C. *Santiago Vidaurri and the Southern Confederacy.* Austin: Texas State Historical Association, 1973.

Viele, Teresa G. *Following the Drum: A Glimpse of Frontier Life.* Lincoln: University of Nebraska Press, 1974.

Vigness, David M. *The Revolutionary Decades.* Austin, Texas: Steck-Vaughn Company, 1965.

Wallace, Lew. *Lew Wallace: An Autobiography.* 2 vols. New York: Harper and Brothers Publishers, 1906.

Washington, Ann R. "Three Restless Men of Violent Times: Carbajal, Cortina, and Ford," in *Roots by the River.* Canyon, Texas: Staked Plains Press, 1978.

Watkins, Sue, ed. *One League to Each Wind: Accounts of Early Surveying in Texas.* Austin, Texas: Von Boeckman–Jones, 1964, reprint 1973.

Wells, Tom H. *Commodore Moore and the Texas Navy.* Austin: University of Texas Press, 1960.

Who's Who in America: Historical Volume 1607–1896. Chicago: A. N. Marquis Company, 1963.

Winkler, John K. *The First Billion: The Stillmans and the National City Bank.* New York: Vanguard Press, 1934.

Woodman, Lyman L. *Cortina: Rogue of the Rio Grande.* San Antonio, Texas: Naylor Company, 1950.

Wright, John. *Recollections of Western Texas.* London: W. & F. G. Cash, 1857.

Zorilla, Juan F., and Carlos G. Salas. *Diccionario Biográfico de Tamaulipas.* Victoria, Mexico: Universidad Autónoma de Tamaulipas, 1984.

ARTICLES

Barker, Eugene C. "Land Speculation as a Cause of the Texas Revolution." *Quarterly of the Texas Historical Association* 10: 76–95, 1906.

Bridges, C. A. "The Knights of the Golden Circle: A Filibustering Fantasy." *Southwestern Historical Quarterly* 44, no. 3 (January 1941): 287–302.

Chance, Joseph E. "South of the Border." *American History* 31, no. 2 (June 1996): 48–55.

Cook, Zoroaster. "Mexican War Reminiscences." *Alabama Historical Quarterly* 19 (1957): 435–60.

Crimmins, M. L., ed. "W. G. Freeman's Report on the Eighth Military Department." *Southwestern Historical Quarterly* 51, 52, 53 (1948–50): 54–58, 167–74, 252–58, 350–57; 100–108, 351–53, 444–47; 71–77, 202–8, 308–19, 443–73.

Davenport, Harbert. "General Jose Maria Carabajal." *Southwestern Historical Quarterly* 55 (1952): 475–83.

de la Cova, Antonio R. "Filibusters and Freemasons: The Sworn Obligation." *Journal of the Early Republic* 17 (spring 1997): 95–120.

Dienst, Alex. "The Navy of the Republic of Texas." *Quarterly of the Texas Historical Association* 13, no. 1 (July 1909): 1–43; 13, no. 2 (October 1909): 85–127.

———. "The Navy of the Republic of Texas, II." *Quarterly of the Texas State Historical Association* 11, no. 4 (1909): 85–127.

Dobie, J. Frank. "Mustang Gray: Fact, Tradition, and Song." *Tone the Bell Easy*. Publications of the Texas Folk-lore Society, no. 10 (1932): 1–15.

Dugan, Frank H. "The 1850 Affair of the Brownsville Separatists." *Southwestern Historical Quarterly* 61 (October 1957): 270–87.

Fornell, Earl W. "Texans and Filibusters in the 1850's." *Southwestern Historical Quarterly* 59, no. 4 (April 1956): 411–28.

Franklin, Ethel M. "Joseph Baker." *Southwestern Historical Quarterly* 36 (1932): 130–43.

Frazer, R. W. "The United States, European, and West Virginia Land and Mining Company." *Pacific Historical Review* 13 (1944): 28–40.

Greene, A. A., trans. "The Battle of Zacatecas." *Texana* 7, no. 3 (1969): 189–200.

May, Robert E. "Young American Males and Filibustering in the Age of Manifest Destiny: The United States Army as a Cultural Mirror." *Journal of American History* 78 (December 1991): 857–86.

Miller, Robert R. "Herman Sturm: Hoosier Secret Agent for Mexico." *Indiana Magazine of History* 58 (1962): 1–15.

———. "Lew Wallace and the French Intervention in Mexico." *Indiana Magazine of History* 59 (1963): 31–50.

Moretta, John. "Jose Maria Jesus Carvajal, United States Foreign Policy and the Filibustering Spirit in Texas, 1846–1853." *East Texas Historical Journal* 33 (fall 1995): 3–22.

Porter, Kenneth W. "The Hawkins Negroes Go to Mexico." *Chronicles of Oklahoma* 24 (1946): 55–58.

———. "The Seminole in Mexico, 1850–1861." *Chronicles of Oklahoma* 19 (1951): 153–68.

———. "Wild Cat's Death and Burial." *Chronicles of Oklahoma* 21 (1943): 41–43.

Rippy, J. Fred. "Border Troubles along the Rio Grande, 1848–1860." *Southwestern Historical Quarterly* 23 (1919): 91–111.

———. "Diplomacy of the United States and Mexico Regarding the Isthmus of Tehuantepec, 1848–1860." *Mississippi Valley Historical Review* 6 (1920): 503–31.

Smith, Justin H. "La República del Río Grande." *American Historical Review* 25 (1920): 660–75.

Spellman, Paul. "Corpus Christi, 1852, People and Politics at the First State Fair of Texas." *South Texas Studies* 6 (1995): 1–19.

Tyler, Ron. "The Callahan Expedition of 1855: Indians or Negroes." *Southwestern Historical Quarterly* 70 (1967): 574–85.

———. "Fugitive Slaves in Mexico." *Journal of Negro History* 57 (January 1972): 1–12.

ARCHIVES

Annual Returns of Rio Grande Lodge No. 81, 1850–51, Masonic Grande Lodge Library and Museum of Texas, Waco.

Center for American History, University of Texas, Béxar Archives.

The Confederate Military Papers of John S. Ford, Nita Stewart Haley Memorial Library and J. Evetts Haley History Center, Midland, Texas.

The Letters of Governor P. H. Bell, Texas State Library and Archives Commission, Austin.

Mississippi Department of Archives and History Papers of John A. Quitman, Jackson.

Missouri Historical Society LaMotte–Coppinger Papers, St. Louis.

The Papers of John Grant Tod, Rosenberg Library, Galveston, Texas.

The Papers of Samuel May Williams, Rosenberg Library, Galveston, Texas.

The Private Collection of Enrique Guerra, Linn, Texas.

Texas General Land Office, Archives Division Texas State Library and Archives Commission, Austin.

Virginia Historical Society Papers of A. P. Hill, Richmond.

MANUSCRIPTS

Brown, Robert B. "Guns over the Border: American Aid to the Juarez Government During the French Intervention." Ph.D. dissertation, University of Michigan, 1957.

Castillo Crimm, Anna C. "Success in Adversity: The Mexican Americans of Victoria County, Texas, 1800–1880." Ph.D. dissertation, University of Texas at Austin, 1994.

Day, James M. "The Writings and Literature of the Texan Mier Expedition." Ph.D. dissertation, Baylor University, 1967.

Ford, John S. "Memoirs of John S. Ford and Reminiscences of Texas History from 1836–1888." Unpublished manuscript.

Goldfinch, Charles W. "Juan N. Cortina 1824–1892: A Re-appraisal." M.A. dissertation, University of Chicago, 1949.

Gore, W. R. "The Life of Henry Lawrence Kinney." M.A. thesis, University of Texas at Austin, 1948.

Graf, LeRoy P. "The Economic History of the Lower Rio Grande Valley, 1820–1875." Ph.D. dissertation, Harvard University, 1942, 4 vols.

Huson, Hobart. "Iron Men: A History of the Republic of the Rio Grande and the Federalist War in Northern Mexico." Unpublished manuscript, Refugio, Texas.

Marcum, Richard T. "Fort Brown, Texas: The History of a Border Post." M.A. thesis, Texas Technological College, Lubbock, 1964.

Mauck, Jeffrey G. "The Gadsden Treaty: The Diplomacy of Transcontinental Transportation." Ph.D. dissertation, Department of History, Indiana University, 1991.

Nuhn, Oradel. "The Public Career of Memucan Hunt." M.A. thesis, University of Texas at Austin, 1940.

Ramirez, Mary Scanlon. "The Everett's of South Texas." Unpublished manuscript, Chepachet, Rhode Island.

Resendez, Andres. "Caught Between Profits and Rituals: National Contestation in Texas and New Mexico." Ph.D. dissertation, University of Chicago, 1997.

Shearer, Ernest C. "Border Diplomatic Relations Between the United States and Mexico, 1848–1860." M.A. thesis, University of Texas at Austin, 1939.

"Trial of Brevet Major R. S. Garnett by a General Court Martial." Privately published, city unknown.

Vigness, David M. "The Republic of the Rio Grande: An Example of Separatism in Northern Mexico." Ph.D. dissertation, University of Texas, 1951.

Wynn, Dennis Joseph. "The San Patricios and the United States–Mexican War of 1846–1848." Ph.D. dissertation, Loyola University, Chicago, 1982.

PRIVATE COMMUNICATION

R. Jean Cobb. Archives and Special Collections, T. W. Phillips Memorial Library. Bethany College. 13 June 1999.

GOVERNMENT DOCUMENTS

The Census of 1850: Texas. 36th Congress, 1st Session, Ex. Doc. No. 52, "Difficulties on Southwestern Frontier."

32d Congress, 1st Session, Ex. Doc. No. 112, Message from the President of the United States, "Information Respecting Disorders and Outrages Committed on the Rio Grande Frontier."

32d Congress, 2d Session, Ex. Doc. No. 1, Message from the President of the United States to Congress, "Reports from the Eighth Military District— Texas."

NATIONAL ARCHIVES

Returns from Fort Brown, Texas, May 1846–February 1861. Microfilm roll #151, microcopy #617.

Returns from Fort Ringgold, Texas, October 1848–April 1861. Microfilm roll #1019, microcopy #617.

Despatches from U.S. Consuls in Monterrey, Mexico, 1849–1906. Seven rolls, microcopy #165.

NEWSPAPERS

American Flag, Matamoros, Mexico, 1846–48.

Charleston [South Carolina] *Courier*, 1849.

Coastal Bend Sun, Corpus Christi, Texas, 1998.

Corpus Christi [Texas] *Gazette*, 1846.

Daily National Intelligencer, Washington, D.C., 1851–52.

Daily Union, Washington, D.C., 1851–52.

Democratic Telegraph and Texas Register, Austin, 1851.

Galveston [Texas] *Journal*, 1854.

Galveston [Texas] *News*, 1854.

Indianola [Texas] *Bulletin*, 1851.

McAllen [Texas] *Monitor*, 1979.

New Orleans Picayune, 1851–59.

Semi-Weekly Journal, Galveston, Texas, 1854.

South-Western American, Austin, Texas, 1852.

Texas State Gazette, Austin, 1852.

PERIODICALS

El Mesteño. A Magazine About Mexican-American Culture and Heritage in South Texas and Mexico. 3, no. 28 (January 2000).

INTERNET

"Treaty of Guadalupe Hidalgo," Monterey County Historical Society, available online at www.dedot.com/mchs/treaty.html. Accessed on 4 May 1999.

Index